# The Responsibility to Protect

This volume is a collection of the key writings of Professor Ramesh Thakur on norms and laws regulating the international use of force.

The adoption of the Responsibility to Protect (R2P) principle by world leaders assembled at the UN summit in 2005 is widely acknowledged to represent one of the great normative advances in international politics since 1945. The author has been involved in this shift from the dominant norm of non-intervention to R2P as an actor, public intellectual and academic and has been a key thinker in this process. These essays represent the author's writings on R2P, including reference to test cases as they arose, such as with Cyclone Nargis in Myanmar in 2008.

Comprising essays by a key thinker and agent in the Responsibility to Protect debates, this book will be of much interest to students of international politics, human rights, international law, war and conflict studies, international security and IR in general.

**Ramesh Thakur** is Professor of International Relations in the Asia–Pacific College of Diplomacy, Australian National University and Adjunct Professor in the Institute for Ethics, Governance and Law at Griffith University in Brisbane, Australia. He was a Commissioner for the International Commission on Intervention and State Sovereignty (ICISS), and one of the principal authors of their report *The Responsibility to Protect* (2001). He was also Senior Adviser on Reforms and Principal Writer of the United Nations Secretary-General's second reform report (2002). A former Senior Vice Rector of the United Nations University and UN Assistant Secretary-General, he is author or editor of over thirty books and 300 articles and book chapters.

**Global Politics and the Responsibility to Protect**
Series Editors: Alex J. Bellamy, *Griffith University*, Sara E. Davies
*Griffith University* and Monica Serrano, *The City University, New York*

The aim of this book series is to gather the best new thinking about the Responsibility to Protect into a core set of volumes that provides a definitive account of the principle, its implementation, and role in crises, that reflects a plurality of views and regional perspectives.

**Global Politics and the Responsibility to Protect**
From words to deeds
*Alex J. Bellamy*

**The Responsibility to Protect**
Norms, laws and international politics
*Ramesh Thakur*

# The Responsibility to Protect

Norms, laws and the use of
force in international politics

**Ramesh Thakur**

Routledge
Taylor & Francis Group

LONDON AND NEW YORK

First published 2011
by Routledge
2 Park Square, Milton Park, Abingdon, Oxon OX14 4RN

Simultaneously published in the USA and Canada
by Routledge
270 Madison Ave, New York, NY 10016

*Routledge is an imprint of the Taylor & Francis Group, an informa business*

© 2011 Ramesh Thakur

The right Ramesh Thakur to be identified as author of this
work has been asserted by him in accordance with sections
77 and 78 of the Copyright, Designs and Patents Act 1988.

Typeset in Bembo by
Florence Production Ltd, Stoodleigh, Devon
Printed and bound in Great Britain by
CPI Antony Rowe, Chippenham, Wiltshire

*British Library Cataloguing in Publication Data*
A catalogue record for this book is available from the British Library

*Library of Congress Cataloging-in-Publication Data*
Thakur, Ramesh Chandra, 1948–
   The responsibility to protect: norms, laws, and the use of force in
   international politics/Ramesh Thakur.
       p. cm.
     1. Intervention (International law)    2. Humanitarian
intervention.    3. Security, International.    4. Conflict management.
   I. Title.
   JZ6368.T53 2010
   327.1'17—dc22                                    2010032365

ISBN 13: 978–0-415–78168–8 (hbk)
ISBN 13: 978–0-415–78169–5 (pbk)

# Contents

# Acknowledgements

I owe a deep debt of gratitude to Mr Andrew Humphrys, Senior Editor at Routledge, for first raising with me the idea of bringing together a collection of my published articles on the responsibility to protect and then for organizing the feedback from the anonymous reviewers regarding the idea and how best to structure the essays. He was professionally efficient and helpful throughout the subsequent process as well. A very warm thank you.

My wife Bernadette once again put up with some crazy hours and work habits as the work neared completion and maintained her supportive good humour throughout. As she has been with me throughout the responsibility to protect journey now for almost exactly a decade, her role and influence in this is considerable.

Ms Debbie Dietrich, my Executive Assistant at the Balsillie School of International Affairs, was her usual efficient self in organizing and collating various material during the course of bringing these essays together. I thank her most warmly for all her help.

Not surprisingly, there was some repetition of phrases over the years in these different publications. Mr Benjamin Weir, Balsillie Fellow in the Balsillie School of International Affairs, diligently read through several drafts to try and catch all such repetitions and excise them, unless they were critical to the arguments in different places. My warmest thanks to him. A second change to them is editorial and stylistic standardization. In every other respect they are reprinted exactly as originally published.

I am grateful to the original publishers of the following material to reprint them in this collection:

- Chapter 2 entitled 'Non-intervention in international relations: a case study', was previously published in *Political Science* 42(1), July 1990, pp. 26–61.
- Chapter 3 entitled 'Kosovo, humanitarian intervention and the challenge of world order' (with Albrecht Schnabel), was previously published as 'Kosovo, the changing contours of world politics and the challenge of world order', and 'Unbridled humanitarianism: between justice, power, and authority' in A. Schnabel and R. Thakur, eds, *Kosovo and the Challenge of Humanitarian Intervention: Selective indignation, collective action, and international*

*citizenship* (Tokyo: United Nations University Press, 2000), pp. 1–16 and 496–504.

- Chapter 4 entitled 'Global norms and international humanitarian law: an Asian perspective', was previously published in *International Review of the Red Cross*, Vol. 83, No. 841, March 2001, pp. 19–44.
- Chapter 5 entitled 'Intervention, sovereignty and the responsibility to protect: experiences from ICISS', was previously published in *Security Dialogue* 33:3 (September 2002), pp. 323–40.
- Chapter 6 entitled 'In defence of the responsibility to protect', was previously published in *International Journal of Human Rights* 7:3 (Autumn 2003), pp. 160–78.
- Chapter 7 entitled 'Collective security and the use of force: reflections on the report of the high-level panel on threats, challenges and change', was previously published in N. Azimi and Chang Li Lin, eds, *United Nations as Peacekeeper and Nation-Builder: Continuity and change – what lies ahead* (Leiden: Martinus Nijhoff for the UN Institute for Training and Research, Geneva and the Institute of Policy Studies, Singapore, 2005), pp. 31–48.
- Chapter 8 entitled 'The responsibility to protect and prosecute: the parallel erosion of sovereignty and impunity' (with Vesselin Popovski), was previously published in G. Z. Capaldo, ed., *The Global Community: Yearbook of international law and jurisprudence 2007*, Vol. 1 (New York: Oxford University Press, 2008), pp. 39–61.
- Chapter 9 entitled 'R2P: from idea to norm – and action?' (with Thomas G. Weiss), was previously published in *Global Responsibility to Protect* 1:1 (January–March 2009), pp. 22–53.
- Chapter 10 entitled 'The responsibility to protect and the North–South divide', was previously published in S. R. Silverburg, ed., *International Law: Readings on contemporary problems and future issues* (Boulder, CO: 2011) and used by permission of Westview Press, a member of the Perseus Books Group. All rights reserved.

Finally, I am grateful to my co-authors for three of the above articles – Albrecht Schnabel (Chapter 3), Vesselin Popovski (Chapter 8) and Thomas G. Weiss (Chapter 9) – for their agreement to have the jointly-written articles published in this volume.

# 1    Introduction

## Norms and laws in international relations

The International Commission on Intervention and State Sovereignty (ICISS) published its landmark report entitled *The Responsibility to Protect* in December 2001.[1] Its central propositions – that sovereignty entails state responsibility as well as rights, that one such responsibility is to protect all people inside a state's sovereign territorial jurisdiction, and that when the state fails to discharge this owing to incapacity, unwillingness or complicity in atrocity crimes being committed, the responsibility trips upwards to the international community acting through the United Nations – resonated immediately and powerfully with many governments and civil society organizations. The principle, commonly referred to as R2P, was unanimously adopted by the largest gathering of heads of state and government meeting at the UN summit in October 2005. Paragraphs 138–40 of the Outcome Document from the summit are worth recalling in full:

> *Responsibility to protect populations from genocide, war crimes, ethnic cleansing, and crimes against humanity*
>
> 138. Each individual State has the responsibility to protect its populations from genocide, war crimes, ethnic cleansing, and crimes against humanity. This responsibility entails the prevention of such crimes, including their incitement, through appropriate and necessary means. We accept that responsibility and will act in accordance with it. The international community should, as appropriate, encourage and help States to exercise this responsibility and support the United Nations in establishing an early warning capability.
>
> 139. The international community, through the United Nations, also has the responsibility to use appropriate diplomatic, humanitarian, and other peaceful means, in accordance with Chapters VI and VIII of the Charter, to help to protect populations from genocide, war crimes, ethnic cleansing, and crimes against humanity. In this context, we are prepared to take collective action, in a timely and decisive manner, through the Security Council, in accordance with the Charter, including Chapter VII, on a case-by-case basis and in cooperation with relevant regional organizations as

appropriate, should peaceful means be inadequate and national authorities are manifestly failing to protect their populations from genocide, war crimes, ethnic cleansing, and crimes against humanity. We stress the need for the General Assembly to continue consideration of the responsibility to protect populations from genocide, war crimes, ethnic cleansing, and crimes against humanity and its implications, bearing in mind the principles of the Charter and international law. We also intend to commit ourselves, as necessary and appropriate, to helping States build capacity to protect their populations from genocide, war crimes, ethnic cleansing, and crimes against humanity and to assisting those which are under stress before crises and conflicts break out.

140. We fully support the mission of the Special Adviser of the Secretary-General on the Prevention of Genocide.[2]

Considering that just six years earlier, a majority of UN member states had rejected the notion of a right of 'humanitarian intervention', this was quite a dramatic turnaround in an astonishingly short span of time. The debate continues in both policy and academic circles on the precise legal status of R2P: does it have any legal status; should we describe it as a principle; has it attained the status of a global norm? Regardless of whether it is a norm or not, there would be general agreement that a normative shift has been taking place from non-intervention, the dominant global norm in 1990 that shielded sovereign states from external intervention, to the responsibility to protect that seeks to qualify the norm of non-intervention in significant respects, albeit under narrow circumstances and tight procedural safeguards.

This book brings together a collection of essays that map that shift. It relies on a lifetime of professional studies of international relations supplemented by an insider's perspective as an ICISS commissioner as well as a senior UN official. As such it combines advocacy and analysis. The essays reflect my personal and professional identity at the intersection of West and East, North and South, and of international relations scholarship and the international policy community.

## Norms

A norm can be defined statistically to mean the pattern of behaviour that is most common or usual; that is, to refer to the 'normal curve': *a widely prevalent pattern of behaviour.*[3] Or it can be defined ethically, to mean a pattern of behaviour that should be followed in accordance with a given value system; that is, to refer to the moral code of a society: *a generally accepted standard of proper behaviour.* In practice, the two different meanings may converge, complement or diverge from each other. For example, corruption among public officials and politicians is ubiquitous and pervasive in India, so much so that citizens who have to engage in dealings with the government become part of the web of corruption as bribe givers. And yet, simultaneously, there is almost universal public revulsion at the level of institutionalized corruption in the country. In other words, corruption is the norm in the statistical sense of the word, while in the ethical sense the norm is the very opposite, public probity.

Whichever definition we choose to adopt between the 'is' and the 'ought', it is clear that norms and laws are alternative mechanisms for regulating human and social behaviour. Human beings are social actors; norms are essential to the functioning and existence of society; therefore social interaction is viewed through normative lenses, from bilateral relations between two individuals to relations among national leaders. Laws and norms do not just shape decisions; the language of norms and laws permits human beings to pursue goals, challenge assertions and justify actions.[4] For example, the Treaty of Versailles was widely perceived as unjust both by Germans and the allies, especially the British. The order established by the treaty therefore lacked legitimacy, which facilitated Hitler's challenge both to the Weimar Republic and the European order, on the one hand, and robbed people in the allied countries of conviction in defending the European order, on the other.

The role and efficacy of norms and laws change at different levels of social and political organization. At the local level, norms are far more important. Village society is governed principally by norms – that is what makes it a society. At the national level, in modern societies laws take over from norms. But there must be a degree of congruence between the laws enacted by a parliament and the prevailing values – norms – of that society. Otherwise, not only will the laws be disregarded; habitual disobedience to particular laws will engender a more generalized disrespect for the system of laws, for the principle of a polity being governed by laws and all its actors – rulers as well as citizens – being subject to the rule of law. For example, as the Western-influenced elite in India banned centuries-old social practices among Hindus, such as dowry and caste discrimination, the net effect was to divorce the legal system from everyday behaviour rather than change entrenched social practices. At the international level, both norms and laws, including 'soft' laws, are at work in shaping the behaviour of different classes of actors. The statistical meaning of norm refers to standard state practice; the evaluative, to standards of state practice.

The most effective form of behaviour regulation is for complete convergence between laws and norms, for example with regard to murder. In international relations, epochal shifts in the generally accepted standards of state behaviour mean that such institutions as slavery and colonialism, common enough in earlier eras, are today proscribed in law. But the international norm had to change before the law did. Conversely, the most problematic is when there is near-total dissonance, as with dowry and caste in India. The reason for the dissonance lies primarily in different moral frameworks of social behaviour.[5] At the international level, one of the most likely arenas for normative dissonance is that of human rights, precisely because of alternative moral frameworks, which define and locate the rights and responsibilities of individuals, community and state vis-à-vis one another.

Norms matter because people – politicians and officials as well as citizens – care about what others think of them. This is why approbation, and its logical corollary shaming, are so effective in regulating social behaviour. In this context the imposition of sanctions, especially those that seek to withhold regional and international community recognition and deny regional and international forums to leaders of states under sanction, can be viewed as the functional equivalent in international society of the technique of ostracism in a local community. To be a member in good standing of a community is to subscribe to its moral framework and core values. And the behavioural prescription is not 'Do X in order to get Y' *à la* rules, but 'You should do X because good people do X' *à la* norms. If the target actor believes that the community of actors relevant to him or her subscribes to that norm, and if the respect of that community is important to the actor, then the norm will have a powerful effect in shaping the structure of incentives and disincentives for his or her behaviour. Brian Greenhill has argued that, owing to socialization effects, international organizations have a surprisingly powerful influence on the human rights practices of member states.[6]

That is, as norms become widely shared in any given in-group, they become embedded in the social institutions of that group. The resulting normative structure thereby influences the definition of state interests and so constrains the pursuit of short-term power or wealth maximization: the absolute gains of neorealism or the relative gains of neoliberalism. In constructivist theories, norms shape both the goals of states (the construction of state interests) and the means employed to achieve those goals. The total range of behaviour that may be possible is wider than the range of behaviour that is conceivable in any social system; norms act as a 'cognitive energy-saver' in narrowing the total range of behaviour to manageable limits.[7]

There is great diversity in moral beliefs around the world. Even so, all of us structure our moral world, as individuals, societies and cultures; and the ways in which we do so are remarkably similar around the world. Courage, piety, compassion, charity, fidelity to family and friends, honesty etc. are virtues in all societies, and their opposites are vices. Cultural diversity is relevant to the application of shared moral precepts in different contexts, which does not negate a deeper unity of moral outlooks.

'Shared ideas, expectations, and beliefs about appropriate behaviour are what give the world structure, order, and stability.' Moreover, 'In an ideational international structure, idea shifts and norm shifts are the main vehicles for system transformation.'[8] Just as the realist is interested in changes in the distribution of capabilities in order to explain system change, so the ideational theorist is interested in norm shifts in order to understand system change.

Norms are standards of appropriate behaviour; rules are specific applications of norms to particular situations, either prescribing or proscribing action to conform with the norm. A society inducts new members into its codes of proper behaviour through processes of socialization to the point where its major ethical principles are internalized by the vast majority of children and adults. This then permits the exceptional cases of challenge to be dealt with through compliance mechanisms that may be social, legal or coercive. Society presupposes socialization just as much as socialization presupposes society, whether at local, national or international levels of analysis.

Collective norms constitute the social identity of actors while simultaneously constituting the rules of the game for regulating their social behaviour. The principle of sovereignty defines what a state is and underpins the entire system of states. The norm of non-intervention, a logical corollary of that principle, helps to regulate the interactions of states in international relations. Similarly, human rights norms increasingly constitute a 'civilized' state in contemporary international society, while regulating the matrix of citizen-state interaction. The human rights norm has also encroached increasingly on the non-intervention norm. Despite that, the definition of the state still entails a necessary reference to the notion of sovereignty.[9]

Norms can be held by individual actors, or shared by a group, or shared universally. By definition, collective norms are shared standards of behaviour. How many actors of a group must share a norm before we can call it a group norm? How many countries must share a norm before it is a global norm? We still do not have adequate conceptual tools and empirical research for a theory of international norms: how they emerge, are diffused globally, consolidated to the point of being internalized by members of the international society and embedded in international institutions. Nor is there agreement on who can legitimately claim to articulate or pinpoint 'global' norms.

A preliminary distinction can be made between 'robust' and 'soft' norms. Annika Björkdahl and Sean McMahon define robustness in terms of specificity (clarity of meaning and comprehension), durability (longevity) and concordance (how widely shared they are in the family of nations).[10] The norm of non-intervention was robust on the combination of the three dimensions at the end of the last century. Conversely, even if there could be said to have been an emerging new norm of intervention, it could only be described as weak on all three dimensions: it was too vague and generalized, lacking clarity on meaning, triggering thresholds and activities, and certification or legitimation agencies and procedures; it was of very recent vintage; and it was characterized by discordance in the international community. That is, to the extent that it existed at all, it was soft.

International norms diffuse neither automatically, uniformly nor consistently. They can be transmitted down into national politics through incorporation into domestic laws or into the policy preferences of political leaders through elite learning. As in life generally, so with norm prominence: success feeds on itself. The crucial question is how contested norms become institutionalized both within and among nations, and the interactive dynamics of the process of institutionalization at the national, regional and global levels. Values held by states and actors regarded as successful and desirable models achieve more prominence than norms held by less successful states. Martha Finnemore and Kathryn Sikkink hold this to be the reason for the greater diffusion of Western norms in contemporary international relations.[11] If so, then the significant power and ideational changes underway in the global order will generate at least some major norm shifts. It is only through state structures – through governments – that international norms can be integrated into domestic standards. Norm diffusion is not in itself, therefore, about the state withering away.

Amitav Acharya, one of the finest theorists of the interrogation of global and Asian norms, makes a useful distinction between norm localization and norm subsidiarity. By norm localization he means the active construction – through discourse, framing, grafting etc. – of foreign ideas by local actors so that a significant congruence develops between global norms and local beliefs and practices.[12] By norm subsidiarity he means the creation by local actors of rules that seek to protect and enhance their autonomy from dominance, neglect, violation, or abuse by the powerful central actors.[13] Thus in norm localization, local actors, whether weak or powerful, are norm-takers who import foreign norms that they view as good and desirable into their regions. In norm subsidiarity, the peripheral and excluded local actors are foreign norm rejectionists and norm creators seeking to export or universalize locally constructed norms to outsiders.

As with laws, so with norms: violations in the particular do not invalidate the general. Specific transgressions of individual laws and norms can be compatible with the principle of a system of laws or norms. If an actor violates the norm of non-intervention, but insists that the action does not constitute non-intervention, or that there were extenuating pressures, then the actor is implicitly endorsing the validity of the norm in principle but rejecting its application or relevance in the specific instance. Alternatively, reaffirmations of an existing norm may suggest, by the very fact of their having to be proclaimed anew, that they are in the process or danger of being weakened.

## The life cycle of norms

Finnemore and Sikkink postulate a three-stage life cycle of norms: the emergence of a new norm and its advocacy by a norm entrepreneur; norm cascade when agreement among a critical mass of actors on an emergent norm creates a tipping point; and norm internalization so that it becomes taken for granted and norm-conforming behaviour is routinized, requiring no further justification.[14] The United Nations provides an organizational platform for advocacy in the first stage, the forum of choice for cascade in the second, and the forum of choice for seeking affirmation, reaffirmation and compliance in the third and final stage.

In the first stage, human agency is critical. For norm advocacy to occur, an actor – the would-be entrepreneur – must have strong notions about appropriate standards of behaviour by fellow-actors in an inclusive social or political community. The actor can range from individuals, such as the founders of Amnesty International and the Red Cross, through transnational advocacy networks, to transnational non-governmental organizations (NGOs) such as

Amnesty International and Greenpeace. The actor must have a strongly developed sense of dissatisfaction about existing standards of international behaviour. For this sense of grievance to be translated into a new norm, the actor must possess rhetorical skills, the ability to communicate moral ideas and arguments, and the diplomatic infrastructure and capacity to convince and coax others to one's moral preferences. The motive can be disinterested morality or self-interested diplomacy. Success will depend less on motivation and more on coalition-building skills: the ability to forge winning coalitions of the willing, the able and the high-minded. (Major powers, by contrast, can coerce or compel compliance.)

Entrepreneurship in the marketplace connotes creative imagination, inventiveness and non-routine responses that produce changes in the methods of production or types of economic organization.[15] Through improvisation and originality, the entrepreneur introduces new goods to the market, or discovers new markets, or spots a gap in the market and moves to fill it with a new product or service.

Norm entrepreneurs in international affairs – Henry Dunant for the norm of international humanitarian law via the international Red Cross movement, Mahatma Gandhi for the norm of non-violence, Peter Benenson for the human rights norm via Amnesty International – spot gaps in the existing normative architecture of world order and engage in moral proselytism in order to fill those gaps. They use organizational platforms – the United Nations in particular but also ad hoc transnational and trans-actor coalitions – from which to launch their crusades; they frame issues by using powerfully resonant language and metaphor; and they lobby state actors for institutionalizing the new norm in international law, in the rules of multilateral organizations, and in national foreign policies. Adjacency, or guilt by association, is an effective technique for delegitimizing a prevailing practice and proselytizing the new norm in its stead. Thus 'female mutilation' resonated more powerfully than 'female circumcision' in efforts to halt and outlaw the practice. Similarly, terms like 'ethnic cleansing', 'genocide' and calls of 'No more Auschwitzes' are powerful rallying calls to action because they are social metaphors deeply imprinted in the collective memory of the moral community to whom the appeal is being made.

Norman Frolich and Joe Oppenheimer write of 'a coordinator of expectations', a political entrepreneur who coordinates the expectations of all members regarding the probable actions of all others.[16] Canada, Norway and others can be said to have performed just such an entrepreneurial role with respect to the Ottawa Treaty on landmines and the Rome Statute establishing the International Criminal Court.[17] Classical diplomacy was about national power in international relations: its location, bases, exercise by, of and for states, and distributional impact on relations between states. New diplomacy is much more fundamentally about authority: its location and sources, its channelling into international norms and regimes, its exercise by states for the people, and distributional impact on the welfare and security of people. This is why norm entrepreneurship is a more useful asset in the new diplomacy of the twenty-first century.[18]

In the transformation of an emergent norm into a global norm, the second stage is critical. Norm cascade (meaning that the norm, after being adopted by a critical mass of actors, cascades through the rest of the population) results from a combination of peer pressure for conformity, the search for increased international legitimacy and the desire of leaders to enhance their self-esteem. Finnemore and Sikkink suggest the threshold of one-third of a group's membership as the point at which norms tip over into a cascade.[19] But they note that some states are more critical than others, either through exemplary effect because of their moral and political standing in the community of nations (what may be called norm swing states), such as South Africa during the presidency of Nelson Mandela; or because of their political weight arising from other considerations (in the cases of China and India, for example, by the ancient trajectory of their civilizations, their continental size, and their billion-strong populations). During the cascade, heroes are emulated, norm-conforming behaviour is praised, and norm-deviating behaviour is held up to international censure (for example, through a resolution in the UN Security Council or General Assembly) and ostracism (sanctions). Thus the European Union has been very explicit in specifying standards of behaviour that are appropriate for any state that wishes to be accepted as part of the in-group: appropriate behaviour, not just geographical location, is essential to a European identity. Before Serbia could be integrated into Europe, for example, the new democratic leadership was required to hand over defeated and disgraced former President Slobodan Milosevic to the International Criminal Tribunal for former Yugoslavia. In turn, international legitimation reinforces the domestic legitimacy of national regimes.

In the Ottawa Treaty banning landmines, *norm generation* by Western middle powers was underpinned by *norm-advocacy* from the NGOs and reinforced by *norm-promoting* standard-setting by the UN Secretary-General when he endorsed the Ottawa process as the negotiating track and the convention that resulted from it.[20] Such norm promotion was a function of his positional leadership.

Once a norm is internalized by most members of international society in the third and final stage, it becomes the prevailing standard against which state behaviour is measured and against which new norms must arise and struggle for support. Governments and civil society groups can and do appeal to prevailing international norms within the context of domestic policy debates in order to buttress their normative preferences. The efficacy of international norms in structuring domestic policy choices will depend on the domestic governmental structure (decision-making system, state-society relations) and the domestic salience of the international norm.[21]

Thus many international norms begin as domestic norms and are externalized and internationalized through the filter of domestic structures and norms by the deliberate actions of norm entrepreneurs. One of the great social movements of the twentieth century, for example, was the effort to emancipate and empower women. Its roots go back to the women's suffrage movement in Western countries. Sometimes, of course, minority adherents of a new domestic norm use international points of reference in the struggle to establish the norm domestically (and also to strengthen their position in the domestic power struggle). Much of the human rights movement in the past several decades has taken this form.

## Human rights: norm diffusion from the West to the rest

During the twentieth century there was growing isomorphism among states with respect to international human rights norms. Despite that, in the early twenty-first century there is neither a homogeneous international society with respect to human rights and humanitarian concerns, nor a unifying normative architecture. Rather, the reality of norm variation attests to the existence of a polymorphic international society.

Thus Risse argues that the human rights norm protects citizens from the state.[22] While this is true, it is truer of Western than developing countries. For in the latter case, the threat of a failed state would be a major derogation of human rights in every sense of the concept – security (freedom from fear) as well as socio-economic (freedom from want). In the words of Assistant Secretary-General Danilo Türk (himself a scholar of international law and subsequently the President of Slovenia), 'The role of the state is essential in the need to ensure respect for and . . . the realization of human rights'.[23]

After independence, the newly decolonized countries engaged simultaneously in the pursuit of state building, nation building and economic development. Sovereignty was the critical shield behind which the triple pursuit was attempted. The path dependence of their colonial history offers a clue as to why sovereignty and its correlative norm of non-intervention are more deeply internalized in the developing country elites than their counterparts in the West. Yet on the other side, fewer and fewer Westerners are impressed any longer with charges of neoimperialism by historical association. Human rights advocacy groups inside the target state can forge alliances of convenience with foreign and international counterparts. Norm-violating governments can choose to deny the validity of global norms and reject critics as agents or stooges of ignorant or ill-intentioned foreigners. But if vulnerable and subjected to sufficient pressure, they may begin to make tactical concessions in order to mollify domestic and international critics, lift aid suspensions, and so on. The discourse has shifted from denying to accepting the validity of the norm, but rejecting specific allegations of norm-violation by questioning the facts and evidence presented by critics, or else insisting that these are isolated incidents and the cases will be investigated and perpetrators will be punished, etc. By such a process of 'self-entrapment',[24] the war for human rights as a universal norm is won though many battles might remain to be fought.

The idea of universal rights is denied by some who insist that moral standards are always culture-specific. Value systems around the world are not merely diverse; often they are antagonistic. Placing the individual at the centre of social thought is a distinctively Western tradition. For many non-Western societies, the relationship between the individual and the community is conceived quite differently, with the individual being placed within and subordinate to the bonds of family and duties of community.[25] Even the social identity of the individual is not conceivable outside his or her sociocultural context. Thus rights to self-determination and national economic development are asserted on behalf of socio-political groups collectively.

The historicist variant of cultural relativism holds that moral precepts cannot be understood in the abstract but must always be located in the experience of particular historical communities. Terry Nardin notes that the hermeneutical importance of context does not lead to the conclusion that a communal worldview can be understood only from within the community, by its members and no one else: 'To understand a system of moral ideas requires neither a standpoint located wholly within that system, nor a single, indisputable standpoint that lies outside it.'[26] We are members of many different ethical communities, and overlapping communities are apt to communicate and appropriate one another's ideas. Acknowledgement of cultural diversity does not lead us down the low road to moral scepticism. Even realism asserts the limits to morality in public life, not its non-existence or total irrelevance. It's just that moral constraints can ethically be set aside for reasons of state, since the first duty of public officials is to defend and advance the interests of states.[27] But it does require us 'to discipline the use of moral language in international affairs'.[28]

The resilience of the opposition to the internationalization of the human conscience lies in the fear that the lofty rhetoric of universal human rights claims merely masks the more mundane and familiar pursuit of national interests by different means. As the 2001 UN world conference on racism at Durban showed, human rights comprise one of the most fiercely contested sectors on the terrain of ideas. The contestation reflects competing conceptions of the good life, the proper relationship between citizen and state, between historical wrongs and present rights, and between correlative rights and obligations. But also embedded in the ferocity of the contestation are power equations and unequal power relations. The voiceless in the human rights debate are the socially marginalized and politically powerless.

NGOs are great champions of global norms as passionate advocates and monitors. They are thus the carriers and transmitters of norms across borders. The international media highlights human rights atrocities selectively, the principle of selectivity extending both to target regimes (think of which Middle Eastern countries are chosen and which are ignored) and to categories of human rights. But from the point of view of developing countries, NGOs and the international media are both within the array of instruments available to Western societies to assert dominance and normative primacy in world affairs. The great transnational NGOs – Amnesty International, Greenpeace, Human Rights Watch, Doctors without Borders (MSF) – are all Western.

Too many Western analysts seem to believe that human rights is a problem only in non-Western countries:

> The diffusion of international norms in the human rights area crucially depends on the establishment and the sustainability of networks among domestic and transnational actors who manage to link up with international regimes, to alert Western [sic] public opinion and Western [sic] governments.[29]

The philosophical antecedents of such beliefs lie in the eighteenth–nineteenth century theory of evolutionary progress through diffusion and acculturation from the West to the rest. The implicit but clear assumption is that when Western and non-Western values diverge, the latter are in the wrong, and it is only a matter of working on them with persuasion and pressure for the problem to be resolved and progress achieved. The cognitive rigidity is shown again in 'Pressure by Western states and international organizations can greatly increase the vulnerability of norm-violating governments to external influences'.[30] Self-evidently, only non-Western governments can be norm-violators; Western governments can only be norm-setters and norm-enforcers.

## The rise and fall of developing countries as norm entrepreneurs

The cold war was a transcendental conflict between two fundamentally incompatible value systems committed to each other's eventual destruction; between the command and free market models of economic production and exchange; and between the United States and Soviet Union as the world's two leading powers. It ended with the comprehensive defeat of Moscow on all three counts. In consequence, to the extent that there is any one binary divide in world politics since the end of the cold war, it is between the industrialized and the developing countries. That is, the axis around which international affairs rotate has been reconfigured from East–West to North–South.[31]

The Non-aligned Movement (NAM) was successful as a norm entrepreneur with regard to decolonization, apartheid, and national liberation movements, but a failure in respect of new international economic and information orders which met their nemesis at the 1981 Cancun summit, colliding head-on with Reaganism and Thatcherism. The organizational platforms used by developing countries in establishing norm prominence for self-determination and racial equality were NAM and the United Nations, with NAM being an effective caucus in the UN forum. The organizational platforms for the unsuccessful effort to promote the norms of new international economic and information orders were the G77 and the UN.

In the 1960s–70s, the heady days of the postcolonial period, international conditions favoured narratives of grievance and claims for redress and assistance. The developing countries were the norm advocates and norm generators, via the UN General Assembly, in delegitimizing colonialism,[32] criminalizing apartheid and legitimizing armed national liberation movements. The central norm underpinning this triple assault on the international political status quo was that of self-determination from European colonial powers. The transnational anti-apartheid movement was made up of domestic, state, intergovernmental and non-governmental actors. It was formed and sustained on the members' shared advocacy of the sibling, but different, norm of racial equality. The growing numbers of people joining the movement in more and more countries led states to redefine interests, even when they had material incentives to the contrary, so that opposition to apartheid in South Africa acquired an intrinsic value in their foreign policies.[33] It was the successor to the anti-slavery movement and the precursor to the global human rights movement. India was a critical entrepreneur in the articulation and diffusion of the norms of self-determination and racial equality despite the opposition of some of the great powers.[34]

Developing countries were less successful in efforts to delegitimize the existing international economic order and replace it with a new one. Indeed with the end of the cold war and the triumph of liberal internationalism, the legacy of the new international economic order (NIEO) movement served in the 1990s to delegitimize the General Assembly and shift the political primacy to the Security Council. With the end of the cold war, NAM lost its conceptual moorings – there was nothing to be non-aligned against – and hence much of its political coherence and relevance.[35] The end of the cold war also marked the triumph of liberal internationalism in economics. In combination, they led to the loss of Third World solidarity. Developing countries abandoned, or at least modified, policies of dirigisme and embraced market friendly policies instead. Solidarity with fellow developing countries gave way to the search for US capital, credits, technology, management and markets. And the drive for market capitalism was underpinned by the norms of private property and contract sanctity. Unlike the principle of sovereignty and the norm of non-intervention, these are not territorially bounded.

Countries that lack the skills and assets to be norm entrepreneurs can still play the role of *norm brokers*. The task of brokers is to introduce entrepreneurs to client consumers and if necessary to mediate between them in efforts to strike a deal. For example, Malaysia played such a role with respect to the UN Convention on the Law of the Sea (UNCLOS). Similarly, South Africa helped to broker the deal at the NPT Review and Extension Conference in New York in 1995, which saw the NPT extended indefinitely in return for a statement of objectives and principles in which the nuclear powers reaffirmed their commitment to a nuclear test ban and disarmament negotiations.

India, an original entrepreneur of the norm of nuclear disarmament, found itself switching to the role of *norm-spoiler* with the Comprehensive Test Ban Treaty (CTBT) in 1996. The reasons for India's opposition to the CTBT need not concern us here; the stated reasons were more of an alibi than an explanation.[36] In reaction to India's spoiling efforts in the Conference on Disarmament (CD) at Geneva, Australia demonstrated *norm entrepreneurship* in bypassing the CD and transferring the stalled CTBT to the General Assembly directly, where it was endorsed with an overwhelming majority. But because the constitutional manoeuvre was viewed in New Delhi as constitutional trickery, the CTBT was condemned for having been born in sin. Because it was illegitimate in Indian eyes, it had no normative bearing on Indian behaviour. Indeed India's 1998 nuclear tests were anticipated in analyses questioning the wisdom of the 1996 move to take the CTBT from the CD in Geneva to the UN in New York.[37]

## The shifting global order

International Relations is shaped by the interplay of power and ideas. The centre of the multilateral order cannot hold if the power and influence embedded in international institutions is significantly misaligned with the distribution of power in the real world.[38] From 1000 to 1800 AD, Asia, Africa and Latin America – today's developing world – accounted for 65–75 per cent of global population and income. Europe rode to world dominance through the industrial revolution, innovations in transport and communications, and the ideology and practice of colonialism, during which the developing countries suffered dramatic relative losses. From 1870 to 1950, Asia's per capita income plummeted from one-half to one-tenth of West European levels.[39]

The demonstration of the clear limits to US and NATO power in Iraq and Afghanistan has made developing countries less fearful of 'superior' Western power. The catalogue of abusive practices in the so-called war on terror and the financial collapse of 2008–9 has made them less respectful of Western values and ideas. As power and influence seep out of the US-led transatlantic order and migrate towards Asia and elsewhere, how, and by whom, will the transition from the Westphalian to a replacement system of structuring world affairs be managed?[40] As China, India and Brazil emerge as important growth centres in the world economy, the age of the West disrespecting the rest's role, relevance and voice is passing. A much needed global moral rebalancing is in train. The importance of Brazil, China and India lies in their future economic potential, which already has translated into present political weight.[41] Westerners have lost their previous capacity to set standards and rules of behaviour for the world. Unless they recognize this reality, there is little prospect of making significant progress in deadlocked international negotiations. Not just the process but the structures and rules of the game for conducting negotiations must be agreed to jointly. This includes the rise and consolidation of new norms of international behaviour by sovereign states.

# 2  Non-intervention in international relations

## A case study[1]

The subject of international intervention tends to be discussed either in the abstract, or else in respect of particular interventions that have occurred, such as the Soviet Union's in Hungary (1956), Czechoslovakia (1968) and Afghanistan (1979–89); India's in Bangladesh (1971); Vietnam's in Cambodia (1978–89); the United States in Grenada (1983). It may be helpful to take an alternative approach. As was the case with Sherlock Holmes' interest in the dogs that did not bark, aspects of the problem of intervention in international politics may be illuminated by an examination of a case where there was no intervention. In this chapter, I intend to do this with regard to the crisis stemming from the military overthrow of legally elected government in Fiji in 1987. Two questions will be explored. First, would intervention have been justified, or even, was non-intervention justified? Second, who should or could have intervened? Between them, the two questions might also direct our attention to the issue of pinning responsibility on some actor for breakdowns of regional order.

The background to the coup lay in the formation of the Fiji Labour Party in 1985 in an effort to break the mould of racial politics that had characterized the country's affairs since independence in 1970. The composition of Parliament was racially fixed, with twenty-two Fijians, twenty-two Indians, and eight Europeans and other races. The Labour Party fought the elections of April 1987 in coalition with the Indian-dominated National Federation Party on a cross-racial platform, promising economic justice and a clean and caring administration: slogans that were particularly appealing to the disproportionate number of ethnic Fijians in the ranks of the poor. Narrow victories in four urban constituencies, where Fijians deserted the ruling Alliance Party, gave the coalition a 28:24 majority in Parliament. Of the twenty-eight coalition members, nineteen were Indian, seven Fijian, and two part-European. Sensitive to racial undercurrents, Labour Prime Minister Dr Timoci Bavadra chose seven Indians, six Fijians, and one part-European in his cabinet. Key Fijian affairs portfolios were allocated to Fijians. The new government had not been in office for a month when third-ranking army officer Lt. Col. Sitiveni Rabuka overthrew it at gunpoint in Parliament itself on 14 May 1987. When negotiations threatened to negate the professed aims of the coup, Rabuka staged another coup in September 1987.

In explaining his motives, Rabuka claimed divine guidance in a mission to save indigenous Fijians from domination by an immigrant group of aliens. Yet not only had Bavadra not given any indication of doing anything to damage Fijian interests, in fact such interests were safeguarded by cast-iron constitutional guarantees. Furthermore, Indians were still in a minority in Parliament. The call to racial arms was not a cause of the coup, but a political strategy of mobilizing support from all Fijians, drawing upon the brotherhood of fellow-Melanesians in the region, and confusing the liberal conscience of those Westerners who suffer from a guilt complex regarding the plight of Maoris, Aborigines, North American Indians, and other pre-Western contact societies marginalized by settler colonies.

The most persuasive explanation of the coup is that it was a refusal by the ruling elite to countenance a loss of power: 'Race was used as a vehicle to return to power a group of people for whom power had become an unbreakable habit.'[2] There were considerable overlapping party, tribal, regional, feudal and family connections between coup leader Rabuka, Alliance's Ratu Sir Kamisese Mara, and Governor-General Sir Penaia Ganilau. There were allegations of financial irregularities by the defeated Alliance government. And there were Fijians in the bureaucracy who backed the coup out of career frustrations.

Suspicions of a ruling elite trying to protect its privileged position were reinforced on 15 September 1988 when cabinet approved a single-house Parliament of seventy-one members, of whom only twenty-two would be Indians. The Fijian Great Council of Chiefs and the eastern islands would have disproportionate weight in choosing Fijian representatives. Christianity would receive special recognition in the proposed new constitution. The role of the military in the politics of Fiji would be formalized, institutionalized and made permanent. The overthrown coalition government condemned the draft constitution as undemocratic, racist and feudal.[3]

## Legitimizing principles of intervention

Five developments are said to have militated against intervention in the post-1945 period: the growth of will and capacity in former colonies to resist intervention; the erosion of the Western will to intervene, post-Indochina and Algeria for France, post-Suez for France and Britain, post-Vietnam for the United States; the enhanced power of the Soviet Union; a general balance of power that works in favour of the targets of intervention against interveners; and a new climate of international legitimacy unfavourable to intervention in general, and to Western intervention in particular.[4] These developments notwithstanding, in practice, the legitimacy of intervention turns upon answers to questions about the four main elements involved in an act of intervention: actor, act, target and purpose. That is, who or what is the subject or intervening *agent*; what is the mode or *form* of intervention; who or what is the putative *object* of intervention, and what degree of legitimacy attaches to the target; and what is the motive for or *goal* of intervention.

Eleven different legitimizing principles of intervention have been offered in recent times:

1  The USSR argued in regard to Czechoslovakia in 1968 that relations within the socialist community could not be the subject of a legal order reflecting capitalist class relations, and that fraternal assistance to a fellow-socialist regime was not intervention. Mikhail Gorbachev's Soviet Union has repudiated this so-called Brezhnev doctrine.

2  Chinese and Soviet assistance to North Vietnam was defended on the argument that counter-intervention, that is intervention to help the victim of original intervention, is not proscribed by international law.

3  Several countries (Israel, the United States in Indochina, South Africa) have sought to justify short military incursions into land territories by invoking the principle of hot pursuit, which was developed in relation to the high seas, that is areas where no sovereign exercises jurisdiction.

4  Israel has also justified military action on the grounds of pre-emptive self-defence, as in June 1967. The same justification was adduced for the strikes on Iraqi nuclear facilities in 1981, and Israel reportedly offered help to India to conduct comparable raids on Pakistan's nuclear installations.[5]

5  Israel has felt no compunction against punitive raids in retaliation for guerrilla/terrorist attacks on it. It has also expanded the right to self-defence to include the right to take military action inside the borders of its neighbours who are incapable of preventing their territories from being used as launching pads for attacks on Israel, for example Lebanon (1978, 1982). The United States used similar justification for its raids on Libya in 1986.

6  In the case of Afghanistan in 1979, Moscow fell back on the argument used by Washington to justify its military presence in South Vietnam in the 1960s: namely, that it was a permissible response to an invitation of the legitimate government. The United States and the Organization of Eastern Caribbean States engaged in the Grenada intervention too claimed that their action was validated by the prior invitation of the Governor-General Sir Paul Scoon.

7  Israel has asserted that the right to self-defence includes the right to take military action anywhere in the world to secure the release of its citizens unlawfully held as hostages, for example the raid on Entebbe airport in 1976. The US explicitly justified its invasion of Grenada in 1983 with reference to securing the safety of its nationals.[6]

8  Since the Second World War, humanitarian concern has frequently been claimed to justify intervention. In the 1970s, India sent troops into Bangladesh in order to protect Bengali–Pakistanis from the oppressive rule of a military dictatorship in West Pakistan; Vietnam sent its troops into Cambodia to get rid of Pol Pot; Tanzania intervened to overthrow Idi Amin in Uganda.[7]

9  Given the importance of self-determination in the contemporary normative order, this principle can be used to justify intervention.

10  The subject of intervention in a civil war, extensively debated during the Vietnam war,[8] is a particularly vexed question.

11  The most immediately acceptable justification for intervention is the collectivist principle; that is, not *why* intervention was undertaken, but *who* took the decision to intervene. Since 1945, the most widely accepted legitimator of international action has been the United Nations, for example in the Korean war, in setting up various peacekeeping forces, in calls for ceasefire, in efforts to end racial discrimination, etc. The intervening organization can also be a regional body.

In other words, while intervention must overcome the presumption of illegitimacy, very few analysts or statesmen would elevate non-intervention to an absolute rule. Modern international society is built around the organizing principle of sovereign statehood. The sovereign equality of states has received its most emphatic affirmation in the modern era of decolonization by the newly independent states in understandable reaction to the age of colonialism. Because the colonial masters were Europeans, the opprobrium extends more easily to perceptions of so-called neocolonial intervention by Europeans than non-Europeans. Yet, paradoxically, the doctrines of sovereign equality and non-interference are distinctively European in origin.[9]

The newer states of the decolonization era are not conservative statists in every respect. In some important areas they are radical revisionists, calling for major restructuring of international political and economic relations in order to achieve a more equitable redistribution of resources and influence. The potentially serious destabilizing consequences of such an 'intruder' role comes from the fact that the revisionist challengers, for the first time in international history, outnumber the entrenched defenders of the status quo.[10] Yet the same countries exert powerful pressures in the opposite direction as states with a vested interest in preserving the normative international order that legitimizes their autonomy. Indeed the lack of 'unconditional legitimacy' for the state-structures and regimes of several of the newer states means that they have a relatively greater stake in international order than the established states. The ambivalent role of the newer states in international relations is thus a result, not of hypocrisy, but of the tension between competing pulls of justice at the level of a marginalized collectivity, and order at the level of individual states preoccupied with stability.

## By invitation

Of the eleven principles that can justify intervention, the first five are not relevant to Fiji, and will form no further part of this discussion. We begin therefore with the sixth. In a speech to the Royal Commonwealth Society in London on 9 December 1983, Prime Minister Tom Adams of Barbados explained that government itself having been destroyed in Grenada, the Governor-General became the constitutional authority in the island. His 'opinion and approval' had been obtained and arrangements made for him to issue a formal invitation to intervene as soon as it was politically safe to do so.[11] Australia, New Zealand and the United Kingdom took a remarkably similar line regarding the Governor-General of Fiji. This begs the question of whether intervention in Fiji would have been justified if Ganilau had requested it. If yes, then the right of the legally elected but illegally overthrown head of government to request external intervention must be even greater. Otherwise we end up with the absurd doctrinal situation that the Governor-General – a nominee of the previous government, related by marriage of children to the defeated Prime Minister, a former Deputy Prime Minister himself, confronting a coup led by a godson – could have legitimately called for external troops to suppress disorder being organized by the overthrown government.

Consent of an existing government can be said to excuse intervention if the government in question is held to represent the free choice of the people.[12] On this criterion, the Bavadra government was the only actor in Fiji entitled to request external intervention for protection/restoration against internal enemies. Spokesmen for the ousted Bavadra government did on occasion urge the introduction of an external peacekeeping force, but were politely ignored. The situation is simplified if a government unmistakably *lacks* popular consent, as was the case with post-coup Fiji in 1987. Elections had been held as recently as a month before the coup, and the government freely chosen by the people was overthrown by force. Whatever else it could rest its claim to autonomy on, Colonel Rabuka's regime could not rest it on a metaphorical social contract. Having explicitly denied the citizens of the state of Fiji their liberty to associate, his regime could not be protected from external interference on the reasoning that it was representative of Fijians exercising their freedom of association. Consequently, external intervention in Fiji could not be delegitimized for exercising coercion on a people. Indeed the latter conclusion would itself need to be established upon empirical, possibly *ex post facto*, investigation as well.

In short, a prescription of absolute state autonomy that rests on the consent theory of the state involves a paradox: how can external intervention be deemed illegitimate if its purpose is to remove a regime that violates the principle of government by consent? Beitz argues that the principle of non-intervention is a derivative of more basic principles of justice: particular cases of potential intervention might involve moral or prudential considerations other than state autonomy. In his view, 'only states whose institutions satisfy appropriate principles of justice can legitimately demand to be respected as autonomous sources of ends'.[13] Applying this to Fiji in 1987, it seems reasonable to conclude that the overthrown Bavadra government did satisfy appropriate principles of justice; Rabuka's military regime did not.

Can the argument be extended to justify intervention when a state is unjust in terms of appropriate principles, and intervention helps to promote the development or re-establishment of those principles? That is, could outside intervention to restore Bavadra's legitimately elected government be defended on this principle? 'The recent history of international relations appears to teach nothing so eloquently as the folly of intervention in the cause of justice.'[14]

Indeed. But . . . first, because recent examples of interventionary expeditions have been flawed, it does not follow that all interventions against unjust states must always be wrong. The principal objection to injustice-remedying intervention is not logical but practical. But even a consequentialist ethic of non-intervention is double-edged. In Fiji, the consequence of non-interference was (1) at the practical level, there was political instability, racial tension and economic damage; and (2) at the theoretical level, time was bought to legitimize the forcible overthrow of the elected government in putative defence of indigenous rights. Prospects for the Fijian economy had looked promising in 1986. The economic situation in the aftermath of the coup-associated upheavals was such that a major study concluded that 'by the end of 1988 Fiji will have lost all the economic gains made since independence. Real per capita income would be back to the 1970 level'.[15] Yet skilled professionals, the very people that Fiji most desperately needed in order to repair the ravages, were leaving in great numbers. Like the story about the person who killed his parents and then sought clemency from the courts for being an orphan, the Fijian government appealed to the UN Development Programme to alleviate the shortages of skilled personnel, and about thirty volunteer doctors had been recruited from China and Thailand by the end of 1988. The racial and security atmosphere remains brittle. Organized political activities have ceased. Instead, there is sullen resentment among the Indians and emerging factional and clan rivalries among Fijian chiefs whose word is law in the village-based society.

What if a nominal executive himself launches a constitutional coup, as happened in Vanuatu in 1988? After a power struggle within the government between Prime Minister Father Walter Lini and cabinet minister Barak Sope, the latter's uncle, President Ati George Sokomanu, in a remarkable political echo of the Fijian Governor-General in May 1987, attempted in 1988 to dissolve Parliament and set up an interim administration. For his troubles, he was arrested, dismissed and on 7 March 1989 imprisoned for six years. The conviction was, however, overturned on 14 April 1989 by the Court of Appeal. In this instance, Australia and New Zealand supported the legitimate government against the challenge of its head of state. Being required to pick winners in power struggles, regardless of the means employed, is not going to be the most satisfactory basis of formulating foreign policy.

### For protecting nationals living abroad

Although the 1945 UN Charter may proscribe the right to use force to protect nationals abroad, in the last century European countries and the United States intervened to protect their nationals living in foreign countries.[16] This was also the putative justification for the US intervention in Grenada. In Fiji in 1987, Australia and New Zealand were prepared to intervene to evacuate endangered nationals. Yet even Australia – officially described as 'the major power in the

South Pacific region'[17] – experienced logistical difficulties in preparing for a possible evacuation of citizens from Fiji. A parliamentary sub-committee report in 1989 expressed disbelief that the difficulties were as minor as had been claimed by the military.[18] New Zealand's armed forces are only one-sixth the size of Australia's.

Since 1945, alongside the creation of a large number of sovereign states, there has also occurred an assertion of ethnic and other sectarian identities. Indeed, Rabuka justified his coup along the lines of protecting ethnic rights. There does not seem to be much discussion of whether the doctrine of protection of nationals can be extended to cover ethnic groups. If a communal group is the object of human rights abuses, then does another state where the same group is in power have the right to be concerned and to intervene if necessary after a critical threshold has been crossed? Few in the West would be comfortable with a norm that compelled Israel to watch helplessly as Jews, say, were massacred yet again in another country. To demand such abstinence is to erode the legitimacy of an international system built upon such intra-national abuse-sanctioning and international help-preventing principles.[19] If the norms of an international system are themselves illegitimate, they cannot possibly serve and survive as behaviour-regulating instruments. For international society to be preserved, states must accept internal obligations corresponding to external rights vis-à-vis other members of that society.

### Humanitarian intervention

It is easy to be cynical about the lip service to human rights by governments that prove ever more ingenious in devising new forms of abuses. But this ought not to be the case. Increasing lip service is testimony enough to the power of the ideology of human rights even in an age of cynicism: hypocrisy is the sincerest tribute to idealism.

While self-determination is an agreed principle of contemporary international order, self-government understood as democracy is not. But intervention on humanitarian grounds – to protect basic political, social, economic and human rights – transcends state sovereignty, for an external actor is intervening to constrict the scope of the sovereign's power internally in relation to its own citizens. In the area of human rights, the exertion of pressure and the application of certain sanctions and coercion is not uncommon today, even though in earlier eras it would have constituted intervention in domestic affairs. Human rights have been transformed from being a matter solely of domestic concern into a matter of legitimate international concern, even though 'a surprising number of Western politicians seem to share the Soviet view that mere verbal concern is tantamount to intervention'.[20]

Twentieth-century developments have generated tension with nineteenth-century practice.[21] Previously, states were not proscribed from ill-treating their own citizens, but outsiders claimed the right to use force to prevent them from doing so. Today's norms restrict the rights of states both to violate citizens' rights arbitrarily and to use force abroad unilaterally. In case of conflict, therefore, should human rights violations justifying external intervention prevail over the doctrine of non-intervention? Akehurst's survey of state practice in Asia and Africa since 1945 leads him to conclude that the doctrine of humanitarian intervention has been invoked but seldom by interveners, and its validity never conceded by the international community. Yet the activities of such transnational organizations as Amnesty International have produced a growing conviction that human rights do have a place in international relations, and this conviction in turn has been deeply corrosive of the inviolate rule of non-intervention. For the record, it is worth recalling that the principle that states alone have rights in international law – which lies at the heart of non-intervention even amidst systematic and extensive abuses of human rights – is a curiously old-fashioned, *European*, belief.

The 'epochal shift in moral law that would ultimately find expression in law'[22] has transformed individuals from objects into subjects, similar to even if not co-equal with states. International concern with human rights prior to the Second World War dwelt on the laws of warfare, slavery, and protection of minorities. The experience of Fascism-Nazism both strengthened the concern and enlarged its scope. In the twentieth century, states have bound themselves, through formal agreements and declarations that form a source of customary law, to refrain from torturing or summarily executing their citizens, from imprisoning citizens without due process of law, from discriminating between citizens on the basis of race, religion or gender. The UN Charter requires member states to cooperate in promoting respect for human rights and fundamental freedoms for all without distinction as to race, sex, language and religion (Articles 1 and 55). The Universal Declaration of Human Rights was adopted by the General Assembly on 10 December 1948, with the aim of providing 'a common standard for achievement for all peoples and all nations'. As the UN itself puts it:

> The Declaration was originally conceived of as a statement of objectives to be achieved by Governments and as such, not part of binding international law. But now, 40 years later, it is accepted by so many States that it is considered to be an international standard against which their behaviour is measured.[23]

The 1966 International Covenants, on Civil and Political Rights, and on Economic, Social and Cultural Rights, came into force in 1976. By 1988 more than half the UN membership had become parties to the two covenants. The 1948 Declaration is the central normative instrument of the international human rights regime; the 1966 Covenants add force and specificity; and collectively they comprise the International Bill of Rights.[24] In addition, the UN has also adopted some fifty other legal instruments on human rights, including declarations and conventions on genocide, torture, racial discrimination and discrimination against women.

Nevertheless, the UN system, which at inception 'seemed destined to be the engine of human rights',[25] has in fact produced little more than a whimper. The organization has been less successful in humanitarian assistance and more successful in promotional and standard-setting activities that affirm, define and clarify the rights of individuals even in the absence of international machinery to enforce them. In the field of peace and security, the legitimizing function of the UN has increased in importance as and because its collective enforcement powers have sunk into desuetude. In the field of human rights, similarly, the norm-generating function of the UN has increased in importance for the lack of power to punish persistent state offenders.

One survey of UN efforts in the realm of human rights identified a threefold evolution from norm-drafting (1945–54) and undifferentiated information dissemination (1954–67), to partial activism since 1967. In the early stages, timidity on the part of member states was matched by self-denying competence on the part of the UN Human Rights Commission, reflecting a 'fierce commitment to inoffensiveness'.[26] By the 1980s, however, 'there was a fragile but persistent movement toward improved supervision of states' policies on human rights'.[27] The Economic and Social Council (ECOSOC) adopted a resolution in 1967 authorizing its sub-organs to scrutinise a pattern of gross violation of human rights; a 1970 resolution authorized sub-organs to examine private communications from individuals and NGOs alleging human rights violations. As a consequence, the UN Human Rights Commission 'has become the world's first intergovernmental body that regularly challenges sovereign nations to explain abusive treatment of their own citizens'.[28]

But Akehurst's survey can also indicate to disinterested readers that the doctrine of non-intervention is a convenient peg on which to hang the vested interests of self-preservation and perpetuation of particularly odious regimes (Idi Amin in Uganda, Pol Pot in Cambodia). The issue of human rights is necessarily politicized and therefore inevitably controversial, touching as it does 'on the very foundations of a regime, on its sources and exercise of power, on its links to its citizens or subjects'.[29] The tension between the intervention-prescribing principle of human rights and the intervention-proscribing principle of sovereignty is contained in the UN Charter itself. Articles 55–6 oblige member states to take joint and separate action in cooperation with the UN to facilitate the achievement of universal human rights around the world; Article 2(7) contains an express prohibition of interference in the domestic affairs of any state.

The difficulty with humanitarian intervention is that the real world is characterized by moral ambiguity. Intervention may be self-serving from the start, or begin as humanitarian but be transformed into self-aggrandizement. The United States may have intervened in Grenada to protect the lives of US citizens; not everyone failed to see the removal of a radical-left regime that resulted from the action. Vietnam may have had cause to lift the shroud of Pol Potism from the Cambodian body politic; its intervention ended as the imposition of Vietnamese rule. India may have intervened to halt the massacre of Bengalis by Pakistani troops; the intervention caused the dismemberment of its major enemy. In the history of post-1947 US foreign policy, any divorce between cold war calculations and disinterested promotion of human rights seems coincidental: even a convinced champion of human rights such as Jimmy Carter could eulogise the record of Ferdinand Marcos on the subject.

Fortunately, the situation in Fiji did not deteriorate to the point where humanitarian intervention was seriously considered. But if race relations were to worsen and degenerate into massacres of Indians – Fijians control the police and virtually monopolize the military – then humanitarian intervention could be put on the agenda.

### In support of self-determination

A state is not conceded absolutely unqualified sovereignty today *qua* state. South Africa and the People's Republic of Kampuchea satisfy the criteria of effective government, people and territory that would entitle them to full-fledged membership of the international community as sovereign states, yet are denied that status. Instead, the constitutive principle of modern international society is the principle of self-determination. Democratic government ranks as the primary principle of governmental legitimacy, so that even regimes which reject democracy in practice seek to emulate it in rhetoric or pretend to defer it until the 'right' conditions obtain for its introduction. Derivatively, this seems to legitimize intervention in support of self-determination, as recognized by the non-aligned movement in justifying assistance to armed national liberation movements that seek to overthrow racist regimes. At the same time, the movement has consistently expressed strong opposition to intervention in the internal affairs of its member states.[30] Once again, therefore, there is a tension between justice and order.

A homogeneous international system can be distinguished from a heterogeneous one according to whether the constitutive units have the same or different principles of legitimacy.[31] A political order is endangered when there are competing principles of internal legitimacy. This is precisely what happened in Fiji, with a clash between ethnic/indigenous rights and race-blind democratic rule. In a heterogeneous international system, imposition of one's preferred ideology upon others is rejected as sufficient justification to intervene in the affairs of sovereign states. Today's international consensus rejects a justification of intervention 'which proceeds from the conviction that a particular nation or people is endowed by God or history with a role or mission that entitles it to impose its will on others for their own betterment'.[32] The interesting thing about Fiji in 1987 was that Colonel Rabuka used remarkably similar justification to overthrow the elected government. If the principle is unacceptable as a defence of international intervention, is it nevertheless permissible in defence of internal military intervention?

The Melanesian island countries of the South Pacific seemed to bristle at the merest suggestion of an Australian–New Zealand led campaign to resist the Rabuka coup. What to Australians and New Zealanders would have been an effort to restore political and civil rights within universally shared values was likely to be rejected and resisted as an ideological assault by the advanced European peoples in the Pacific. Yet if the existing international order is delegitimized, then the weaker members of the international community have the most to lose if the normative proscription on intervention is abandoned. It is therefore in their self-interest to help preserve the existing order with its core organizing principle of sovereign statehood based on self-determination. But this means that they must be prepared to identify and act against violations of the self-determination principle, or else suffer an erosion of credibility and legitimacy. Unfortunately, it does seem to be the case that 'attempts to preserve the *status quo*, even if accompanied by measures of the utmost brutality, appear to be viewed with greater tolerance by the opposite camp than forcible efforts towards a change'.[33]

The coup can be interpreted as a rejection of liberalism for another, deeper reason. I have argued that the coup was a reactionary revolt by the entrenched traditional elite against loss of office. Liberal democracy is a powerful tool in the hands of individuals and groups engaged in the struggle to move from an ascriptive to an achievementalistic society. Ethnic Fijians of professional education and occupation in general favoured the Fiji Labour Party over the old race-based Alliance Party, and were prepared to challenge the traditional power and authority of hereditary chiefs.

Liberals face yet another dilemma. Liberalism is predicated on a tolerance of diversity, and so favours peaceful coexistence among different political systems. It also sees violence and war, which would be the predictable results of intervention, as the gravest threats to international order; and international order is the condition of liberty. On the other hand, liberalism is also universalistic, being predicated on the belief that certain values transcend the confines of space and time. Human rights and some other ethical values are not bound by territorial jurisdictions: they belong to all men and women in all situations as individuals. Liberalism therefore contains the seeds of a theory of the just intervention.

In addition to the dangers of a widened war, there is a second pragmatic objection to intervention aimed at facilitating self-determination. The international community is not agreed, and is not likely to be agreed in the foreseeable future, on the appropriate unit of self-determination. The practical difficulties are sufficient to convince one analyst that 'the need for prudence overwhelms . . . the moral argument for intervention'.[34] Liberal sentiments contain the seeds of a tension also between supporting minority rights and indigenous rights if the two should come into conflict, as indeed they did in Fiji.[35] Indeed, the principle of national self-determination, which has received near-universal legitimation by now, would make it difficult to reject calls for secession by Indians and Fijians in western Fiji.

## Intervention in Civil War

The Charter of the United Nations draws an untenably sharp distinction between domestic and external affairs, and consequently fails to address the type of intervention that has been the most common since the Second World War, namely intervention on behalf of parties engaged in a civil war. President Woodrow Wilson had urged a policy of national self-determination after the First World War in the belief that different nations could not live together in one state. Ethnicity remains a neglected dimension of international conflict.[36] The theory of the plural society, most commonly associated with the economist J. S. Furnival, postulates difficulties for separate communities co-existing within one political unit. In a plural society, rules of international morality apply, and the society will disintegrate unless an external force (that is, a colonial power) counteracts the absence of social cohesion. The theory of the plural society was further developed by the anthropologist M. G. Smith.[37] While acknowledging the consociational possibility of diverse collectivities holding equivalent or complementary rights and status in the public domain, Smith argued that either this would lead to assimilative union or the dominant group would try to alter the distribution of power and influence to its segmental advantage. In other words, if different peoples come into contact within one political unit, then violent conflict is the route to political change.[38]

The evolution of Fiji as a plural society has its origins in British colonial policy. Britain, having acquired Fiji as a colony in 1874, undertook contradictory policies of protecting the Fijian way of life while importing indentured labour from India to work the lucrative sugar plantations. In 1987, Indians outnumbered Fijians 48.6:42.4 per cent.[39] Electoral arrangements of independent Fiji institutionalized the racial divide; the politics of race was reinforced by social, economic and military differences that bred mutually reinforcing but antagonistic stereotypes. Rabuka and his cohorts attracted considerable sympathy for the argument that an Indian-dominated government did violence to the notion of a Fijian nation-state. If in fact Indians were to be conceded political parity, he argued, then the state of Fiji would necessarily cease to be a Fijian nation. This is why ethnic Indians could not be admitted to equality with ethnic Fijians.

The legitimate government of a country can be regarded as entitled to ask for outside help. Vanuatu received such help from Papua New Guinea (PNG) at its very independence in 1980, and more recently from Australia in 1988 in combating threats from disaffected dissidents within the ruling party. The 1980 events helped to generate a sense of Melanesian identity that has flowered into the so-called Melanesian Spearhead Group (PNG, the Solomon Islands and Vanuatu) within the South Pacific Forum. The group, generally more radical and anti-nuclear than the Polynesians, and sympathetic to the coup in Fiji rather than to arguments about its destabilizing potential, formalized its relationship in a Joint Declaration of Principles in 1988.

The policy implications of this for Indians in Fiji are not very stability-enhancing. Seemingly the most acceptable route to receiving external assistance would be for the Indians to start a full-scale civil war in Fiji. In rejecting violence, Bavadra may have paid the price of being too gentlemanly.

### Collective intervention

A feature unique to the post-1945 era has been the agreement by almost all the states of the international system on a single set of principles of international life as expressed in the UN Charter. The role of the United Nations as an international actor in its own right has perhaps been less salient than its role as a systemic modifier of state behaviour.[40] One of the major instruments for modifying the external behaviour of member states has been the codification of emergent and nascent norms to reflect the changing international system. In Resolution 2131 of 21 December 1965, the General Assembly pronounced on the Inadmissibility of Intervention in the Domestic Affairs of States and the Protection of their Independence and Sovereignty. Yet the competence of individual states and the international community to involve themselves in human rights within the jurisdiction of other states remains one of the most keenly contested themes at the United Nations.

While the rules of sovereignty, equality and non-interference may have originated in Europe, the belief that the three-pronged protection of national frontiers was inimical to the progressive development of international organization has its strongest impulse in Europe as well. The contradiction of the illegitimacy of intervention and the legitimacy of self-help can be resolved by reference to collective intervention. Unilateral intervention, being manifestly self-interested, is illegitimate, whereas collective intervention occurs after authorization by an international body having widespread legitimacy.[41] Governments are seldom impartial and never act contrary to perceptions of self-interest. Unilateral intervention is usually aimed at changing the political balance in the target country in the intervening country's favour; collective intervention is informed by community purposes. Only representative regional or universal international organizations can be regarded as the actual or potential embodiment of a wider international interest. Intervention authorized by such regional or universal organizations might conceivably escape the taint of partiality.

It helps too to distinguish collective from multilateral intervention. Collective intervention designates intervention by a non-discriminatory, regionally or internationally representative organization with a virtually universal membership within its defining boundaries. Organizations with such a comprehensive regional or international membership have not displayed a notable zeal for intervening in the affairs of member states. An inhibiting consideration always is the fear that the tiger of intervention, once let loose, may turn on the rider: today's intervener could become the object of tomorrow's intervention. The numerical majority of any collective organization, almost by definition, will be the smaller states, suspicious of the motives of the most powerful in their midst and reluctant to sanction interference by the powerful against fellow weaklings.

However, there is another consideration. If collective organizations will not authorize collective intervention against regimes that flout the most elementary norms of legitimate governmental behaviour, then pressures will intensify for unilateral intervention. Yet even in the case of an intervention that few have had the heart to condemn – for example, the Tanzanian intervention to remove Idi Amin from Uganda – the Organization of African Unity (OAU) as the appropriate regional, or the UN as the general international organization, failed to give collective sanction. Tanzania acted alone – on the principle of self-help – because collective organizations were divided on the issue. That is, an important means of keeping self-interested unilateral intervention in check may be to utilize the instrument of collective intervention when warranted.

The United Nations system in practice has emphasized abortion to the neglect of prophylaxis in its primary role of maintaining international peace and security. In 1988, a Special Committee on the Strengthening of the Role of the Organization approved a draft Declaration on the prevention and removal of disputes and situations likely to threaten international peace and security.[42] If the United Nations is serious about reversing its fierce commitment to inaction in its prophylactic role, then it will need to acknowledge and act upon the reality that injustice arouses resentment, which in turn breeds instability. The UN has also seen its credibility diminished in Western nations in recent times because of perceptions of bias in its human rights coverage, with its protestations being seen as anti-Western, anti-democratic and pro-Soviet.[43] The UN system has devoted disproportionate attention to racial discrimination to the neglect of other human rights, and to the pariah regimes of Chile, Israel and South Africa to the neglect of other regimes also deserving international condemnation.[44]

Human rights activities of international organizations can be divided into three categories. The UN has been impartial and remarkably successful in a standard-setting role; guilty of bias and only selectively (in regard both to rights and regimes) successful in monitoring human rights abuses; and feeble and ineffectual in enforcement. The fact that the UN lacks effective enforcement power means that its standard-setting role depends entirely upon the authority of the organization as the conscience of humanity; the authority of the UN is in part a function of its legitimacy; perceptions of bias in human rights monitoring have served to erode the credibility of UN-sourced human rights promotional activities in general: 'Politics controls; equity suffers.'[45] The contrast with Amnesty International, a non-governmental organization (NGO), is instructive. Amnesty International reports carry a ring of authority because the organization – not being a voluntary association of governments – has not been wilfully myopic in the UN mould in investigating and judging human rights abuses around the world without discrimination on grounds of race, religion or ideological belief.[46] Thus where the UN has feared to tread into racial sensitivities in Fiji, Amnesty International's annual report detailed human rights violations by post-coup regimes in Fiji.[47]

Because the authority of the UN derives from legitimacy rather than power, it is important that its actions be seen to be impartial. Unbiased UN pronouncements can strike a responsive chord in powerful segments within a society that is the subject of critical international scrutiny. World opinion is more likely to exercise some influence, however weak and uneven, by this means more than through direct impact on national governments. That is, domestic political repercussions of the power of international embarrassment should not be underestimated. But in general, standard-setting priorities mean that UN influence is likely to be long-term, and therefore not particularly efficacious in protecting individuals against human rights abuses.[48]

Regional organizations are confined largely to managing conflicts in which there is a challenge to a consensual norm.[49] The South Pacific Forum was set up in 1971 as the symbol and instrument of regional decision-making in Oceania. With a membership of fifteen,[50] it meets annually in private session, although a *communiqué* is issued at the conclusion as the public record of the main items of discussion. From the start the Forum has functioned without a written constitution or formal agreement relating to its purpose, membership or conduct of meetings. Decisions are arrived at by consensus, a formal vote not having been regarded as either necessary or desirable. When it met in Apia in the last week of May 1987, there were no official delegates from Fiji's military regime; two ministers from the deposed Bavadra government were refused even observer status. Open debate over the coup was considered a potential threat to Forum harmony and so avoided, and the sensitivity of the crisis was evident in the fact that it was omitted from the draft agenda for the Forum meeting. A subsequent *communiqué* expressed 'deep concern and anguish' at the events in Fiji, and offered the assistance of a regional eminent persons' group, comprising the prime ministers of Australia and the Solomon Islands and the Director of the South Pacific Bureau for Economic Cooperation (SPEC), to help the Governor-General resolve the crisis. The offer was not taken up. The 1988 Forum *communiqué* was conspicuously silent on Fiji. Yet the coup in Fiji significantly expanded potential sources of instability in the region; diminished regional self-confidence and unity and hence also the region's influence in world forums; and retarded prospects for the region's economic development because of setbacks to the Fijian economy.

During a visit to New Zealand in 1988, Bavadra said that the region cannot continue to avoid an unavoidable problem, but must face up to it. The way that the South Pacific Forum has run away from the problem of the overthrow of the legitimate government of a member country, he said, was a shameful abdication of regional responsibility.[51] Regional organizations, like their universal counterparts, are standing diplomatic conferences propelled into action by common, converging and conflicting interests of member governments. With regard to the crisis in Fiji in 1987, such pragmatic calculations would seem to suggest that Australia and New Zealand would have constituted a subordinate coalition (possibly of two) in the South Pacific Forum in asserting that the coup violated consensual norms of regional politics. The post-coup regime of Fiji was more likely to be successful in mobilizing a dormant dominant coalition to the point of view that ancestral rights of indigenous ethnic groups needed protection against encroachment and usurpation by immigrant settlers. On this issue, there is an obvious and fundamental cleavage between Australia and New Zealand, on the one hand, and the Forum Island Countries (FIC), on the other.

One possibility would be for the Forum to initiate studies on drafting and adopting a South Pacific Charter on Human Rights as a regional response to international norms. It could in time establish a supranational Court and Commission on Human Rights for the whole region, modelled perhaps on the European precedents. To the extent that this would offer protection for the rights of Aborigines and Maoris in Australia–New Zealand against potentially racist regimes in power in these countries, perhaps the FICs could be more easily persuaded of the merits of the proposal. It is interesting that at the UN, Third World states have formed diplomatic coalitions with the West to make possible some international movement on human rights protection.[52] States that are suspect in their internal legitimacy are particularly vulnerable to the denial of regional and international legitimacy. Supranational censure of human rights violations, with the added threat of further UN exposure if the violations persist, could prove especially effective in the case of the transparent microstates of the South Pacific.

The Fiji-centred ripples soon spread to the Commonwealth of Nations. In the immediate aftermath of the May coup, India's Prime Minister Rajiv Gandhi had sent emissaries to Britain, Australia and New Zealand to explore the prospects of imposing collective sanctions against the military regime. The search proved fruitless. At the Vancouver Commonwealth Heads of Government meeting in October, however, Gandhi, strongly supported by Canadian Prime Minister Brian Mulroney, insisted that the Commonwealth could not condone the Rabuka regime. By becoming a republic on 1 October 1987, Fiji automatically lost its Commonwealth membership. The Vancouver meeting issued a statement on Fiji in which Commonwealth leaders 'viewed with sadness the developments in Fiji and hoped for a resolution of the problem by the people of Fiji on a basis consistent with the principles that have guided the Commonwealth'.[53]

In the final analysis, the Commonwealth's response was to sustain the failure of collective action. The Vancouver meeting 'fudged' the issue by failing to dispense a sharp and unequivocal warning to Fiji that readmission would be contingent upon a racially balanced constitution emerging for the republic. The result was that the organization not only lost a member; it also suffered a loss of credibility and influence. According to a former New Zealand diplomat, Fiji administrator and Commonwealth official, Fiji showed 'a fatal flaw in the fine phrases about Commonwealth principles, influence and action'.[54]

The sanction of non-recognition can also be regarded as a form of collective intervention.[55] In the 1980s, the UN General Assembly adopted, by overwhelming votes, resolutions calling for the withdrawal of Vietnamese troops from Cambodia and Soviet troops from Afghanistan. The question of diplomatic relations is in normal circumstances solely a concern of individual states and a function of their individual policies of recognition. But when the same policy is channelled through an international organization, the instrument of recognition is transformed into a weapon of collective non-recognition and is intended to exert pressure on particular regimes for the attainment of goals that the wider community regards as a collective good.

Trade and military sanctions can be regarded as intervention on an ascending scale by collective forums.[56] 'Soft' intervention has become endemic since 1945 by becoming embedded in the structure of the international system. Links of trade and investment of former colonies to international economic transactions have been strengthened in the past few decades, producing enhanced transparency of national societies, polities and economies. That is, most of the world's countries have become even more deeply vulnerable to economic and political – not to say strategic – decisions taken by and for foreigners meeting in foreign locations.

Foreign aid and capital investment too constitute intervention;[57] but because these occur with the consent of target governments, the pejorative label of intervention is not usually attached to them. Yet withdrawal of aid and investment because of changes in certain circumstances in recipient countries can be ferociously attacked as intervention in internal affairs. Tourism is another important prop of the Fijian economy. About two-fifths of tourists to Fiji are from Australia, and one-quarter from New Zealand. Fiji's trading partners and aid donors are shown in Table 2.1. It documents the diverse range of countries that would have to participate in collective measures against Fiji for economic coercion to be effective, and the range of potential alternative trading partners for Fiji if it retaliated against sanctions-imposing states. There was little possibility that Britain would have participated in trade sanctions; Hong

*Table 2.1* Fiji's external trade and sources of aid, 1986 (per cent)

|  | Exports | Imports | ODA |
| --- | --- | --- | --- |
| Australia | 11.42 | 29.40 | 42.7 |
| Canada | 1.27 | 1.13 | 0.9 |
| Hong Kong | 0.33 | 2.00 | |
| India | 0.03 | 1.22 | |
| Japan | 6.30 | 11.00 | 34.0 |
| Malaysia | 6.16 | 0.40 | |
| New Zealand | 2.76 | 16.30 | 7.0 |
| Singapore | 0.04 | 9.41 | |
| South Korea | 0.12 | 1.90 | |
| UK | 32.10 | 3.24 | 4.9 |
| US | 4.72* | 4.07* | 3.1 |

*1985

Sources: *Direction of Trade Statistics Yearbook 1988* (Washington DC: IMF, 1988), p. 177, for trade figures; *Australia's Relations with the South Pacific* (Canberra: Australian Government Publishing Service, 1989), p. 77, for Official Development Assistance (ODA) figures.

Kong, Indonesia, Japan, Malaysia, Singapore, South Korea and Taiwan would all happily have taken up any slack in Fiji's trading requirements.

## Unilateral intervention

It was noted above that pressures for unilateral intervention will intensify if such action is felt to be necessary and just but is not forthcoming from appropriate international organizations. Unilateral intervention is a matter of national foreign policy. According to Rosenau, 'the attempt to modify behavior across national boundaries is perhaps the purest of all political acts'. In foreign policy, behavioural compliance cannot be secured by appeal to common ties of culture or history or the authority of legitimating structures. Instead, foreign policy behaviour must rely solely on manipulation of symbols, and 'requires a balance between the use of persuasion on the one hand and the use or threat of force on the other'.[58]

### *Australia and New Zealand*

Regionally, the collapse of democratic government in Fiji does not seem to have caused much concern beyond Australia and New Zealand. Australian Defence Minister Kim Beazley – described as having no hang-ups about military power and as having gone 'over the top' after the 14 May coup in Fiji – notes that, 'We are not in this region as policeman in any shape or form. But we are technically the most skilled military power in the area.'[59] Foreign Minister Gareth Evans has spoken of Australia's 'significant influence' in Fiji: as its largest economic partner, its largest bilateral aid donor and as 'an important neighbour whose voice has traditionally carried weight across a wide spectrum of Fiji's political and social leadership'. Consequently, the South Pacific for Australia 'must be a region of the highest foreign policy and security significance: we have fundamental, long-standing and largely unchanging interests here'.[60] The same comments apply to New Zealand, with appropriate scaling down.

Australia and New Zealand could have claimed a right to intervene on grounds of propinquity as frontline states; on grounds of protecting their own political identities as parliamentary democratic governments in an international system of self-help; on grounds, in such a system, of protecting their demographic identities as settler societies under threat from assertive indigenous claims; on grounds of pre-emptive damage limitation from an uncontrolled influx of Indian refugees from Fiji if the situation went out of control; and on grounds of protecting their own nationals if their safety had been threatened. Had in fact the situation deteriorated into widespread violence, they would have had some responsibility as the major regional powers to intervene both to protect their own nationals and from broader humanitarian motives. Their regional pre-eminence could also be said to have obliged them to organize regional and international opposition to undesirable developments in a proximate area. Their ability to intervene politically, economically and militarily, however, was not self-evident and was contingent on the particular correlation of forces in the region and beyond.[61]

For contesting nations that have moved past the point of dialogue, it has been argued that within certain limits, 'gunboat diplomacy may be one of the few viable options short of war'. The conditions for effective gunboat diplomacy are 'a definitive, deterrent display of force undertaken by an assailant who has engaged in war in the victim's region and who is militarily prepared and politically stable compared with the victim'.[62] Australia and New Zealand satisfied all but one of these conditions; and that remaining condition – of having used force before – would have been available for subsequent use had they resorted to gunboat diplomacy in 1987. That is, for gunboat diplomacy too success feeds on itself, and failure is self-magnifying.

For New Zealand the issue was a South Pacific one in which it was cast in a leading role. On affairs in its own region, New Zealand was advice-giver, not advice-receiver. And its right to be advice-giver was recognized by other countries. From the start New Zealand, like Australia, acted on the assumption of an expansive view of the role of a Governor-General and qualified view of the rights of a parliamentary majority. Both legalism and realism pointed to accepting that the Governor-General of Fiji was its formal and legitimate ruler. Australian–New Zealand–British support for the Governor-General as the repository of constitutional authority is open to challenge on constitutional grounds.[63] But foreign service officials are skilled in the arts of negotiation leading to compromise outcomes in the short and medium term. They are trained to manage problems of international relations in the immediate context, not to grapple with constitutional implications for their own form of government. For better or worse, outside countries had to maintain links with whatever regime was in power in Suva; strident criticism would achieve nothing constructive but could imperil future relations; cautious diplomacy could ameliorate the effects of military rule and perhaps, eventually, guide the country back towards some form of parliamentary democracy.

Constitutional monarchy in Fiji was detached from constitutional democracy, and that detachment was upheld as being within the powers of a Governor-General. As long as Sir Penaia retained his governor-generalship, New Zealand and Australia followed a strategy of appeasement: accept things as they are, for the time being at least, for fear of worse. It was with murmurs of approval from New Zealand in particular that the Governor-General of Fiji saved his own office by renouncing overthrown democracy,[64] and subsequent endorsement by the Queen received the explicit public support of the New Zealand government.

But to overlook the racial and anti-democratic elements of the regime was to accept long-term instability in the region. A distinguished British study group reported that political stability is enhanced in a state which promotes freedom of speech and assembly, enables peaceful changes of leadership by a democratic process and respects human rights.[65] In Fiji, as elsewhere, one half of the population is not going to accept a permanent condition of second-class citizenship based on racial discrimination. Exodus of Indians is depriving Fiji of the very skilled people needed to repair the ravaged country. Nearly 4,500 people emigrated from Fiji in the year to July 1989, and both the public service and other agencies expressed concern about the effects of the brain drain.[66]

There is another long-term damage to Australia and New Zealand, along with Canada and the United States. To accept the legitimacy of the post-coup government in Fiji was to accept the legitimacy of violent overthrow of settler governments by indigenous peoples at present in the numerical minority. The ultimate obscenity of indigenous rights was of course Hitler's Nazi Germany. Even short of that, liberal consciences would be stirred if a Western country, say Britain, were to enact discrimination against non-whites into law on the grounds that they were aliens, that is, non-indigenes. Liberal consciences are less easily agitated if the racists are non-whites. Yet the fact remains that if Fiji-Indians, the majority of whom are third or fourth-generation natives of Fiji, can be denied roughly equal rights in Fiji and such denial is accepted by Australians and New Zealanders, then no *principled* defence is left against the claims to sovereign paramountcy by Aborigines and Maoris regardless of their fewer numbers. Indeed the latter have greater equivalent justice on their side, if we consider the example of land rights. In Fiji, four-fifths of the land was owned by ethnic Fijians, and only 1.7 per cent by Indians; and the balance could not have been altered within the 1970 constitution without the overwhelming consent of the Fijian community. Aborigines and Maoris can only dream of land ownership on such a scale.

The noticeable cooling of New Zealand Prime Minister David Lange's ardour after his initial passionate denunciations may have been influenced by fears of an influx of Fiji-Indian refugees and its impact upon the not too distant 1987 general election. Lange's own constituency of Mangere in Auckland has a significant Pacific Island population. With the dramatic lengthening of queues outside the New Zealand High Commission in Suva of would-be Indian immigrants who faced communal disenfranchisement, perhaps it dawned on Lange that Fiji's racial tensions could end up being transferred to Auckland.[67]

By 1988 Australia and New Zealand had shuffled back towards re-establishing links with Fiji, motivated in part by having to recognize reality, and in part by fear of an isolated Fiji turning to other potential friends and allies. In February, Australia announced reactivation of $10m aid programme in non-military categories and New Zealand announced a resumption of 'dialogue' and non-military aid, with the appointment of a new ambassador to Fiji on 28 March 1988. Nevertheless, a year later, Foreign Minister Russell Marshall deeply regretted that 'we are not in a position to restore in full the range of dealings and interaction with Fiji, that New Zealand enjoyed and valued in the past'.[68] Both countries faced a familiar but intractable dilemma in efforts at linking aid to progress towards non-racial democracy. The implementation of the aid programme, Australia announced in February 1988, would be influenced by political, constitutional, economic, social and human rights developments in Fiji, as well as by Fiji government priorities. To proceed with aid thereafter would be an implicit endorsement of the *status quo* in Fiji and render indirect assistance to a government to ameliorate the disastrous economic consequences of its own actions. A decision not to proceed with aid would inflame and alienate the regime in power even further while drawing criticism from other regional states that Australia was trying to buy influence with aid. Claiming that progress had been achieved in Fiji, Australia announced a partial implementation of the aid package in November 1988. A parliamentary sub-committee subsequently questioned the official assessment of progress, noted that aid to countries outside the region was not tied to human rights records and pointed out that in effect Fiji had ended up being rewarded by extra allocations in comparison to other regional countries that had remained democratic. For all these reasons, the committee concluded that Australia had been unwise to try to use aid as a lever.[69]

The Fiji crisis was instrumental in Australia changing its policy on recognition of states and governments. Australia's old policy had led it into the anomalous situation of continuing to have dealings with the state of Fiji while not recognizing the government in effective control there. In an effort to rescue Australia from the embarrassment of such anomalies, on 19 January 1988 Foreign Minister Bill Hayden announced a new policy of recognizing states, not governments; the practice of formal recognition or derecognition of governments would be discontinued.[70] This was commonly interpreted as an indication of Australian desire to re-establish relations with Fiji, which was done by re-appointing an ambassador on 3 March 1988. The reappointment was explained also as a gesture of approval for steps in the direction of re-establishing parliamentary government in Fiji.[71] Yet the steps were not race-blind. And, whether or not Canberra intended it, reappointment of an ambassador was interpreted in Suva and other capitals as a retreat from the earlier stance of public disapproval: a perception reinforced by Hayden's comments in January 1988 that the new policy on recognition would not herald the establishment of formal relations with Najibullah's Afghanistan or Hun Sen's Cambodia.[72]

During a visit to New Zealand in 1988, Bavadra said that Australia and New Zealand are major trading partners of Fiji and therefore in a position to exert pressure.[73] On the other side, during a stopover in Australia in November 1988, President Ratu Sir Penaia Ganilau of the Republic of Fiji warned that if Australia tried to use aid as a lever to force changes in Fiji's proposed new constitution, Fiji would look to Asia for help.[74] This hints at a remarkable phenomenon: aid is an instrument to be used by the recipient against the donor, but not the other way round. More seriously, it also raises an interesting question about the motives and objectives of aid. If aid is given out of a sense of responsibility towards fellow human beings regardless of political boundaries – charity may begin at home, but it should not stop at the border – then does the responsibility towards one half of the recipient population cease at the dictate of the recipient government? Does the donor country owe obligations to the government or to the people of recipient countries? At times the primary objective of aid seems to be not so much to help people as to appease governments, to buy them off from doing something worse; perhaps to placate their sense of outrage at having been criticized for any action. The 'old' human rights imposed negative obligations of non-interference on others; the 'new' human rights impose positive obligations on others to provide an individual with a need that s/he cannot satisfy alone.[75] The demand for aid from other countries is grounded in the new rights, while the insistence on absolute non-interference is grounded in the old rights applied to states not individuals: in short, good old-fashioned double standards apply.

What would Australia and New Zealand stand to lose if Fiji turned to alternative sources of aid? It does not seem self-evident that New Zealand's vital interests would be irreparably damaged if its share of aid to Fiji was replaced by assistance from Singapore, which now has a higher GNP per capita than New Zealand. This is in addition to the challenge posed by the cynical theory of foreign aid, which views it either as exploitative of 'recipient' countries or at best a development retardant that has turned a number of previously self-respecting countries into aid junkies.

### US and UK

Australian and New Zealand opposition to the coup should perhaps have been firmer and more assertive both on grounds of justice and long-term pragmatism and self-interest. The United States is an over-the-horizon presence rather than a regional power in the South Pacific and few of its interests were directly engaged. US strategic interest in the Pacific is concentrated on Northeast and Southeast Asia. Direct interest in the South Pacific is limited to Micronesian territories and American Samoa. Derivative interests include containment of Soviet power projection capability and defeat of meddlesome Libyan intrusions if they should occur. The security objective of strategic denial of the region to the USSR has been successfully pursued through a policy of political ties and economic assistance.

In more general terms, US ideological interest is better served by democratic, non-discriminatory government and regional stability everywhere. The coup in Fiji militated against all these. On the other hand, elements in Washington would not have been totally displeased to see a strongly anti-Soviet regime take over from a government that was soft on Soviet communism. Had Bavadra joined New Zealand in banning US ship visits nationally and pursuing a more active anti-nuclear policy regionally, he would have added to US discomfort in the South Pacific. The low-profile US response to developments in Fiji in 1987 reflected both the low salience of the region and the ambivalence of cross-cutting derivative ideological and security interests.

The United States had ability but not right nor responsibility to intervene. Britain could have claimed a right to intervene as the colonial power that imported Indians into Fiji and brokered the constitutional formula leading to independence. It could also be deemed to have residual responsibility to intervene on both counts. But by 1987 its capacity to intervene in distant Fiji was virtually nil. In fact Britain did not seem to be unduly agitated by the overthrow of the Bavadra government and continues to express qualified understanding of the situation. At the Commonwealth meeting in Vancouver, Prime Minister Margaret Thatcher explained that Britain recognized states, not governments, and that it was wrong to abandon countries in their hour of greatest need. Ratu Mara went to London in late March 1988. Refused an audience with the Queen, he was able to talk to her secretary, had 'cordial talks' with Mrs Thatcher, and secured a resumption of British training of Fijian army officers. Mrs Thatcher expressed her 'most earnest hope' that a basis would be found for readmitting Fiji into the Commonwealth.[76]

### The Crown

A queen who risks losing her kingdom has a clear right and responsibility to act. But how the Queen could act to shape the course of events in Fiji was not equally clear. The Queen's sympathy seemed to be with Bavadra,[77] yet, in the weeks after the coup in May 1987, in effect she helped Governor-General Ganilau lay a cloak of legitimacy over an illegitimate Rabuka government. Ganilau used different sources of authority for different constituencies: to the Indians and outsiders he spoke as Governor-General, deriving authority from the constitution; to the Queen he spoke as Sir Penaia, exercising influence as her vice-regal representative; to Fijians he spoke as high chief, grounding authority in tradition. He pardoned the coup leader who had committed treason against the Queen; he promoted the army officer who had rebelled against the two senior army chiefs; and he gave command of the Royal Fiji Military Forces to an officer who had violated his oath of allegiance to the Queen. The de facto position of Colonel Rabuka as the military strongman of Fiji was legitimized by the Governor-General and the latter's actions received royal assent.

By her reactions to the coup the Queen could help or hinder democracy and set precedents for the future in all the realms in which she has a Governor-General. When Bavadra flew to London in June 1987 to seek help from his Queen, she not only refused to see him – she publicly snubbed him. Tea and sympathy with Her Majesty's Private Secretary was inadequate recompense for the fatal body-blow to the Prime Minister's democratic authority.

A constitution without its democratic component was regrettable; without its monarchical component it was deplorable. Colonel Rabuka's proposed republic in late September prompted more overt royal intervention – 'by the standards of Buckingham Palace . . . an extraordinary venture into politics'. Thanks to inept censorship, a royal statement was translated into Fijian and broadcast on Fijian radio on 30 September: 'The Queen would be deeply saddened if those bonds of mutual loyalty and affection, which have so long held the Fijian people and the British monarchy together, were to be severed.'[78]

If the Queen had put full royal authority behind her elected prime minister in the first place, instructed the Governor-General to deal firmly with the treason committed by Colonel Rabuka and to restore the Bavadra government and been unequivocal in communicating the message that failure to comply would lead to loss of knighthoods for Governor-General and former Prime Minister Mara, then the balance could well have been tilted just enough to reverse the coup without bloodshed.

### India

The Western states were concerned about developments in Fiji for a mixture of ideological and instrumental reasons. A country that could not accept the turn of events in Fiji for affective reasons was India. Until 1987, India had consistently maintained that while 'persons of Indian origin who have taken the nationality of the countries of their domicile should identify themselves with the country of their adoption, the Government of India continues to respond to their need to maintain cultural contacts with India and remains alive to their interest and welfare'.[79] India was caught in a major policy cleft with the coup in Fiji. If India intervened to help Fiji-Indians, its actions would retrospectively confirm the Rabuka diagnosis that Fiji-Indians were Indians not Fijians. Regardless of all that had happened prior to May 1987, the position of Indians in Fiji post-intervention by India would become logically and practically impossible, unless India was prepared to maintain a permanent military garrison in Fiji, and that was out of the question. Even talk of a possible Indian intervention would simply exacerbate Fijian anxieties and heighten their distrust of Fiji-Indians. And there would be the clear and present danger of counter-intervention by the Melanesian Spearhead Group to help the inevitable Fijian resistance movement, possibly with support and assistance from Australia and New Zealand. In short, Indian intervention, far from resolving inter-communal conflict in Fiji, would in fact have aggravated it.

Initially, therefore, Indian spokesmen could do little beyond expressing condemnation.[80] Subsequently, once Fiji became a republic in October 1987, India was able to ensure that Fiji's membership of the Commonwealth lapsed: it requires the unanimous consent of all members to readmit a country to the Commonwealth. The irony lies in the fact that the formula that allows republican status to be compatible with Commonwealth membership was worked out to benefit India.

India's right to intervene would have been a function of ethnic ties that transcend national frontiers; its responsibility was equally a function of obligations that governments owe to fellow groups who are the target of hostile attention *qua* group identity; but its capacity to intervene forcefully or economically was circumscribed by geographical separation and lack of significant commercial contacts. India is not exceptional in being concerned about the safety and welfare of its own ethnic groups wherever they may be in the world. Pan-ethnic causes are commonly held in higher esteem than technicalities of international law and several governments have seen it as both their duty and their right to be involved in the problems of fellow-ethnics in foreign countries. But as long as Fiji-Indians were not being subjected to mass detentions/tortures/killings, India was compelled to restrict expressions of concern to diplomatic channels.

Senior Indian diplomats believe, with the benefit of hindsight, that perhaps 'India should have pushed much harder' from the beginning.[81] But it was not easy for India to decide upon the right mix of statements that would exert diplomatic pressure without, on the one hand, appearing to interfere in another country's sovereign affairs or, on the other hand, cornering India into a position of having to consider military intervention or risk public international humiliation. India argued that opposition to the overthrow of democracy and racial discrimination should have been a matter of principled concern to all countries. Suppression and denial of legitimate rights are the seeds of disturbance and unrest, not peace and stability. Sending troops was out of the question, as much by virtue of principle as because of logistics. India suspended trade and technical cooperation with Fiji and recalled its High Commissioner in Suva for consultations. But India lacked any levers with which to move Rabuka's Fiji. Australia and New Zealand were approached by India precisely because they were viewed as possessing the most leverage over Fiji.

The Commonwealth is a multiracial association of which India's Jawaharlal Nehru was a principal architect and in which the voice of the world's largest democracy has always been listened to with respect. The new Fijian regime was overtly racist,[82] and the victims of that racism were Indians. Yet India had little influence on Commonwealth responses to the coup. For the Queen and her advisers the issue was a constitutional one: whether, how and to what end she should intervene and the character of her relationship with her representative in Fiji. On such matters she could not take counsel from republican India. If she were to heed any messages from outside Britain, they would be constitutional not political messages and from her governments and Governors-General in Australia and New Zealand, and the latter at least readily sent its messages. India, a country outside the region and sensitive to anti-Indian racism, was not one whose message would be sought out or especially appreciated.

In a statement to the Rajya Sabha (the Council of States, India's upper house of Parliament) in November 1987, Minister of State for External Affairs K. Natwar Singh was reported to have expressed disappointment with Australian and New Zealand responses to the coup in Fiji (he had travelled to the two countries after the September reimposition of military rule). Indian unhappiness with Britain was even greater and there was a danger of seeping recognition of the military junta in the course of time, for example with countries such as France and Malaysia getting interested in Fiji. The hints of a possible Indian intervention in the confused situation in Fiji drew a public response from New Zealand Foreign Minister Russell Marshall. Praising the standard of New Zealand intelligence on Fiji (which had signally failed to anticipate events in May and September), on 20 November 1987 Marshall said that he would be communicating assessments of an improving situation in Fiji to New Delhi. He described the Indian concern about Fiji-Indians as 'understandable' and acknowledged that India had to follow the hardest line of any of the Commonwealth countries. He revealed that India had several times floated, in private as well as publicly, the possibility of outside intervention and that he would be pressing upon the Indian government through normal diplomatic channels how unwise outside intervention would be.[83]

## Conclusion

By world standards, Fiji is a small country incapable of defending itself against any major attack. Yet in the end it managed to get away with violating present day norms in regard to the relationship between elected government and national defence forces. Such failure of will, capacity or legitimating instruments will have a doubly corrosive effect on international order. On the one hand, it encourages revisionists to challenge the existing order because they reject its legitimacy; on the other, it saps the resolve of many to defend the existing order against challenges from revisionists if they do not believe it to be worth defending.

While political theory is concerned with the theory of the good life, international theory concentrates upon the theory of survival.[84] Exclusive focus on survival to the neglect of the international good life is sharpened by the insistence that the state has certain absolute rights as a separate political association and leads in turn to the conviction that international cooperation is grounded in calculated interests rather than transcendental obligations. Even when some theorists do venture into a philosophical discussion of extranational obligations that human beings have in respect of non-citizens, they are concerned generally with the structure of international relations.[85] The present chapter, a discourse on a problem of foreign policy, has sought to demonstrate the need for a theory of action.

The degree of legitimacy accorded to intervention will usually turn on the answers to such questions as the purpose, the means, the exhaustion of other avenues of redress against grievances, the proportionality of the riposte to the initiating provocation, and the agency of authorization. The example of Vanuatu in 1980 and 1988, and the assistance provided by Australia to help the government of PNG combat the threat of secession by Bougainville in 1990, indicate that intervention is not an absolute proscription even in the South Pacific. If the state has the right to seek external assistance, then do not its citizens have such rights? Or must we continue to accept the nineteenth-century notion that only states can be the subjects of international law?

A perennial difficulty in trying to justify intervention is that: 'The use of force as a sanction for a breach of an international obligation may do more harm than the breach of the international obligation; the cure is often worse than the disease.'[86] It may well be the case that the use of force for humanitarian reasons and for protecting one's nationals abroad have been abused only too frequently to find ready acceptance. But this is a prudential rather than a principled prohibition of intervention. That is, it may be morally or legally justified to intervene under appropriate conditions, but the costs to the intervener or the larger international community may exceed the expected or desired benefits.

The answer to this is that there is a difference between morally permissible and morally required. The task in any specific crisis is to locate the correct point on the continuum between non-intervention, permitted intervention and obligated intervention. I have also tried to indicate why the calculation can never be divorced from considerations of legitimacy and justice: of the target state, of the instruments of intervention and of the agents of intervention. If justice can be expected to triumph from the internal interplay of forces in due course, intervention cannot be justified. If injustice can be expected to be institutionalized and made structurally permanent if a state is left to its own devices and designs, intervention cannot be regarded as impermissible. But whether it is thereby wise or required will depend upon a cluster of other calculations of countervailing principles and pragmatism.

Even at the prudential level, there is a danger that when force is not used under justifying circumstances, the cases of abuse will acquire a permanent majority. This is why there is 'a need to identify more precisely the principles governing the circumstances in which intervention is justified and the form that it should take'.[87] At present, humanitarian intervention will be tolerated and accorded de facto legitimacy, its unlawfulness notwithstanding, if: the use of outside force is confined to capturing or repelling the abusers; democratic elections under international (for example Commonwealth or UN) supervision are speedily held, with all competing factions being given the opportunity to campaign for their causes; the individual intervener is superseded by an international peacekeeping operation, or at least it withdraws its troops from the target state after completion of an internationally recognized act of self-determination.

The arguments against intervention hold up less easily in principle than in pragmatism. But we could at least be clear and honest about this. This would include being prepared to accept the consequences of such a position, namely, that intervention is right if one can get away with it (which after all is the position in regard to internal military intervention). India had the capacity and will to intervene to restore legitimate government to the Maldives in November 1988 and suffered no lasting adverse effects in the region or beyond in consequence.[88] We can and should resist the self-serving claim of governments that they have a natural (divine, *pace* Rabuka?)[89] right to be cruel and monstrous to their own subjects.

In regard to the consequences of intervention, it should be emphasized that a decision not to intervene can have momentous consequences for certain groups or individuals too. 'The principle of non-interference in the internal affairs of sovereign states, while protecting them from the use of force from without, simply sanctifies the rule of force from within.'[90] Western powers in effect, even if not in intention, helped the cause of Franco by refusing to intervene in the Spanish civil war (1936–9). A prescriptive theory of international morality will therefore concern itself not only with moral restraints on actors (individuals, groups, states, regional and international organizations), but also the moral goals of statecraft. International relations 'is a domain of moral choice' where 'diversity does not vitiate or preclude efforts at moral reasoning'.[91] And international relations is the 'domain in which, much more than domestic politics, one pays a penalty for behaving decently'.[92] Political philosophy has traditionally merged its pursuit of the good life with the search for the good state. But as the latent conceptualizations of a self-sufficient and impermeable state have proven increasingly inadequate depictions of international reality, 'traditional ethical–political concerns could not but be transported from the level of the state to the level of the international system itself'.[93]

And if judgements of whether or not to intervene are going to turn on practicalities, then it is not clear – or at least not publicly clear – that Australia and New Zealand engaged in any feasibility study of intervention against the Rabuka coup in 1987. If India had supplied the troops out of ethnic and democratic calculations, Australia and New Zealand the logistics out of regional-democratic calculations, Britain and the United States the diplomatic support to express solidarity with democratic principles, then was a reversal of the coup beyond contemplation?

What this chapter does point up is the need for guidelines for intervention in a world in which non-intervention is in practice impossible: guidelines for determining the nature and gravity of threats that would justify external military intervention and for determining the conditions that would trigger economic and humanitarian intervention. Such guidelines can be grounded in the neo-liberal framework of Hedley Bull, who in *The Anarchical Society*[94] elaborates upon a statist conception of international morality in which the international order is a society of states in which social and cultural underpinnings ameliorate anarchy and conflict. Or they can be grounded in more radical alternatives to the realist approach that identify or anticipate the emergence of a world society or community.[95]

# 3 Kosovo, humanitarian intervention and the challenge of world order[1]

*Ramesh Thakur and Albrecht Schnabel*

We live in troubled times. The Kosovo war confronted us with an abiding series of challenges regarding humanitarian intervention: Is it morally just, legally permissible, militarily feasible and politically doable? If there are massive human rights atrocities, can sovereignty be forfeited – either temporarily or for a limited part of territory – on humanitarian grounds? Is the sovereignty of individual human beings any less inviolate than that of countries as collective entities? Is the use of force to settle international disputes justified outside the United Nations framework and without the prior authorization of the UN Security Council? What happens when the different lessons of the twentieth century, encapsulated in such slogans as 'No More Wars' and 'No More Auschwitzes', come into collision? Who decides (and following what rules of procedure and evidence) that mass atrocities have been committed and by which party? Similarly, who decides what the appropriate response should be?

To supporters, the North Atlantic Treaty Organization (NATO) cured Europe of the Milosevic-borne disease of ethnic cleansing. The spectre of racial genocide had come back to haunt Europe from the dark days of the Second World War. The challenge to the humane values of European civilization had to be met and met decisively. Military action outside the UN framework was not NATO's preferred option of choice. Rather, its resort to force was a critical comment on the institutional hurdles to effective and timely action by the United Nations. The lacuna in the architecture of the security management of world order that was starkly highlighted by NATO bombing needs to be filled.

To critics, however, 'the NATO cure greatly worsened the Milosevic disease'.[2] The trickle of refugees before the war turned into a flood during it and afterwards the Serbs were ethnically cleansed by the Albanians in revenge attacks. By the end of 1999, a quarter of a million Serbs, Romanies, Slavic Muslims and other minorities had fled from Kosovo. The Serbian population of Pristina, the capital of Kosovo, had dwindled from around 20,000 to 800, consisting mainly of elderly people too infirm to escape.[3]

The Kosovo war has the potential to be a defining moment in post-cold war history. It could restructure the pattern of international relations by reshaping the relationship between regional security organizations and the

United Nations, major powers in East and West, friends and allies within those camps and between force and diplomacy. It may also call into question the unipolar moment that has prevailed since the end of the cold war. Moreover, the normative, operational and structural questions that are raised by the Kosovo crisis will have long-term consequences for the way in which we understand and interpret world politics. For instance, can the UN Security Council veto now effectively be circumvented to launch selective enforcement operations? How can the humanitarian imperative be reconciled with the principle of state sovereignty;[4] are we witnessing the end to absolute principles in the international legal framework and, if so, at what cost? Under what conditions do such absolute principles lose their legitimacy? We will come back to these and other key questions. First it is necessary to situate the Kosovo crisis in the context of the changing contours of world politics since the end of the cold war.

## The loss of post-cold war innocence

The end of the cold war offered new and exciting opportunities for international and regional organizations to underpin and underwrite international, national and human security. In the absence of overarching ideological divisions, the emphasis shifted to creating and strengthening the bases of cooperative framework among various security providers. There was recognition of the fact that for effective security provision to be realized, coordination, collaboration and cooperation are necessary between nonstate, state and interstate actors. Regional cooperation among groups of states to address common and shared threats and challenges became an important imperative, perhaps more important than common defence mechanisms against a real, perceived or potential enemy.

The Gulf War seemed to herald the dawn of a 'New World Order': major and smaller powers collaborated across the East–West divide to punish an aggressor (Iraq) who had attacked another sovereign state. Indeed the international community and, for the first time, both the United States and the Soviet Union collaborated in expelling Iraq from Kuwait. They even went so far as to establish safe areas under international military control for Iraq's Kurdish and Shiite communities. This was followed by international sanctions against Iraq in an attempt to force that country into an unconditional surrender of its programme to build weapons of mass destruction. The international community had united to enforce global norms and standards.

In the Gulf War, world-order motives were intertwined with strategic interests related to free and secure access to oil reserves and the containment of Iraq as a potential regional hegemon. Ulterior motives were harder to ascribe to international involvement in Somalia, another example of new world order hopes being dashed. Some 300,000 people had died there as a result of internal war, drought and famine. When humanitarian aid agencies were on the verge of leaving the country for safety reasons, the international community sent protection troops to allow them to continue their work. The 'CNN' effect,

where agitated TV-watching public opinion would pressure political representatives to take action in defence of human justice and dignity, was identified
as a major driving force for assertive humanitarian foreign policies of major
states. However, in the end both the United States and the United Nations
failed to bring peace to Somalia. The violent death of a group of US Rangers
caused a 'reverse CNN effect' and the US government felt pressured to
withdraw its troops in the face of the growing risk of casualties. President
Bill Clinton's Presidential Decision Directive 25 was to set the conditions and
limitations for future peace support operations: unless the national interest was
at stake, allies could be engaged, there was a safe exit strategy and clear mandate
and the force was under US command, no American soldier would again
be exposed to peacekeeping operations in situations where there was no peace
to keep.

Rwanda became the symbol of international indifference and callousness.
Hundreds of thousands of Rwandans were slaughtered despite ample
forewarning to the UN and the major powers of the genocide that was about
to unfold: ignorance was not an alibi for inaction. If the Gulf War marked the
birth of the new world order, Somalia was the slide into the new world disorder
and Rwanda marked the loss of innocence after the end of the cold war.

Worse was to follow for world conscience in Srebrenica in a tragedy that,
in the words of the official UN report, 'will haunt our history forever'.[5] The
horror in Yugoslavia unfolded in the context of a confused international
community, an undecided and incoherent Europe, and an indecisive United
Nations. The UN became involved in a quagmire. It attempted to manage a
conflict that turned out to be unmanageable. The UN Protection Force in
former Yugoslavia (UNPROFOR) became involved in internal wars, created
not necessarily by history and primordial fears and hatred, as so often assumed,
but by calculating, shrewd and power-hungry politicians who knew how to
manipulate a confused populace.

The political vacuum and economic downfall in a dissolving Yugoslavia was
filled by nationalist propaganda and rhetoric. Serbia fought wars to save the
greater Yugoslavia, Croats fought Bosnian Muslims and then Serbs, Bosnians
fought Croats and Serbs. One ethnic group cleansed another group whenever
it seemed to serve the war interest. The UN suffered one of its worst post-
cold war blows with the fall of the 'Safe Area' of Srebrenica in July 1995. A
peacekeeping operation in a theatre where there was no peace to keep,
UNPROFOR offered neither safety to the local people, solace to the displaced
and dispossessed, nor even the consolation to the international community of
having done the job to the best of their ability. It remains a stain on world
conscience for passivity in the face of the calculated return of 'evil' to Europe.

As the war seemed to be grinding to a stalemate, Srebrenica shamed NATO
into bombing Bosnian Serb positions, which led in turn to the Dayton Accord
(1995). The General Framework Agreement for the Former Yugoslavia was
signed in Paris in January 1996. NATO's Stabilization Force (SFOR) and
Implementation Force (IFOR) troops, along with the Organization for Security

and Cooperation in Europe (OSCE) as the main civilian peace-builder and a minor involvement of the UN, have thus far assured slow but gradual progress in providing for basic stability and the rebuilding of Bosnia–Herzegovina.

## The Kosovo Crisis

Just like Slovenia, Croatia, Macedonia and Bosnia, Kosovo too desired to gain independence in the wake of the dissolution of Josip Tito's Yugoslavia. While the other communities resorted to force in their bid for independence, the much smaller autonomous region of Kosovo invested in diplomacy and negotiation. Its non-violent approach was not rewarded. Kosovo lost the little autonomy it had and, along with Montenegro and Serbia, became an integral part of 'rump-Yugoslavia'. Its predominantly Albanian population was suppressed by a small Serb elite and was forced to develop its own 'shadow state', including its own governing structures, schools and health care system. It continued to hope for eventual support from the international community in its bid for liberation from Serb control, either in the form of full autonomy within Yugoslavia or complete separation and independence.

Concluding that their concerns had been disregarded at Dayton, some radicalized Kosovars began to support the development of a paramilitary underground force known as the Kosovo Liberation Army (KLA). Serbia's war against the KLA escalated between the years 1996–8, with increasingly serious repercussions for Kosovo's civilian population. The international community became increasingly involved. Disagreements about the future of Kosovo, with the United States insisting on the inviolability of rump-Yugoslavia and others favouring a potentially independent Kosovo, made it difficult for the West to oppose Yugoslav President Slobodan Milosevic's campaign against the KLA. Numerous diplomatic missions and threats of military intervention were eventually followed by a Security Council-sanctioned deployment of more than 1,000 OSCE observers throughout Kosovo and, later, a peace conference in Rambouillet, France, attended by all conflict parties. The conference produced a draft peace agreement that was eventually signed by the Kosovo Albanian delegation. Following the Serb refusal to sign the deal, NATO threatened and then began bombing Serb military facilities throughout Kosovo and Yugoslavia.

After NATO bombing began on 24 March 1999, the situation on the ground as well as in the international arena deteriorated rapidly. Despite the bombing, Serb forces managed to continue and intensify their war against the KLA and the civilian population in Kosovo. A substantial number of Kosovo's Albanian population fled to Montenegro, Macedonia and Albania or became displaced within Kosovo. During almost three months of bombing, Serb military and paramilitary forces terrorized the Albanian population in Kosovo, drove hundreds of thousands out of the country, committed atrocities against the local population and fought a relentless war against the KLA. Yugoslavia bitterly denounced NATO strikes as illegal aggression on a sovereign state. Its traditional ally Russia strongly opposed NATO's war against Yugoslavia and distanced itself from previous *rapprochement* with the West. China was deeply wounded by the bombing of its embassy in Belgrade and became increasingly alienated in its relations with the West.

The UN found itself sidelined by NATO: Security Council sanction for the bombing was neither sought nor given. Secretary-General Kofi Annan, who had been Under-Secretary-General for Peacekeeping Operations at the time of the Srebrenica tragedy, was torn between criticism of the illegality of NATO actions and sympathy for the victims of Serb atrocities. He also had to be mindful of the negative repercussions of any harsh criticism for already shaky UN–US relations.

With the assistance of Russia and through the involvement of the G-8 (the group of seven industrialized states plus Russia), whose mediation was accepted by Belgrade, the war was eventually brought to an end and Yugoslav troops were withdrawn from Kosovo. A UN-led peacekeeping mission established a de facto protectorate in Kosovo, supported by a military presence (KFOR) with a large NATO component but also a Russian element. Most refugees returned home. Ethnic cleansing in reverse broke out in the form of atrocities against local Serb and Roma populations. At the end of 1999, ethnic tensions in Kosovo remained high, most Serbs had fled, the KLA had been officially disarmed (but not removed from substantial local power and influence) and the peace was a very fragile one, dependent on extensive outside presence. But goals had metamorphosed during the war, so that the initial war aims were not the benchmarks against which the outcome at the conclusion of the war was judged to have been a great success.

## Kosovo, Yugoslavia and the Wider Balkans

History is a contested terrain. Myths can be vital components of nationhood and so myth-making becomes an important tool in the social construction of political identity. Even when analysts make the utmost effort to be dispassionate and objective, they can still disagree fundamentally on the interpretation of a common history. The unfolding situation in Kosovo itself has been tragic and, indeed, one of confusion. What is the price for independence that might never happen anyway? NATO's quick and forceful response to the refusal of Belgrade to agree to every stipulation of the Rambouillet peace agreement was welcomed by many as a strong show of outside support for the Kosovar victims. Nevertheless, NATO's refusal at the start even to consider the deployment of ground troops, its insistence on the territorial integrity of Yugoslavia and the immediate withdrawal of all OSCE presence and most foreign journalists and diplomats from the battleground of NATO air raids, made this a mixed blessing at best. Moreover, Belgrade's immediate launch of a major offensive against the KLA and its civilian 'supporters' tragically aggravated the crisis on the ground and worsened the plight of the victims.

Most Kosovars found themselves driven out of their homes and across borders into miserable refugee camps in Macedonia or Albania. Some were given the opportunity to move on to Western countries. The Kosovar political elite became deeply divided. The KLA continued to fight Serb forces in the quest for eventual independence and political control over Kosovo. Meanwhile, Serb looting and NATO bombing slowly but systematically destroyed Kosovo's infrastructure. For many Kosovars it is very difficult to comprehend what has happened and to understand who actually won or lost the Kosovo war.

Many Serbs are just as bewildered by what happened in 1999. Of course, Milosevic supporters were strongly opposed to NATO bombing, done without UN support and in direct violation of Yugoslavia's sovereignty. In their opinion they were attacked by an outside world which failed to understand that military action in Kosovo only served to suppress a terrorist military organization, the oppression of Serbs living in Kosovo and the protection of Serbia's cultural heritage. For them, as for Milosevic, Kosovo – the 'cradle of Serb nationalism' – could not and should not be surrendered. Moreover, governments respond with great violence to secessionist uprisings all around the world and few of these conflicts have ever resulted in the draconian punishment handed down on Belgrade. Even moderate Serbs were outraged at the Western community's response to Serb action against Kosovars, while no attention was given to Croatia's expulsion of several hundred thousand Serbs from the Krajina region only a few years earlier.

Opponents of Milosevic's rule over Serbia were sympathetic to the Kosovars' plight, but they too pointed to the double standard applied by NATO in its punishment of Serb offensives in Kosovo while many conflicts of much larger scale and worse atrocities escaped international censure or retaliation. Such reasoning does not, of course, excuse Belgrade's operations in Kosovo. Milosevic was quite successful in reaching his goals, namely the expulsion of a majority of Albanians, at least in the short run. Less military action and more diplomacy could have possibly achieved faster and less destructive results, without producing an essentially emptied Kosovo at the end of the air campaigns.

Neighbouring countries suffered under the pressure of the refugee influx, disruption in trade and tourism and decelerated foreign investment into a region that was, yet again, in turmoil. Countries such as Macedonia and Albania pleaded for international aid to accommodate the mass influx of expelled and fleeing Kosovars. Moreover, attention was diverted from Bosnia, a still-unstable country in continuing need of assistance from the European and international communities and their key security and economic organizations. An alienated people and government of Yugoslavia and a further destabilized Balkans portend continuing volatility in the region. On the other side of the Black Sea, Armenia, Georgia and Azerbaijan pondered what the impact of NATO's actions would be on their own situations. Would NATO come to the rescue of Nagorno–Karabakh or Abkhazia? Would NATO's actions set a precedent that would legitimize unilateral intervention by the Commonwealth of Independent States (CIS) under Russian leadership?

## Major external actors: a return to cold war fault lines?

In April 1999, members of the newly-enlarged NATO gathered in Washington to celebrate fifty years of peace-maintenance by the collective defence organization – when the alliance was engaged in an offensive war against a non-member. Rueful Russians could be forgiven for concluding that, after all, the Warsaw Pact had contained NATO, rather than the reverse. Washington had seemingly lost faith in quiet diplomacy and conflict management undertaken by international organizations. Congress used the opportunity to ask for and push through long-demanded increases of the defence budget and the US and NATO had yet another opportunity (in addition to their ongoing engagement in Iraq) to test the evolving strategy of zero-casualty air wars against enemies that employ mainly ground forces – a strategy that many find morally repugnant.

The Clinton administration defended NATO operations, their huge costs and the even larger costs of the subsequent reconstruction of Kosovo, on the argument that something had to be done to oppose totalitarian leaders and stop ethnic cleansing and oppression. Yet reliable inferences could *not* be drawn on the application of those principles to other conflict theatres.

Russia and China were bitterly opposed to NATO's handling of the crisis. Conscious perhaps of their own 'Kosovos', they were wary of the alliance's self-proclaimed authority to secure peace and stability in a globalizing world. In the wake of NATO's actions in Kosovo, they froze relations with the United States and other NATO members. Russia, upset about yet more evidence of its waning world role and the ease with which the West can bypass Russian preferences in international affairs, was ultimately instrumental in finding a diplomatic face-saving solution to end the conflict. On the other hand, heavy reliance on Western assistance in attempts to bring its sliding economic situation under control allowed for little more than verbal condemnation of Western action. NATO's bombing of the Chinese Embassy in Belgrade in particular greatly damaged Sino–US relations and gave China considerable scope for some serious introspection.

The major European NATO allies showed steadfast support for the bombings. While Britain's traditional 'special relationship' with the US cuts across party lines and France was pushing for more action by European powers, the German government faced greater problems. The first Socialist–Green coalition government had to justify Germany's first military involvement after the Second World War, with a Green Foreign Minister and Socialist Defence Minister going out of their way to ensure internal cohesion and support for alliance policies.

Smaller NATO members played along, with little official opposition. This is somewhat surprising given the traditional focus of NATO's northern European members on non-violent and political approaches to conflict management. Italy, Turkey and Greece felt less comfortable with the handling of this conflict. Italy has been torn between its allegiance to NATO, its major-power aspirations, internal political divisions and the fear of a destabilized Albania. Turkey's own Kurdish conflict and various Turkish–Greek disputes, as well as Greece's Orthodox affinity to the Serbs, made it difficult for these countries to give wholehearted support to NATO. Moreover, there is the prospect of greater Islamic influence in the Balkans, especially if an independent Kosovo should join Albania. While Turkey would welcome this, other countries in the region, such as Bulgaria, Macedonia and Greece, are quite wary of such a development.

The alliance's newest members – Poland, the Czech Republic and Hungary – were torn between loyalty to their new partners and uneasiness over the changing focus of NATO strategy and activity. Hungary's position was the most uncomfortable, as it was worried about the significant Hungarian minority living in Serbia and as it is the only NATO country that directly borders on Yugoslavia. Moreover, these countries had joined NATO to protect themselves from military adventurers, not to join them.

The Kosovo conflict had a wider international resonance that was not fully appreciated by the West. The Islamic world interpreted the conflict with mixed emotions. On the one hand, a Muslim population was indeed defended by a mainly Christian alliance. On the other hand, the fact remains that a regional military alliance acted without Security Council approval to defend its value system by force and Islamic groups have too often been victims of such patterns of behaviour in the past not to feel uneasy. In Latin America, Kosovo has been discussed in the context of changing political and legal interpretations of the right of intervention in humanitarian crises. The debate on Kosovo in South Africa is particularly interesting as the country is currently Chair of the Non-Aligned Movement. Moreover, Africa has seen much conflict that has attracted neither the interest nor the compassion from the West comparable to Kosovo. Self-admitting members of the exclusive nuclear club, such as India, ask if NATO would have attacked Yugoslavia if it possessed an extensive nuclear arsenal backed by ballistic missiles. Is NATO's action in Kosovo an example of neo-imperialism against which the developing world has to defend itself?

## Military lessons

Military power is a brutal, ugly instrument and should only be used sparingly and as an instrument of last resort. But once the decision is made, then from an operational and humanitarian point of view (because only so can military personnel, facilities and assets be most forcefully hit and civilian casualties be minimized), maximum force should be applied to achieve the goal of defeating the enemy as swiftly as possible.

Relying on threats as a bluff transformed a humanitarian crisis into a humanitarian catastrophe when the bluff was called. Fundamental policy differences between the Allies led to a lowest common denominator approach to achieving military objectives. Excluding ground forces from the beginning was a serious mistake and reflected an inability to grasp the integrated nature of modern military power. Uncertainty about the possible use of ground forces should have been preserved. Air strikes did not prevent widespread atrocities against civilians on the ground in Kosovo nor the mass exodus of refugees into neighbouring countries. The resulting bloody mess also served to harden the bitter divide between the different communities in the region.

High altitude, zero-casualty air war shifted 'the entire burden of risk and harm' to life and limb completely to the target society, 'including the supposed beneficiaries and innocent civilians'.[6] Expanding the list of bombing targets, such as water and electricity infrastructure and broadcasting stations, reversed progressive trends in the laws of war over the course of the twentieth century. And bombing mistakes, the increased risk of which was deliberately accepted by political leaders in order to minimize risks to their own soldiers, 'caused the finger of criminality to be pointed in NATO's direction'.[7]

## Long-term conceptual challenges

Kosovo raises many conceptual challenges that could redefine our understanding of international affairs and global order. Justice may well triumph eventually, but at what cost to peace and stability? And can a just order be secured in the midst of collapsing pillars of the international order? NATO's actions in Kosovo and the strong affirmation of a new world role for it proclaimed at the fiftieth anniversary meeting, suggest that regional organizations can reinterpret, on a case-by-case basis, the UN prerogative to sanction the international use of force. This is an important step for an organization that has been redefining its own purpose from that of being a collective defence alliance to that of global perhaps, but certainly out-of-area, peace enforcer. NATO is not based on an equal partnership. Of all members, the US imprint on NATO's strategy, actions and preferences is the heaviest.

If NATO's intervention in Kosovo was legitimate, a similar course of action could then also be justified by organizations such as the CIS (with its hegemon Russia), the Economic Community of West African States (ECOWAS, with Nigeria as the hegemon), or the South Asian Association for Regional Cooperation (SAARC, with India as the hegemon). Would NATO leaders be comfortable with a parallel situation where the Arab League claimed the commensurate right to determine on its own, without UN authorization, that Israel was guilty of gross human rights atrocities against its Palestinian citizens and therefore the Arab League would intervene with military force in their defence? While, on the one hand, it will be easier to initiate humanitarian interventions and other regional security operations under regional mandates and operational control, this also suggests a devolution of the previous UN domain to authorize the use of force.

Humanitarian intervention has increasingly been used and abused as justification for Chapter VII missions of the UN as well as multilateral forces under and beyond the mandate of Security Council resolutions. Yugoslavia was bombed over an internal conflict that seems minor in its local and regional effects compared, for instance, to Chechnya, Tibet, or Kashmir. However, Yugoslavia's history of treachery and war in the Balkans between 1991 and 1995 brought little sympathy for it when it received 'a taste of its own medicine'. Given the large number of conflicts throughout the world that will not see any significant international involvement to protect and punish civilian atrocities and other 'collateral' damage resulting from major armed conflicts, it is unlikely that Kosovo will redefine our approach to humanitarian intervention. The humanitarian imperative is not likely to be enshrined as a legitimate validation of regional and international military interventions. This relates, of course, directly to the question of sovereignty. Was state sovereignty challenged more seriously in 1999 than in the early days of the post-cold war era, in the aftermath of the Gulf War, or during the UN-authorized missions in Haiti and former Yugoslavia? The concept has become more dynamic and evolutionary throughout much of the twentieth century, but it will still stand as a major pillar of interstate relations.

Public opinion, both within the conflict region and in the outside world, became an important instrument in a war that was as much one of rhetoric as of arms. On all sides, in the news, official statements and public discussion, public and major political figures were eager to throw out yet another, more dramatic, historical metaphor in their attempts to rally public opinion behind the government. The determination to avoid another Munich led to the folly of Vietnam. The insistence on 'No More Vietnams', it was said, would have produced another Munich in Kosovo. Will we see a neo-Vietnam syndrome emerging from the ashes of Kosovo for the new era? If history is a contested terrain, then the twentieth century is crowded with metaphors that seek to encapsulate the larger meanings of formative historical events. The utility of historical analogies in American discourse is a worthy topic in its own right.

Major media outlets in the West were quick to support NATO's mission and did much to bolster public support for the operation. Tales of horror committed by Serb forces against Kosovars captured the headlines for many weeks without break. While much of that, although not all, later turned out to be true, little or no attention was given to the atrocities committed by the KLA. Overall, the one-sidedness of major news agencies' reporting on Operation Allied Forces made the media a powerful ally in NATO's war against Slobodan Milosevic. However, it also added to growing antagonism among the Serb people who, tapping easily into Western broadcasts through private satellite dishes and Internet access, concluded that Westerners too are victims of state-sponsored propaganda.

Non-governmental organizations (NGOs) have been of crucial importance both in the shaping of public opinion throughout the Kosovo conflict and in direct assistance to the people caught in the crossfire of the war. They too were torn between support for effective action to stop Serb violence in Kosovo and commitment to non-violent means of conflict resolution.

## International citizenship

Why is it that some conflicts, such as the one in Kosovo, receive so much support from the international community while others do not? One possible answer points to the powerful alliance between NGOs and the internationally dominant Western media as the catalyst to humanitarian intervention. Must the response to humanitarian tragedies be highly selective? Have we returned to the days of Clausewitz, where the use of force was considered the logical extension of politics by other means? Or did NATO strikes portend a discontinuation of policy by other means? Bearing in mind that war itself is a great humanitarian tragedy, at which point, under what conditions and subject to what safeguards can armed humanitarian intervention be justified in an era in which absolute non-intervention is morally not permissible but universal application of humanitarian interventionism is physically impossible?

One of the most important lessons of the Kosovo conflict is the power of norms in justifying the use of force. If it does indeed become practice to defend norms with military force, we could eventually end up with another cold war of mutually exclusive norms not dissimilar to the competing ideologies of the old cold war. On the other hand, if a large enough portion of the international community shares these norms and if solidarity can override strategic thinking, then what we saw in Kosovo may indeed become a potent feature of a newly emerging international society. Such an international society would inculcate a sense of global responsibility in international citizens, possibly through international organizations such as the United Nations.

## The legacy of Kosovo for the United Nations

What, then, is the role and place of the United Nations? Has it been permanently sidelined in its efforts to navigate states through the choppy waters of war and peace in a more complex, congested and volatile post-cold war environment? Has it sacrificed human and group rights at the altar of state sovereignty and the territorial inviolability of member states? Has the Security Council finally proven to be of little use in a world in which old antagonisms between Council members resurface and taint their judgements on global issues? These are difficult questions. Given the failure of NATO to simply *force* its preferences onto Yugoslavia and the importance of active Russian and acquiescent Chinese diplomacy in bringing the conflict to an end, one wonders if the post-conflict constellation of powers and the political solutions available, differ so dramatically from the pre-war situation.

In their addresses to the opening of the annual session of the United Nations General Assembly in September 1999, both US President Bill Clinton and UN Secretary-General Kofi Annan referred to the issue of the need for humanitarian intervention to avert or stop mass killings and to the debate on whether regional organizations can act to intervene in this way only with the authorization of the UN. In retrospect, there are five lines of response to the relationship between the NATO action in Kosovo and the United Nations.

The first is the simple claim that NATO acted illegally in terms of the Charter of the United Nations, state practice and on prudential grounds. This line of argument was articulated most forcefully by China, Russia and India (as well as Serbia). Under the UN Charter, states are committed to settling their disputes by peaceful means (Art. 2.3) and refraining from the threat or use of force against the territorial integrity or political independence of any state (Art. 2.4). Furthermore, Article 53(1) empowers the Security Council to 'utilize . . . regional arrangements or agencies for enforcement action *under its authority. But no enforcement action shall be taken under regional arrangements or by regional agencies without the authorization of the Security Council'*, with the sole exception of action against enemy states during the Second World War (emphasis added).

Neither the UN Charter nor the corpus of modern international law incorporates the right to humanitarian intervention. State practice in the past two centuries and especially since 1945, provides only a handful of genuine cases of humanitarian intervention at best and on most assessments none at all. Moreover, on prudential grounds, the scope for abusing such a right is so great as to argue strongly against its creation. According to the weight of legal opinion and authority, the prohibition on the use of force has become a peremptory norm of international law from which no derogation is permitted and NATO was not permitted to contract out at a regional level. In this view, in circumventing the anticipated UN veto NATO repudiated the universally agreed-on rules of the game when the likely outcome was not to its liking. The prospects of a world order based on the rule of law are no brighter. The overriding message is not that force has been put to the service of law, but that might is right.

By contrast, NATO leaders argued that the campaign against Serbia took place in the context of a history of defiance of UN resolutions by President Milosevic. Over the years, the UN Security Council had become increasingly more specific in focusing on human-rights violations by the Milosevic regime, not by both sides; and increasingly coercive in the use of language threatening unspecified response by the international community. While NATO action was not explicitly authorized by the UN, therefore, it was an implicit evolution from UN resolutions and certainly not prohibited by any UN resolution.

A third response is that Serbian atrocities in Kosovo challenged some of the cherished basic values of the United Nations. The Charter is a dynamic compromise between state interests and human rights. Had Milosevic been allowed to get away with his murderous campaign of ethnic cleansing, the net result would have been a fundamental erosion of the idealistic base on which the UN structure rests. NATO action was not a regression to old-style balance-of-power politics, but a progression to new-age community of power. After all, in values, orientation and financial contributions, some of the NATO countries, for example Canada and the northern Europeans, represent the best UN citizen-states.

Interestingly enough, support for this line of argument can be found in the official UN report, published after the Kosovo War ended, on the fall of Srebrenica in 1995. Acknowledging at least partial responsibility for the tragedy, the report in effect concludes that the UN peacekeeping philosophy of neutrality and non-violence were unsuited to the conflict in Bosnia where there was a systematic attempt to terrorize, expel or murder an entire people in a deliberate campaign of ethnic cleansing. The approach of the international community was wholly inadequate to the Serb campaign of ethnic cleansing and mass murder, which culminated in Srebrenica. Evil must be recognized as such and confronted by the international community; the UN commitment to ending conflicts, far from precluding moral judgement, makes it all the more necessary. One key paragraph from the report is worth quoting in its entirety:

> The cardinal lesson of Srebrenica is that a deliberate and systematic attempt to terrorize, expel or murder an entire people must be met decisively with all necessary means and with the political will to carry the policy through to its logical conclusion. In the Balkans, in this decade, this lesson has had to be learned not once, but twice. In both instances, in Bosnia and in Kosovo, the international community tried to reach a negotiated settlement with an unscrupulous and murderous regime. In both instances it required the use of force to bring a halt to the planned and systematic killing and expulsion of civilians.[8]

The fourth strand is that while NATO made war, it still needed the UN to help secure the peace. Far from discrediting the UN permanently, the Kosovo War showed that a UN role remains indispensable even for the most powerful military alliance in history. The Kosovo experience will have made all countries even more reluctant to engage in military hostilities outside the UN framework, as confirmed by the way in which the force for East Timor was assembled and authorized only and quite deliberately, under Security Council auspices.

Fifth and finally, some argue that the sequence of events shows that the real centre of international political and economic gravity has shifted from the UN Security Council to the G-8 countries plus China. That was the forum in which the critical negotiations were held and the crucial compromises and decisions made. This reflects the failure to reform the UN Security Council in composition and procedure, as a result of which it no longer mirrors the world as it really is. In essence, therefore, the 'G-8 plus' is the Security Council as it ought to be.

The counter to this, however, is that the permanent membership of the Security Council is already weighted disproportionately towards the industrialized countries. The shift of the decision-making locus to the 'G-8 plus' disenfranchises the developing countries even more. If this trend continues, the UN will lose credibility and legitimacy in most of the world – and hence any remaining effectiveness.

## Of norms and laws

In today's dangerously unstable world full of complex conflicts, we face the painful dilemma of being damned if we do and damned if we don't. The bottom-line question is this: Faced with another Holocaust or Rwanda-type genocide on the one hand and a Security Council veto on the other, what would we do? Because there is no clear answer to this poignant question within the existing consensus as embodied in the UN Charter, a new consensus on humanitarian intervention is urgently needed.

Part of that consensus must include promotion of discussion and agreement about, first, the point at which a state forfeits its sovereignty and second, the voluntary suspension of veto power in the Security Council in exceptional circumstances so that the support of a majority of the great powers is all that is required to permit states to engage in humanitarian war. It is good that the international system can tear down the walls of state sovereignty in cases where states kill their own people.

The UN Charter balance between state sovereignty, with the corollary of non-intervention, and human rights, with the corollary of international concern, tilted a little in the 1990s and is delicately poised at the start of the new millennium. The days when a tyrant could shelter behind the norm of non-intervention from the outside in order to use maximum brutal force inside territorial borders are past. The indictment of Yugoslav President Slobodan Milosevic as a war criminal, as well as the arrest of former Chilean President August Pinochet while on a visit to Britain, shows the inexorable shift from the culture of impunity of yesteryears to a culture of accountability at the dawn of the twenty-first century.

The UN system, however, needs to be ready, willing and able to confront humanitarian catastrophes wherever they occur. The unavoidability of selectivity should not become an alibi for the strong using force against the weak. That will only heighten disorder. One veto should not override the rest of humanity. Otherwise we might see more NATO-style actions with less or no UN involvement – and thus less order and less justice in the global community. Formal amendment of the UN Charter is neither feasible in the foreseeable future nor necessary. In the 1990s, the veto-wielding powers generally abstained from the use and misuse of that power. The history of Russian and Chinese policy in the 1990s in the Security Council with respect to Milosevic is essentially one of cooperation, not obstructionism. The major powers need to return to the shared management of a troubled world order.

The UN is committed to the protection of the territorial integrity, political independence and sovereignty of all its member states, including Yugoslavia. The Security Council lies at the heart of the international law-enforcement system. The justification for bypassing it to launch an offensive war remains problematic and the precedent that was set remains deeply troubling. NATO acted essentially within the normative and moral framework of the West. That was the source both of its strength and weakness.

By fighting and defeating Serbia, NATO became the tool of the KLA policy of inciting Serb reprisals through terrorist attacks in order to provoke NATO intervention.[9] In his Millennium Report, UN Secretary-General Kofi Annan notes that his call for a debate on the challenge of humanitarian intervention had led to fears that the concept 'might encourage secessionist movements deliberately to provoke governments into committing gross violations of human rights in order to trigger external interventions that would aid their cause'.[10]

Communities bitterly divided for centuries cannot be forced by outsiders to live together peacefully. The Kosovo war further radicalized both communities and squeezed out moderates. The interests of nationalists on both sides lie in still more conflict. Since the war, there has been a persistent threat of ethnic cleansing of Serbs by the Albanians. The lack of international solidarity and effective action further entrenches the victim mentality among Serbs and undermines prospects of long-term stability. The KLA by another name wants to liberate 'Eastern Kosovo' from Serbia, while Serbia wants NATO to withdraw from Kosovo in humiliating failure.

Security Council Resolution 1244 called for the demilitarization of the KLA. An agreement with the UN and the Kosovo Force (KFOR) in September 1999 led to the formal dissolution of the KLA. In reality, the high command structure and symbol of the KLA were replicated in the new Kosovo Protection Corps. As the Serbs pulled out of Kosovo and the state structures of administration collapsed, the power vacuum was filled by a mixture of KLA cadres and criminal organizations. A year later, pledges of administrative and financial support, for example the provision of police forces and judicial personnel, remained largely unfulfilled. In a milieu where local judges earn less than drivers on UN duty, a judge with a valid driver's licence faces difficult career choices.

Another lesson that has been reinforced is that it is easier to bomb than to build. The willingness of the strong to fund a campaign of destruction stands in marked contrast of the reluctance of the rich – who happen to be the same group of countries – to find far less money for reconstruction. In turn this seriously, if retrospectively, undermines the humanitarian claims for having gone to war.

### UN authority and legitimacy

Many of today's wars are nasty, brutish, anything but short and mainly internal. The world community cannot help all victims, but must step in where it can make a difference. However, unless the member states of the UN agree on some broad principles to guide interventions in similar circumstances, the Kosovo precedent will have dangerously undermined world order. Not being able to act everywhere can never be a reason for not acting where effective intervention is both possible and urgently needed. Selective indignation is inevitable, for we simply cannot intervene everywhere, every time. But community support for selective intervention will quickly dissipate if the only criterion of selection is friends versus adversaries.

In addition, we must still pursue policies of effective indignation. Humanitarian intervention must be collective, not unilateral. And it must be legitimate, not in violation of the agreed rules that comprise the foundations of world order.

The core of the UN influence in world affairs rests in its identity as the only authoritative representative of the international community. When we affirm the existence of an international society, an international system and world institutions, questions immediately arise as to the possibility and nature of international authority. *International society* exists only to the extent that member states observe limits on their freedom of action in pursuing national interests and acknowledge the authority of these limits. The UN is a community-building institution; to strengthen its structure and function is to provide it with greater community-building authority. The United Nations was to be the framework within which members of the international system negotiated agreements on the empirical rules of behaviour and the legal norms of proper conduct in order to preserve the semblance of society.

That is, the community-sanctioning authority to settle issues of international peace and security has been transferred, over the course of the last two centuries, from the great powers in concert to the United Nations. Acceptance of the United Nations as the authoritative expositor of values in international society is demonstrated by the fact that even non-compliance with Council or Assembly directives is defended by efforts to show the error, unfairness or illegality of the collective decision. Every such effort, whether it succeeds or fails in its immediate task, is a confirmation, not a negation, of the *right* of the United Nations to engage in collective decision-making.

The decisions of the United Nations command authority because they are the outcome of an international political process of the assertion and reconciliation of national interests. It is the political process that authenticates UN resolutions and converts them into authoritative prescriptions for the common good of humanity. 'Authority' signifies the capacity to create and enforce rights and obligations that are accepted as legitimate and binding by members of an all-inclusive society who are subject to the authority. 'Power' is different from 'authority' to the extent that it is the capacity simply to enforce a particular form of behaviour. Authority, even when associated with power or force, necessarily connotes 'legitimacy'. That is, authority is distinct from power to the extent that it entails acceptance of right *by those to whom it is applied*.

Both authority and power are important in the regulation of human behaviour. The function of either term is to stress its role of conduct regulation *in contrast* to alternative means of controlling behaviour. In particular, authority and power are used to distinguish each other in the exercise of influence. The concept of authority is used to clarify ways in which behaviour is regulated *without* recourse to power; a recourse to power is made necessary to enforce conformity when authority has broken down. Thus the use of power indicates both a failure of authority and the determination to restore it. The failure of UN authority was reflected in the refusal of Milosevic to heed a succession of Security Council resolutions. The recourse to force by NATO was an effort to restore the UN authority in the Balkans that was crumbling under the sustained challenge from Serbia.

The concept of legitimacy acts as the connecting link between the exercise of authority and the recourse to power. In the case of the NATO campaign against Milosevic, the prior authorization of NATO by the UN Security Council as its enforcement arm earlier in the 1990s, plus the evolutionary nature of Security Council resolutions directed at Serbia, meant that NATO could claim to be acting at least in a 'semi-permissive' legal environment.

Segments of international society have diffused, fragmented and multiple layers of authority patterns. The central role of the United Nations as the applicator of legitimacy suggests that international society as a whole is characterized by congruence of authority. The reason for this is that the United Nations is the only truly global institution of a general purpose that approximates universality. The UN represents the idea that unbridled nationalism and the raw interplay of power must be mediated and moderated in an international framework. It is the centre for harmonizing national interests and forging the international interest. The role of custodian of collective legitimacy enables the United Nations, through its resolutions, to promulgate authoritative standards of state behaviour or codes of conduct against which to measure the compliance of governments.

Being the indispensable power can tempt one into being indisposed to accept the constraints of multilateral diplomacy. But being indispensable does not confer the authority to dispense with the legitimacy of the UN as the only entity that can speak in the name of the international community. The reason for much disquiet around the world with the precedent of NATO action in Kosovo was not because their abhorrence of ethnic cleansing is any less. Rather, it was because of their dissent from a world order that permits or tolerates unilateral behaviour by the strong and their preference for an order in which principles and values are embedded in universally applicable norms and the rough edges of power are softened by institutionalized multilateralism.

## Conclusion

It may take some time before we can fully comprehend the meaning of Kosovo. The consequences of the 1999 war for it will keep students of international relations – and no doubt policy makers – busy for years to come. If Kosovo turns out to be an anomaly, little will have changed. However, if the Kosovo conflict signifies a well-planned and intentional strategy on the part of the main actors, it will have serious and long-lasting consequences. Moreover, much of the UN role in world politics will hinge on the fallout from Kosovo. As the only truly representative body of the world community, the UN will have to apply the lessons learned to reaffirm or reformulate the basic rules and principles of international order and international organization.

Critics of the Kosovo war must concede the many positive accomplishments.[11] Almost a million of Kosovo's displaced inhabitants returned to their homeland. Milosevic was thrown out of Kosovo and has been confined to his lair in Serbia. The credibility of NATO was preserved; the transformation of its role from collective defence of members against attack from the outside, into the more diffused role of peace-enforcement throughout Europe, was validated; and Washington remains firmly anchored to Europe.

The achievements notwithstanding, one year after its 'successful' military campaign in the Balkans, NATO's choices in Kosovo had seemingly narrowed to policy failure (abandon the dream of a multiethnic society living peacefully together) or policy disaster (defeat at the hands of sullen and resentful Serbs and increasingly hostile Albanians waging a guerrilla war of independence). A week before the anniversary of the start of the NATO air strikes, an influential US newspaper was already arguing that 'The United States has endured more than its share of bitter experience with quagmires. . . . It's time to prepare for an early American exit'.[12] In the meantime, an analysis from the equally influential International Institute for Strategic Studies in London argued that UN Security Resolution 1244 had created a conundrum by formally recognizing Yugoslav sovereignty over Kosovo while simultaneously instructing the UN Mission in Kosovo (UNMIK) to establish the institutions of substantial autonomy and self-government in the province. 'As a result of this impasse, troops from NATO countries look set to stay in Kosovo for decades.'[13]

The KLA is unlikely to compromise on its goal of complete independence. If NATO resists, it will be viewed and treated as an occupying force. If NATO withdraws in exasperation, Serbia might attempt to reconquer Kosovo, regardless of whether or not Milosevic was still in power in Belgrade. The threat of renewed fighting might prompt the major European NATO leaders to stay the course. But Kosovo in 1999 showed that NATO still needs firm US political leadership and military assets. How long US patience will last in the face of the continuing impasse and escalating tensions in Kosovo remains anybody's guess.

The current situation in Kosovo can only be an interim solution – in the form of an open-ended protectorate. The only lasting solution is a political settlement that reconciles legitimate ethnic Albanian interests about the future of the province and long-term peace with Serbia in the wider context of regional peace, security and order in the Balkans.

Similarly, the example of a regional organization invoking the mantle of the international community in order to launch a humanitarian war can only be a partial and halting solution. Because the antecedents are not beyond question, the precedent-setting value must remain limited. The urge to humanitarian intervention by powerful regional organizations must be bridled by the legitimating authority of the international organization. The only just and lasting resolution of the challenge of humanitarian intervention would be a new consensus proclaimed by the peoples of the world through their governments at the United Nations and embodied in its Charter.

The United Nations lies at the interface of power-based realism and values-based idealism. This is a creative tension that must be resolved in specific cases without abandoning either the sense of realism or the aspiration to an ideal world. The Kosovo learning curve shows that the UN ideal can neither be fully attained nor abandoned. Like most organizations, the UN too is condemned to an eternal credibility gap between aspiration and performance. The real challenge is to ensure that the gap does not widen, but stays within a narrow band. Only the UN can legitimately authorize military action on behalf of the entire international community, instead of a select few. But the UN does not have its own military and police forces and a multinational coalition of allies can offer a more credible and efficient military force when robust action is needed and warranted. What will be increasingly needed in future is partnerships of the able, the willing and the high-minded with the duly authorized. Anything else risks violating due process. East Timor offers a better model than Kosovo of a more prudential and effective multilateral intervention blessed by the UN Security Council. But without the lead of Kosovo, would East Timor have followed?

# 4 Global norms and international humanitarian law

## An Asian perspective[1]

International humanitarian law is defined as 'the principles and rules regulating the means and methods of warfare as well as the humanitarian protection of the civilian population, of sick and wounded combatants and of prisoners of war'.[2] As such, international humanitarian law is on the one hand something more and of a higher order than norms. On the other hand, it is of a lower order and of a lesser scope in coverage than other parts of international law. In this chapter, I shall explore aspects of contemporary international humanitarian law and international norms as an Asian commentator.

An important preliminary point to note is that all three concepts in the equation – Asia, international humanitarian law and general international law – remain, as concepts, essentially contested. A second preliminary comment, equally significant in terms of its political ramifications, is that all three concepts are essentially non-Asian in origin and frames of reference. This does not mean that they lack validity or relevance in this part of the world. It does mean that, to the extent that norms and laws are mechanisms for regulating the social behaviour of human beings interacting with one another as organized groups, the socio-political construction of Asia, global norms and international humanitarian law cannot simply be dismissed. The argument must instead be confronted, addressed and to the extent possible, answered.

In the age of colonialism, most Asians became the victims of Western superiority in the organization and weaponry of warfare. The danger today, I argue, is that they could continue to be the objects but not the authors of norms and laws that are supposedly international. But a world order in which Asians and other developing countries are *norm-takers*, while the Western countries are the *norm-setters* and *norm-enforcers*, will not be viable because the division of labour is based neither on comparative advantages – Asia, no less than other continents, is home to some of the world's oldest civilizations with their own distinctive value-systems – nor on equity. The risk is under-appreciated because the international discourse in turn is dominated by Western, in particular Anglo–American, scholarship.[3] Asian and African voices are largely silent.

## The Western roots of international humanitarian law and global norms

Of the three concepts – Asia, international humanitarian law and general international law – the first is the least problematic despite having its roots in Europe. Asia is a geographical construct (hence its unproblematic politics) devised by Europeans to differentiate the self from the other. In some minds the distinction is sharpened to 'us civilized insiders' versus the 'heathen outsiders'. In reality the continent is far too diverse in virtually all respects – language, scripts, religion, culture, politics, economics, legacies of literary and philosophical discourse – to connote much practical content as a collective entity. Arguably, 'West' Asians have more in common with Europeans than with 'East' Asians. It is difficult to trace a sense of common Asian identity either among the people or the cultural, political or commercial elites. Asia simply does not have the theory, history or practice of European integration. Asians lack the sense of regionalism that is evident, in however rudimentary a form, among Africans and Latin Americans. In other words, of all the inhabited continents Asia is the only one that does not have a sense of constituting one distinct identity. It is not surprising, therefore, that Asia has the least developed pan-continental institutions (political, economic, even sporting) of any of the inhabited continents.

### *International humanitarian law*[4]

To the extent that Asians are bound by shared institutions, laws and norms, they are at the international rather than the continental level. International society is anarchic but not lawless. Anarchy indicates the absence of central government; *society* indicates the existence of shared norms and values.[5] Most norms and principles of international law are obeyed most of the time by most states.

The radically different roots of international humanitarian law are to be found in the tradition of *just war*, which focused not simply upon the circumstances leading to the initiation of hostilities (*jus ad bellum*) but also on the conduct of hostilities themselves (*jus in bello*).[6] This tradition, expressed most forcefully in Hugo Grotius's *De Jure Belli ac Pacis* (1625), was amenable to justification in both religious and secular terms, and found resonance in the political traditions of other faiths, such as Islam. Yet in its concrete form international humanitarian law was very much a product of the Enlightenment, which witnessed the rise of individualism as a counterpoint to the potency of *raison d'état* as sufficient justification for the unconstrained use of force. With regard to humanity in warfare, until the decisive shifts in social values, economic activity and political structures that came in the late eighteenth and early nineteenth centuries the 'barbarous' East, as represented in literature by notorious figures such as Tamerlane, had no reason to feel morally inferior to the 'civilized' West, whose leaders during the Thirty Years War showed an equal indifference to the sufferings of foot soldiers and non-combatants.

A watershed event in the law's development, although its full significance became clear only in retrospect, was the Battle of Solferino of 1859. Fought by the Austro–Hungarian Empire and the Kingdom of Sardinia against France, the battle would have disappeared into the oblivion of obscure footnotes had it not been witnessed by a young Swiss businessman, Jean-Henry Dunant, who captured its horrors in a powerful memoir.[7] Dunant became the driving force behind the adoption in 1864 of the Geneva Convention for the Amelioration of the Condition of the Wounded in Armies in the Field. He devoted his energies to the establishment of what is now the International Red Cross and Red Crescent Movement, which continues to play a major role in the development and dissemination of international humanitarian law. Other hands took up the task of developing instruments to regulate the conduct of war, and two major streams of law developed:[8] the *Law of The Hague*, taking its name from the First and Second Hague Peace Conferences held in 1899 and 1907, which resulted in a number of treaties and declarations concerned with the conduct of hostilities; and the *Law of Geneva*, taking its name in particular from the 1864 Convention and subsequent treaties adapting the law to changed circumstances and culminating in the four Geneva Conventions of 12 August 1949 on the protection of war victims. The *Law of Geneva* deals with the wounded, sick and shipwrecked, prisoners of war, and protected civilians, and even imposes limitations on what is permissible in armed conflicts 'not of an international character'.[9]

Treaties are a major source of international humanitarian law and are recognized as such in Article 38(1) of the Statute of the International Court of Justice. Underpinned by the principles set out in the 1969 Vienna Convention on the Law of Treaties, their force derives from their reflecting the free consent of states to be bound by particular rules. Such consent no more compromises the sovereignty of the state than entering into a contract compromises the autonomy of an individual: it simply reflects the societal as opposed to the anarchical dimension of the international system.

Another important source is custom. One of the most famous passages in the laws of armed conflict – the so-called *Martens Clause* – is generally regarded as a codified statement of customary law, and as set out in the Preamble to the 1907 Hague Convention respecting the Laws and Customs of War on Land provides that inhabitants and belligerents 'remain under the protection and the rule of the principles of the law of nations, as they result from the usages established among civilized peoples, from the laws of humanity, and the dictates of the public conscience'. Furthermore, two of the most important principles governing the conduct of hostilities, namely *proportionality* and *discrimination* , are fundamentally customary in character,[10] although they have been reflected in the shape of various codified texts.

Custom has typically been traced back to two elements: a pattern of behaviour on the part of states, and a psychological dimension (*opinio juris sive necessitatis*). Analysts also recognize the possibility of 'instant custom', in which evidence of a sufficiently powerful *opinio juris* can compensate for the absence of long-standing state practice. Resolutions of the UN General Assembly are clearly candidates for attention in this respect: almost three decades ago, Richard Falk highlighted them in arguing for 'a trend from consent to consensus as the basis of international legal obligations'.[11] More recently, the expression 'soft law' has emerged as a way of describing the prescriptions contained in such resolutions. It is a useful expression for characterizing rules that are technically non-binding as a matter of international law, but secure a high level of compliance.[12] The international system is replete with such rules, and while clothed in legalistic form, their efficacy derives from extra-legal considerations. Yet they are no less potent on this account. D. W. Greig has argued that such technically non-binding norms should be labelled 'soft rules', and that the term 'soft law' should be reserved for provisions that are technically binding, but give rise to obligations that are 'vague or inchoate'.[13] Again, 'soft law' in Greig's sense is not necessarily without effect in international relations: it may play a role in setting standards that states should attempt to honour if they are not to meet with disapproval (muted or vocal) from other states or from interest groups within their own territory.

It should also be noted that while states can exempt themselves from customary legal prohibitions by pointing to a sustained pattern of objection, this will not protect them from being deemed to have committed violations of a peremptory norm of general international law (*jus cogens*), which Article 53 of the 1969 Vienna Convention on the Law of Treaties defines as 'a norm accepted and recognized by the international community of states as a whole as a norm from which no derogation is permitted and which can be modified only by a subsequent norm of general international law having the same character'. Linehan has argued that the norms which attract the clearest support for status as *jus cogens* 'are the prohibition on the use of force, the right to self-determination and the prohibitions against genocide, racial discrimination, slavery, and piracy on the high seas'.[14]

### The Ottawa Treaty as an example

Because we have dealt with this subject elsewhere,[15] I do not propose to discuss at length here the implications of the Ottawa Treaty banning the manufacture, transfer and use of antipersonnel landmines.[16] Briefly, our argument is that the Ottawa Treaty makes more sense as a normative advance in international humanitarian law than as an arms control treaty. It purports to ban an entire class of weapons already in general and widespread use. As such, it is without precedent in the history of arms control and disarmament. But it is also fatally flawed from the point of view of an arms control regime. This is so with respect to adherents: states that are among the most relevant to the landmines issue, including China, India, Pakistan and the United States, are not party to the treaty. It is just as true with respect to verification machinery: the Ottawa Treaty contains no monitoring, inspection and compliance clauses. What the Ottawa Treaty seeks to do, and succeeds in doing, is to establish a new norm against landmines. And it anathematizes this class of weapons by pointing to the inhumane nature of the damage wrought by them when used *as designed to be used* (much like cigarettes). They are victim-activated, they cannot tell a soldier from a child, they cause injuries years after conflicts have ended, and so on. That is, they are contrary to international humanitarian law.

The example of the Ottawa Treaty begs the question of the process by which norms emerge and are globalized. How are they articulated and consolidated? Who interprets them, and who has the right to monitor them to ensure and, if necessary, enforce compliance? We know very little about the answers to these questions. Certainly the fact that the Ottawa Treaty was negotiated outside the United Nations Conference on Disarmament in Geneva, the world's only authentic and duly authorized standing multilateral forum on arms control, affected its legitimacy in the minds of some Asian leaders. Equally important, since they were not involved in drafting the clauses of the treaty, will they consider themselves morally bound by its prohibitionary *norms*? And if they do not, then what are the implications for the efficacy of the Ottawa Treaty in general?

The *norm-setters* behind the Ottawa Treaty were Canada, Norway and Austria. Norm generation by Western middle powers was reinforced by standard-setting by the UN Secretary-General when he endorsed the Ottawa process as the negotiating track and the convention that resulted from it. Asian nations were essentially consumers, neither producers nor retailers, of the new norm. The Canadians, for example, led the effort to proselytize Asian countries through two major back-to-back conferences and workshops in the region in July 1997 in Sydney and Manila.[17]

## Human rights as a global norm

Part of the reason for the gathering strength of the anti-nuclear movement in the early and mid-1980s lay in the feeling that the two superpowers held the fate of humanity hostage to their bilateral relations. The logic of nuclear deterrence gave humanity the right to voice its preferences about the nuclear equation: 'no annihilation without representation.' International humanitarian law is concerned with protection of the humanitarian norm in the midst of armed conflict. What if the war itself is being fought over humanitarian norms?

Before that question can be answered, it must be contextualized within the broader global human rights norm. The Charter of the United Nations is the embodiment of the international political and moral code. It encapsulates the international consensus and articulates best-practice international behaviour by states and regional and international organizations. In 1948, conscious of the atrocities committed by the Nazis while the world looked silently away, the United Nations adopted the Universal Declaration of Human Rights. On a par with other great historical documents such as the French Declaration of the Rights of Man and the American Declaration of Independence, this was the first *international* affirmation of the rights held in common by all.

The Universal Declaration is a startlingly bold proclamation of the human rights norm. The two 1966 Covenants[18] added force and specificity, affirming both civil-political and social–economic–cultural rights without privileging either. Together they mapped out the international human rights agenda, established the benchmark for state conduct, inspired provisions in many national laws and international conventions, and provided a beacon of hope to many whose rights had been snuffed out by brutal regimes.

A right is a claim, an entitlement that may neither be conferred nor denied by anyone else. A human right, owing to every person simply as a human being, is inherently universal. Held only by human beings, but equally by all, it does not flow from any office, rank or relationship.

The idea of universal rights is denied by some who insist that moral standards are always culture-specific. If value relativism were to be accepted *in extremis*, then no tyrant – Adolf Hitler, Josef Stalin, Idi Amin, Pol Pot – could be criticized by outsiders for any action. Relativism is often the first refuge of repressive governments. The false dichotomy between development and human rights is usually a smokescreen for corruption and cronyism. Relativism merely requires an acknowledgement that each culture has its own moral system. Government behaviour is still open to evaluation by the moral code of its own society. Internal moral standards can be congruent with international conventions. Because moral precepts vary from culture to culture does not mean that different peoples do not hold some values in common. Few if any moral systems proscribe the act of killing absolutely under all circumstances. At different times, in different societies, war, capital punishment or abortion may or may not be morally permissible. Yet for every society, murder itself is always wrong. All societies require retribution to be proportionate to the wrong done. Every society prizes children, the link between succeeding generations of human civilization; every culture abhors their abuse.

The doctrine of national security has been especially corrosive of human rights. It is used frequently by governments, charged with the responsibility to protect citizens, to assault them instead. Under military rule, the instrument of protection from without becomes the means of attack from within.

An argument sometimes invoked for a policy of 'See Nothing, Hear Nothing, Do Nothing' is that an activist concern would merely worsen the plight of victims. Prisoners of conscience beg to disagree. It is important to them to know that they have not been forgotten.[19] Lack of open criticism is grist to the propaganda mill of repressive regimes.

The United Nations – an organization of, by and for member states – has been impartial and successful in a standard-setting role, selectively successful in monitoring abuses, but feeble in enforcement. Governments usually subordinate considerations of UN effectiveness to the principle of non-interference.

The modesty of UN achievement should not blind us to its reality. The 1948 Universal Declaration embodies the moral code, political consensus and legal synthesis of human rights. The world has grown vastly more complex in the fifty years since. The simplicity of language belies the passion of conviction underpinning them: its elegance has been the font of inspiration down the decades, its provisions comprise the vocabulary of complaint. Activists and non-governmental organizations (NGOs) use the Human Rights Declaration as the concrete point of reference against which to judge state conduct. The 1966 Covenants require the submission of periodic reports by signatory countries, and so entail the creation of long-term national infrastructures for the protection and promotion of human rights. United Nations efforts are greatly helped by NGOs and other elements of civil society. NGOs work to protect victims and contribute to the development and promotion of social commitment and enactment of laws reflecting the more enlightened human rights culture.

Between them, the UN and NGOs have achieved many successes. National laws and international instruments have been improved, many political prisoners have been freed and some abuse victims have been compensated. The United Nations has helped also by creating the post of a High Commissioner for Human Rights who has given the UN campaign a human face and a more public profile. The most recent advances on international human rights, such as the Ottawa Treaty banning landmines and the Rome Treaty establishing the International Criminal Court,[20] are the progressive incorporation of wartime behaviour within the prohibitionary provisions of international humanitarian law.

### Not quite universal

And yet – of the fifty-one founding members of the United Nations in 1945, only eight were geographically Asian: China, India, Iran, Iraq, Lebanon, Philippines, Saudi Arabia and Syria. As can be seen, of these only three are from Asia proper (the others belonging more to the Middle East than Asia in political terms). Even from within this tiny group of three, one (India) was still a British colony. If the UN Charter articulates the 'global' political norm of its time, then why should Asians feel bound by it? Today, Asia accounts for more than half the world's population. But Asian countries make up only 26 per cent of the UN membership, and only 20 per cent of the UN Security Council's membership.[21] Thus the organization under-represents Asian countries, and seriously under-represents Asian peoples. Once again, therefore, why should UN-sourced 'global' norms be construed as having binding effects on Asian internal and international behaviour?

Asians are neither amused nor mindful at being lectured on universal human values by those who failed to practice the same during European colonialism[22] and now urge them to cooperate in promoting 'global' human rights norms. The displacement and ethnic cleansing of indigenous populations was carried out with such ruthless efficiency that the place of settler societies such as Australia, Canada and the United States in contemporary international society is accepted as a given. The superiority of Western ways has remained a constant theme over the past few centuries, only the universal truths of Christianity have been replaced by the universal rights of humankind. Mahatma Gandhi, asked what he thought of European civilization, is said to have replied, 'I think it is a very good idea'. Gandhi of course had a pronounced sense of mischief. But the story, even if apocryphal, serves to illustrate the resentment of people whose societies are backed by centuries of civilization against presumptuous preaching by Westerners.

Western countries, including the United States, are quite happy to use Amnesty International reports as a lever with which to nudge other countries on human rights. But they are outraged at the idea that their own human rights record, for example with respect to the racial bias in the death penalty, might merit independent international scrutiny. The major Anglophile outpost in Asia is Australia. At the same time as many Australians preach universalism to Asians, Australia rejects the right of the United Nations or any outsider to comment on the plight of Aborigines. Between 1910 and 1970, 100,000 Australian aboriginal children were taken from their families and placed in white foster homes. The goal was to wipe out the 40,000-year old Aboriginal culture through detribalization: assimilating the children into European civilization while the adults died out. The result was dispossession, dislocation and devastation of Australia's first inhabitants.

The official inquiry into the 'stolen generation', chaired by Judge Sir Ronald Wilson, President of the Human Rights Commission, listened to the stories of 535 aborigines and received written submissions from another 1,000.[23] The 689-page report into the sorry saga used a UN definition – the deliberate extermination of a culture of one group through the forcible transfer of its children to another group – to conclude that the policy was one of genocide. The collective pain inflicted on two generations of Aborigines adds to the distress over their current plight. Their life expectancy is significantly lower than that of other Australians; their infant mortality is four times higher; they are grossly over-represented in the prisons; too many die in custody.

The report is compelling, painful, even harrowing. Many children were used as free labour or sex objects by those responsible for rescuing them from their primitive culture. Rape, child abuse, beatings and mental breakdowns were commonplace. One family engaged in ritual grieving over its stolen child every sunrise for thirty-two years. Publication of the report provoked shame and controversy. It avoided assigning guilt, preferring healing to retribution. Opposition leader Kim Beazley broke down and wept in parliament at the memory of the case studies. The government reacted angrily to the emotive charge of genocide and rejected the recommendations for an official apology, reparation and an annual 'sorry day'. In 2000, the government threatened to curtail cooperation with UN human rights agencies and inquiries because of their presumptuousness in investigating human rights in Australia. When Australians preach to Asians on human rights, they revive memories of the White Australia policy on immigration, whose structural continuity can be seen in parts of detention practices of illegal immigrants to this day.[24]

Australia is not alone in acting as though only non-Westerners should be targets of norms that are supposedly universal. Which rights that Westerners hold dear would they be prepared to give up in the name of universalism? Or is the concept of universalism just a one-way street – what we Westerners have is ours, what you heathens have is open to negotiation? Similarly, where is the borderline between universal norms of environmental, labour and children's rights protection, and disguised trade protection measures (i.e., non-tariff barriers)?

In other words, even if we agree on universal human rights, the question remains of the agency and procedure for determining what they are, how they apply in specific circumstances and cases, what the proper remedies might be to breaches, and who decides, following what rules of procedure and evidence. With world realities as they are today, the political calculus – relations based on military might and economic power, not to mention the nuisance value of NGOs – cannot be taken out. As far as many Asians are concerned, *that* is the problem.

## From human rights to 'humanitarian intervention'

The problem becomes more intractable when we slip across from human rights to armed intervention for humanitarian reasons. In international affairs, intervention can be defined broadly to mean just about anything that is done or said about an independent political entity by someone who is not a member of that entity. Or it can be defined narrowly to mean coercive interference by one state in the affairs of another state through the employment or threat of force. In medicine, it is commonly used to describe action taken to arrest and cure pathological conditions. In law-enforcement, it is an accepted part of the repertoire of community policing. In humanitarian crises, 'low-level' humanitarian intervention to help with emergency relief and assistance, as indeed epitomized by the ICRC, is welcome and uncontroversial. At the high-politics end of international security, however, the term is used pejoratively to connote action that is illegitimate within the prevailing legal or normative order. Together, the two (range of meanings and impermissibility) produce the strange result that nations agree that intervention is unlawful, but disagree on what precisely is intervention.

Contrary to what many European governments claimed, the application of a right of 'humanitarian intervention' in Kosovo was not self-evidently (self-righteously?) based in law or morality. During the Security Council debate on Kosovo in 1999, for example, the Sino-Russian draft resolution condemning bombing by the NATO forces was defeated by a vote of twelve to three. Yet the Indian Ambassador claimed that since China, Russia and India had opposed the bombing, the representatives of half of humanity were opposed to the action.

Contemporary norms prohibit ill-treatment of citizens by their own states. But they also prohibit interference in the internal affairs of states. The UN Charter reflects this tension.

Venerable commentators assert that, 'Intervention has become the new norm [in] a climate in which non-intervention appears as a dereliction of duty, requiring explanation, excuse or apology.'[25] The assertion can be challenged both on empirical and doctrinal grounds. Claude's claim is surely easy to refute empirically. In 1999, intervention took place in just two cases (Kosovo and East Timor) from a universe of several where it could have been justified across Asia and Africa. Even East Timor is an arguable example. Since Indonesia's annexation had not been legally recognized by the UN, the international community could not legally be said to have intervened in internal Indonesian affairs.

But what of Claude's claim with regard to the ethical meaning of norms? Can we separate power politics from decisions that were made in Kosovo? The Kosovo campaign was a very good illustration of how different norms can come into conflict, and of the lack of institutional mechanisms for resolving such tension in the existing world order.

The doctrine of national sovereignty in its absolute and unqualified form, which gave rulers protection against attack from without while engaged within in the most brutal assault on their own citizens, has gone with the wind. But we cannot accept the doctrine that any one state or coalition can decide when to intervene with force in the internal affairs of other countries, for down that path lies total chaos. The Kosovo war was a major setback to the cause of slowly but steadily outlawing the use of force in solving disputes except under UN authorization. The argument that NATO had no intention to set a precedent is less relevant than that its actions were interpreted by others as having set a dangerous precedent.

The Russian and Chinese draft resolution of March 1999 condemning NATO action received the support of only one other member of the Security Council, Namibia; the remaining twelve members voted against it. (Although India was granted permission to speak in the debate, it was not at that time a member of the Security Council.)

Faced with the controversy arising from different first principles, we come back to the same set of operational dilemmas: who decides, by what right and authority, following what rules of procedure and evidence, that atrocities have been committed requiring external intervention? How do we weigh in the balance the costs of not doing anything against the international and long-term consequences of going to war without due process?

If NATO can do so with regard to Kosovo without authorization by the Security Council, then why not the Arab League with regard to Palestine today? To say that they lack the power or military capacity to do so is to say that might is right. Similarly, would we accept former or present Israeli leaders being put on trial for crimes against humanity by a tribunal that was set up essentially by the Arab League, funded by them and dependent on them for collecting crucial evidence through national intelligence assets and for enforcement of arrest warrants? How plausible is the argument that the decade-old sanctions on Iraq are responsible for one of the great human atrocities of our times – more deaths than caused by all the weapons of mass destruction throughout the twentieth century,[26] in violation of the laws of war requirements of proportionality and of discrimination between combatants and civilians?[27] Who is to decide the answer to this question and, if the answer is in the affirmative, what is to be done against the perpetrators?

Many Asian countries are former colonies who achieved independence on the back of extensive and protracted nationalist struggles against the major European powers. The party and leaders at the forefront of the fight for independence helped to establish the new states and shape and guide the founding principles of foreign policies. The anti-colonial impulse in their world view was instilled in their countries' foreign policies and survives as a powerful sentiment in the corporate memory of the Asian elites. For most Westerners, NATO is an alliance of democracies and as such a standing validation of the democratic peace thesis. For most Asian ex-colonies, however, the most notable feature of NATO is that it is a military alliance of former colonial powers: every former European colonial power is a member of NATO. It is simply not possible to understand the strength of India's reaction to the 1999 war in Kosovo without first appreciating the significance of the trauma of historical input: countries that in previous centuries had carved up Africa and Asia were now carving up central Europe and pursuing familiar policies of divide-and-leave. NATO and Europe do not own the copyright on moral outrage. For many Asians, the norm of non-intervention remains a moral imperative, not simply a legal inconvenience to be discarded at the whim and will of the West. They were morally outraged at its violation by NATO in 1999. Even Japan, the staunchest of US Asian allies, neither condemned (because it understood the provocation) nor condoned (because it was unhappy with the circumvention of the UN) NATO bombing.

## United Nations and norm generation

The Kosovo war brought to a head the risk of the world's pre-eminent international organization and indispensable power marching down separate paths with potentially fatal consequences for world order.

Intervention that is authorized by the United Nations entails the presumption of legitimacy, that which is not so authorized bears the presumption of illegitimacy. But there are exceptions to both parts of the proposition. In the United Nations system, the normative centre of gravity is the General Assembly, but the geopolitical centre of gravity and the enforcement body is the Security Council in which the Asian peoples are grossly under-represented. The preferences of the two can be at odds.

There is an additional caveat. In national systems, bills passed into law by the legislature and actions of the executive arm of government can be found, by judicial review, to violate constitutionally guaranteed rights of citizens. In principle, Security Council resolutions could similarly violate the rights of member states guaranteed by the UN Charter. But there is no mechanism to hold the Security Council to independent international judicial account for its actions. Given the unrepresentative nature of the Council, there are occasional tremors of apprehension among developing countries about the potential for the UN, which they see as the best protection that the weak have against the strong in international affairs, to become instead the instrument for legitimating the actions of the strong against the weak. Thus authorization by the United Nations is not a sufficient condition of international legitimacy. Conversely, it may not even be a necessary condition: simply because the UN has not authorized it does not mean that a particular intervention in any given instance is automatically illegitimate. But the overwhelming majority of such cases over time will be deemed to be illegitimate.

## Conclusion

The status of law is not as clear-cut in international relations as it is in domestic systems. International humanitarian law neither develops nor operates in a vacuum. It has to be placed within its particular temporal and political contexts. In particular, norms and international law are the two end points on the continuum along which international humanitarian law needs to be located. International law and international norms provide mutual underpinnings to each other. International law as we know it was a product of the European states system and even international humanitarian law has its roots essentially in Europe.

The threshold of the new millennium is also the cusp of a new era in world affairs. The business of the world has changed almost beyond recognition over the course of the last one hundred years. There are many more players today, and their patterns of interaction are far more complex. The locus of power and influence is shifting. The demands and expectations made on governments and international organizations by the people of the world can no longer be satisfied through isolated and self-contained efforts. The international policy-making stage is increasingly congested as private and public non-state players jostle alongside national governments in setting and implementing the agenda of the new century. The multitude of new players adds depth and texture to the increasingly rich tapestry of international civil society.

In today's seamless world, political frontiers have become less salient both for international organizations, whose rights and duties can extend beyond borders, and for member states, whose responsibilities within borders can be held to international scrutiny. The gradual erosion of the once sacrosanct principle of national sovereignty is rooted today in the reality of global interdependence: no country is an island unto itself any more. Ours is a world of major cities and agglomerations, with nodes of financial and economic power and their globally wired transport and communications networks. Cumulatively, they span an increasingly interconnected and interactive world characterized more by technology-driven exchange and communication than by territorial borders and political separation.

In a world in such a state of flux, there are problems enough with efforts to provide philosophical underpinnings to global norms. The difficulties multiply when we move to the operational realm of giving policy shape and content to them.

Norms are effective as a behaviour-regulating mechanism only if they are accepted as legitimate by the target player – whether Israel, India, Japan or the United States. We, as the international community, need in every particular instance either:

- to forge a genuine normative consensus; or
- to make realistic assessments of our capacity to coerce recalcitrant players versus their capacity to break out of the constraining regime.

Rules and regulations that have already attained the status of binding provisions of international humanitarian law do not need the same requirement of internalization by the intended target countries. But there is the very grave danger that 'cherry picking' articles of international humanitarian law or of other parts of international law to suit one's partisan interests of the day will undermine respect for the principle of world order founded on law. That is to say, the normative consensus on which law rests will begin to fray and the international order will risk collapsing. The dangers of this are magnified because of the potentially competing and conflicting norms and principles at play on most controversial/important issues, such as landmines, nuclear weapons or intervention for humanitarian reasons.

In many Asian minds, there is bemusement at the confusion. But there is also resentment that, yet again, Asians seem to be consigned to being norm-and-law-takers, not setters; that they have not been made equal partners in the management of regimes in which international norms and laws are embedded.

# 5 Intervention, sovereignty and the responsibility to protect

## Experiences from ICISS[1]

The debate on intervention was ignited in the closing years of the last century by the critical gap between the needs and distress felt in the real world in Somalia, Rwanda, Srebrenica and East Timor, and the codified instruments and modalities for managing world order. There has been a parallel gap, no less critical, between the codified best practice of international behaviour as articulated in the UN Charter and actual state practice as it has evolved in the fifty-seven years since the Charter was signed. The responsibility for protecting the lives and promoting the welfare of citizens lies first and foremost with the sovereign state. There is a gap – a responsibility deficit – if the state proves unable or unwilling to protect citizens, or itself becomes the perpetrator of violence against its own citizens. Can the slack in responsibility be picked up by agents outside the country concerned? If so, by whom, under what authority, in what circumstances and subject to what procedural and operational safeguards?

The community-sanctioning authority to settle issues of international peace and security was transferred from the great powers in concert in the nineteenth century to the United Nations in the twentieth century. While Rwanda in 1994 stands as the symbol of international inaction in the face of genocide, Kosovo in 1999 raised many questions about the consequences of action when the international community is divided in the face of a humanitarian tragedy. The United Nations is the only organization with universally accepted authority to validate such operations. But the only military coalition with the capacity to engage in robust and sustained enforcement action, in and outside its area of operations, is the North Atlantic Treaty Organization (NATO). In 1999, on the one hand, there were claims of a compelling humanitarian tragedy in Kosovo that was an affront to an internationalized human conscience. On the other hand, there was every prospect of Security Council action being blocked by one or two vetoes. But this was never put to the test and NATO launched a 'humanitarian war' without UN authorization and in doing so posed a fundamental challenge to the normative architecture of world order.[2]

The dilemma can be summarized thus:

- To respect sovereignty all the time is to risk being complicit in humanitarian tragedies sometimes.

- To argue that the UN Security Council must give its consent to international intervention for humanitarian purposes is to risk policy paralysis by handing over the agenda either to the passivity and apathy of the Council as a whole, or to the most obstructionist member of the Council, including any one of the five permanent members determined to use the veto clause.
- To use force without UN authorization is to violate international law and undermine world order based on the centrality of the UN as the custodian of world conscience and the Security Council as the guardian of world peace.

Under the impact of contrasting experiences in Rwanda[3] and Kosovo, Secretary-General Kofi Annan challenged member states to come up with a new consensus on the competing visions of national and popular sovereignty. Responding to the challenge, Canadian Foreign Minister Lloyd Axworthy set up the ICISS to wrestle with the whole gamut of difficult and complex issues involved in the debate.

The Report of the Commission,[4] published with formal presentation to Annan on 18 December 2001, seeks to achieve three things. First, it seeks to reposition the existing normative consensus on the subject by replacing the language of humanitarian intervention with the concept of the responsibility to protect. Second, it seeks to locate that responsibility with state authorities at the national and the Security Council at the global levels respectively. Third, it seeks to ensure that when intervention for human protection purposes does take place, it is carried out with efficiency, effectiveness and due authority, process and diligence.

This chapter is devoted principally to an exposition of the first of the three goals.[5] The key to the attempt to move the existing consensus forward is a change in the conceptual vocabulary, from the right and duty of 'humanitarian intervention' to the responsibility to protect. The mandate of ICISS was to eschew polemics and find a formula for reconciling the urge to humanitarian intervention with the persisting reality of state sovereignty. The concept of the responsibility to protect does just that. The rest of the article is divided into five parts. The next section describes the added value of the Commission's work. In the two sections after that, relatively greater attention is paid to elaborating the concepts of the responsibility to protect and sovereignty as responsibility. The fourth section alludes briefly to other parts of the Commission's report, while the fifth and final section considers the tension between UN and great power responsibility to protect deriving from lawful authority and military capacity.

## Added value of ICISS

There is already a vast literature on the subject that ICISS was set up to address.[6] Why bother with another study? What could we do that would be a substantial advance? We believe that ICISS has six distinguishing features: balance, outreach, independence, comprehensiveness, innovativeness and political realism.

The Commission was balanced in composition, starting with the co–chairs, with regard to professional backgrounds (former heads of state and cabinet ministers, UN officials, generals, scholars, journalists), continents-cum-civilizations, industrialized-developing country perspectives and initial starting positions on the intervention-sovereignty debate.[7] Mohamed Sahnoun wears the inherited wisdom of an entire continent very lightly on his shoulders and has long and great experience as a national and UN diplomat. He has a wonderful and seemingly inexhaustible repertoire of African animal stories with a moral for every occasion. Gareth Evans is as passionate about justice and human security as Sahnoun and driven by a restless energy that is astonishingly creative when harnessed to a pet cause. The excellent personal chemistry between the Commissioners, combined with their willingness to listen to one another and adapt and evolve their thinking, without necessarily giving up bottom lines, enabled us to come up with a unanimous report that is more than a collection of clichés and platitudes. If just twelve reasonable, experienced and intelligent people had failed to come to an agreed report, the prospects of the international community forging a new consensus on the contentious subject of military interventions would have been bleak indeed.

The willingness to listen and adapt was put to the test in an extensive outreach exercise that was one of the most valuable parts of the ICISS process. Commission meetings and round tables were held in almost all continents and major capitals, involving continent-wide representatives, over 200 in total, from all sectors and cross-section of views.[8] The Report reflects a genuine effort to incorporate many of the views that were expressed in Cairo, New Delhi and Santiago as well as Beijing, London, Paris and Washington. The views presented during the outreach exercise were sometimes used as tie-breakers during deadlocked discussions in the Commission.

There would not have been much point to the regional consultations if the Commission was working to a secret agenda. If the Canadian government had a hidden agenda and a predetermined outcome for ICISS, as mooted by some, they neglected to tell the Commissioners. ICISS was notable for the lack of 'shrinking violets' and this reinforced the independent nature of the Commission. The Report reflects our combined and collective thinking as it evolved over the year's deliberations.

The Report is comprehensive in three senses. First, it includes separate chapters on prevention, intervention, reconstruction, lawful authority and the operational dimension of military interventions. The 'responsibility to protect' provides conceptual, normative and operational linkages between assistance, intervention and reconstruction. The inputs from the round table discussions contributed greatly to the comprehensiveness of the Commission's final product, which consists of a supplementary research volume in addition to the main report.[9] The Commission was assisted by a Secretariat provided by

Canada's foreign ministry, plus a research team under the co-direction of Stanlake Samkange and Thomas W. Weiss. While the primary responsibility for the second volume lay with Weiss and Don Hubert, they were helped by several especially commissioned essays plus submissions and contributions from over fifty specialists. The research volume is supported by an extensive and annotated bibliography that contains more than 2,200 entries and the entire report and volume is available in a CD-ROM that is key-worded and indexed to facilitate ease of research.

Fifth, the 'Responsibility to Protect' formulation is, we believe, genuinely innovative, as was 'sustainable development' of the Bruntdland Commission whose success in reconciling the previously opposed concepts of development (which is exploitative) and conservation had formed an inspiring model for us from the start of our deliberations. (Co-chair Sahnoun was a member of the Brundtland Commission.)

Sixth, the ICISS discussions and report were always grounded in political realism. For example, we were not interested in solving all the world's problems, but stuck narrowly to our mandate. Thus we resisted the temptation to recast our Report in the light of the terrorist attacks of 11 September 2001, concluding that horrific and urgent as the latter was, self-defence is conceptually and operationally distinct from the protection of at-risk foreign populations. Similarly, we resisted the temptation to urge amendments to the UN Charter, for example with respect to the composition and functioning of the Security Council.

In retrospect, as a final contextual comment, the one-year timeframe was probably a very useful discipline. This meant the momentum never flagged, we worked to a tight deadline and we remembered where we had got to at the last meeting and the progress that had already been made.

## Shifting the terms of the debate

'Humanitarian Intervention' is what humanitarian agencies such as the International Committee of the Red Cross (ICRC) and the UN High Commissioner for Refugees (UNHCR) do; they object to the phrase being appropriated by states engaged in military intervention. 'Humanitarian Intervention' conveys to most Western minds the idea that the principle underlying the intervention is not self-interested power politics but the disinterested one of protecting human life. It conjures up in many non-Western minds historical memories of the strong imposing their will on the weak in the name of the prevailing universal principles of the day, from the civilizing mission of spreading Christianity to the cultivation and promotion of human rights.

The traditional terms of the debate focus attention on the claims, rights and prerogatives of the potentially intervening states much more so than on the urgent needs of the intended, putative beneficiaries of the action. By focusing on the 'right to intervene' they do not adequately take into account the prevention and follow-up assistance components of external action. The phrase 'humanitarian intervention' is used to trump sovereignty with intervention at the outset of the debate: it loads the dice in favour of intervention before the argument has even begun, by labelling and delegitimizing dissent as anti-humanitarian.

Where humanitarian intervention raises fears of domination based on the international power hierarchy, the responsibility to protect encapsulates the element of international solidarity. Moreover, it implies an evaluation of the issues from the point of view of those seeking or needing support, rather than those who may be considering intervention. Our preferred terminology refocuses the international searchlight back on the duty to protect the villager from murder, the woman from rape and the child from starvation and being orphaned.

## Sovereignty

Crucially, the responsibility to protect acknowledges that responsibility rests primarily with the state concerned; only if the state is unable or unwilling to fulfil this responsibility, or is itself the perpetrator, does it become the responsibility of others to act in its place. In many cases, the state seeks to acquit its responsibility in full and active partnership with representatives of the international community. Thus the responsibility to protect is more of a linking concept that bridges the divide between the international community and the sovereign state, whereas the language of the right or duty to intervene is inherently more confrontational.

Internally, sovereignty refers to the exclusive competence of the state to make authoritative decisions of government with regard to all people and resources within its territory. Externally, it means the legal identity of the state in international law, an equality of status with all other states and the claim to be the sole official agent acting in international relations on behalf of a society. *National sovereignty* locates the state as the ultimate seat of power and authority, unconstrained by internal or external checks; *constitutional sovereignty* holds that the power and authority of the state are not absolute but contingent and constrained.[10] Domestically, power sharing between the executive, legislature and judiciary, at federal and provincial levels, is regulated by constitutional arrangements and practices. Internationally, states are constrained by globally legitimated institutions and practices.

Sovereignty has its philosophical and political roots in European thought and practice. Ironically, while aspects of sovereignty are being progressively superseded in the construction of the increasingly borderless European Union, some of its most passionate defenders are to be found among developing countries (although the United States is second to none in the jealous defence of national sovereignty against international encroachments).

At one level, the developing countries' attachment to sovereignty is deeply emotional. The colonial experience traumatized many of them and the long shadows cast by this are yet to disappear. In the age of colonialism, most Afro-

Asians and Latin Americans became the victims of Western superiority in the organization and weaponry of warfare. Most developing countries are former colonies who achieved independence on the back of extensive and protracted nationalist struggles against the major European powers. The anti-colonial impulse in their worldview survives as a powerful sentiment in the collective consciousness of the nation. The continuing scars in the collective memory are difficult for many Westerners to comprehend and come to terms with.

At another level, the commitment to sovereignty is functional. The state is the cornerstone of the international system. State sovereignty provides order, stability and predictability in international relations. It mediates relations between the strong and weak, rich and poor and former colonizers and colonized. With independence and following the globalization of the norm of self-determination, the principle of state sovereignty was the constitutional device used by newly decolonized countries to try to reconstitute disrupted societies and polities and to restart arrested economic development. As Mohammed Ayoob notes, the developing countries typically sought order within and justice among states. By contrast, the industrialized Western countries have given primacy to order among and justice (that is, civil-political human rights) within states.[11]

The Commission's core principle is that state sovereignty implies responsibility,[12] and the primary responsibility for the protection of its people lies with the state itself. But if it should default, a residual, fallback responsibility also lies with the broader community of states. Where a population is suffering serious harm, as a result of internal war, insurgency, repression or state failure and the government in question is unwilling or unable to halt or avert it, the principle of non-intervention yields to the international responsibility to protect. The foundations of that responsibility lie in obligations inherent in the concept of sovereignty; the responsibility of the Security Council for the maintenance of international peace and security; specific legal obligations under human rights and human protection declarations, covenants and treaties, international humanitarian law and national law; and the developing practice of states, regional organizations and the Security Council itself.[13]

If sovereignty becomes an obstacle to the realization of freedom, then it can, should and must be discarded. But sovereignty need not be such an obstacle. While some elements of sovereignty have devolved downwards and inwards to civil society within the state, others have been subsumed in transnational flows, activities and institutions across borders. In today's seamless world, political frontiers have become less salient both for international organizations, whose rights and duties can extend beyond borders and for member states, whose responsibilities within borders can be held to international scrutiny.

The steady erosion of the once sacrosanct principle of national sovereignty is rooted in the reality of global interdependence: no *country* is an island unto itself anymore. The increasing internationalization of the world has widened the gap between the legal status and actual reality of states acting and interacting in the international arena. As a result of agreements that they have signed voluntarily, states now accept many external obligations and international scrutiny. The norms of human rights and international humanitarian law in particular are widely acknowledged and honoured in and among states. As memories of colonialism dim and become increasingly distant, the salience of sovereignty correspondingly diminishes. Citizens and domestic groups instead begin to use the international human rights norm and cross-national global coalitions to subject the actions of their own governments to increasingly critical scrutiny.

For these reasons and based on changes in the real world and evolving best practice international behaviour, the Commission concluded that it is necessary and useful to reconceptualize sovereignty as responsibility. This has a threefold significance. First, it implies that the state authorities are responsible *for* the functions of protecting the safety and lives of citizens and promotion of their welfare. Second, it suggests that the national political authorities are responsible *to* the citizens internally and to the international community through the UN. And third, it means that the agents of state are responsible for their actions, that is to say, they are *accountable* for their acts of commission and omission. Would-be perpetrators of mass atrocities should fear the growth of universal justice as a result of which they will ultimately have nowhere else to run, no place left to hide.

The UN Charter is itself an example of an international obligation voluntarily accepted by member states. On the one hand, in granting membership to the UN, the international community welcomes the signatory state as a responsible member of the community of nations. On the other hand, the state itself, in signing the Charter, accepts the responsibilities of membership flowing from that signature. The United Nations is the symbol and the arena for the shared management of pooled sovereignty.

## Doing it right, doing it well

### Conflict prevention and peacebuilding

Action in support of the responsibility to protect necessarily involves and calls for a broad range and wide variety of measures and responses in fulfilment of the accompanying duty to assist. These may include development assistance to help prevent conflict from occurring, intensifying, spreading, or persisting; rebuilding support to help prevent conflict from recurring; and, in extraordinary cases, military intervention to protect at-risk civilians from harm.

Prevention is the single most important dimension of the responsibility to protect, so prevention options should always be exhausted before intervention is contemplated. Moreover, the exercise of the responsibility to prevent and react should always involve less intrusive and coercive measures being considered (although not necessarily attempted) before more coercive and intrusive ones are applied. The responsibility to prevent requires addressing both the root causes and direct causes of internal conflict and other man-made crises putting populations at risk. The responsibility to react requires us to respond to situations of compelling human need with appropriate measures, which may include coercive measures such as sanctions and international prosecution and in extreme cases military intervention. The responsibility to rebuild requires us to provide, particularly after a military intervention, full assistance with recovery, reconstruction and reconciliation, addressing the causes of the harm the intervention was designed to halt or avert.

## Threshold criteria and cautionary principles

Military intervention for human protection purposes is an exceptional and extraordinary measure. To be warranted, there must be serious and irreparable harm occurring to human beings, or imminently likely to occur, of the following kind:

- large-scale loss of life due to deliberate state action, neglect or inability to act, or a failed state situation; or
- large-scale ethnic cleansing, actual or apprehended, whether carried out by killing, forced expulsion, acts of terror or rape.

We concluded that it would be futile to try to anticipate every contingency and provide a uniform checklist for intervention. Rather, the decision on intervention would have to be a matter of careful judgement on a case-by-case basis. Even when the just cause threshold is crossed of conscience-shocking loss of life or ethnic cleansing, intervention must be guided by the cautionary principles of right intention, last resort, proportional means and reasonable prospects.[14] The primary purpose of the intervention, whatever other motives intervening states may have, must be to halt or avert human suffering. Right intention is better assured with multilateral operations, clearly supported by regional opinion and the victims concerned. Military intervention can only be justified when every non-military option for the prevention or peaceful resolution of the crisis has been explored, with reasonable grounds for believing that lesser measures would not have succeeded. The scale, duration and intensity of the planned military intervention should be the minimum necessary to secure the defined human protection objective. And there must be a reasonable chance of success in halting or averting the suffering that has justified the intervention, with the consequences of action not likely to be worse than the consequences of inaction. Military intervention against major powers is ruled out, therefore, not as a matter of double standards at the level of principles, but due to a prudential consequentialism: under no conceivable circumstances would humanitarian goals be advanced by launching an external military intervention against Russia in order to protect, say, the people of Chechnya.

Finally, the Report also seeks to identify the operational principles to guide interventions. The chapter outlining these should be of particular interest to military staff colleges.

### Right authority and due process

War is itself a major humanitarian tragedy that can be justified only under the most compelling circumstances regarding the provocation, the likelihood of success – bearing in mind that goals are metamorphosed in the crucible of war once started – and the consequences that may reasonably be predicted. And the burden of proof rests on the proponents of force, not on dissenters. The sense of moral outrage provoked by humanitarian atrocities must always be tempered by an appreciation of the limits of power, a concern for international institution-building and a sensitivity to the law of unintended and perverse consequences. The NATO intervention in Kosovo in 1999 remains hotly disputed over the question of whether it triggered more carnage than it averted.

Intervention for human protection purposes occurs so that those condemned to die in fear may be rescued to live in hope instead. Even so, military intervention, even for humanitarian purposes, is just a nicer way of referring to the use of deadly force on a massive scale. Given the enormous normative presumption against the use of deadly force to settle international quarrels, who has the right to authorize such force? On what basis, for what purpose and subject to what safeguards and limitations? In other words, even if we agree that military intervention may sometimes be necessary and unavoidable in order to protect innocent people from life-threatening danger by interposing an outside force between actual and apprehended victims and perpetrators, key questions remain about agency, lawfulness and legitimacy: that is, about international authority that can override national authority.

Attempts to enforce authority can only be made by the legitimate agents of that authority. What distinguishes rule enforcement by criminal thugs from that by police officers is precisely the principle of legitimacy. The chief con-temporary institution for building, consolidating and using the authority of the international community is the United Nations. Set up as the principal element of order and stability in the revolutionary post-World War world, it was meant to be the framework within which members of the international system negotiated agreements on the rules of behaviour and the legal norms of proper conduct in order to preserve the society of states.

The Commission concluded that there is no better nor more appropriate body than the Security Council to authorize military intervention for human protection purposes. Those calling for an intervention should formally request such authorization, or have the Council raise the matter on its own initiative, or have the Secretary-General raise it under Article 99 of the UN Charter.

## UN authority and great power capacity

The formal authority for maintaining international peace and security is thus vested in the Security Council. But the burden of responsibility, from having the power to make the most difference, often falls on the United States and other leading powers. The conceptual connecting rod that links power to authority is legitimacy. The legitimacy of the Security Council as the authoritative validator of international security action has been subject to a steady erosion as it has been perceived as being unrepresentative in composition, undemocratic in operation, unaccountable to anyone 'below' (e.g. the General Assembly) or 'above' (e.g. the World Court) and ineffective in results. Western countries often chafe at the ineffectual performance legitimacy of the Council and their desire to resist the Council's role as the sole validator of the international use of force is the product of this dissatisfaction at its perceived sorry record. On the other hand, if it were to become increasingly activist, interventionist and effective, then the erosion of representational and procedural legitimacy would lead many developing countries to question the authority of the Council even more forcefully.

The UN is just as powerful a symbol of what member states must not do. In the field of state-citizen relations *within* territorial borders, the totality of Charter clauses and instruments such as the Universal Declaration of Human Rights restrict the authority of states to cause harm to their own people. In the sphere of military action *across* borders, UN membership imposes the obligation on the major powers to abjure unilateral intervention in favour of collectively authorized international intervention.

The legal debate on a clear, consistent and workable set of codified criteria for intervention is largely sterile. The political debate quickly degenerates from rational discussion to highly charged polemics. Morally, many fear that any codification of the rules of intervention would relegitimize the use of force in international relations. This would be a major step backward, in that over the course of the twentieth century the international community placed increasing legislative and normative fetters on the recourse to military force as a means of settling international disputes. The United Nations is both the symbol and the major instrument for moderating the use of force in international relations, not blessing it and sanctifying a major expansion in its permissive scope.

The response from those with little patience for claims of UN primacy (let alone monopoly) on the legitimate use of international force is that the UN system of collective security was fatally flawed from the start. Peace was preserved and justice advanced by the operation of institutions and the pursuit of values by coalitions of the right minded, able and willing to defend the international order against all challenges.

The real debate is between those who support the development of guidelines for use by the Security Council in authorizing international intervention but remain firmly opposed to criteria for circumventing the UN and those who wish to retain the right to unilateral intervention. The first group, comprising mainly (but neither exclusively nor all) developing countries, is fearful that the norm of non-intervention could become a roadkill on the highway of international power politics, taking us back to the nineteenth-century system of a concert of great powers.

Among those who wish to retain the flexibility to launch military intervention without UN authorization if necessary, there is a further division of opinion between those who would like a 'doctrine' approach and others who want merely an 'exception' approach[15] – a signposted emergency exit from the existing norms as embedded in the UN Charter.

Yet another variation would be to distinguish a 'red light' from the entrenched 'green light' approach. Under the latter, intervention may not proceed until and unless it has been duly authorized by the Security Council. Under the former, interventions can take place unless and until specifically prohibited by the Council. In Kosovo in 1999, a draft resolution condemning NATO bombing was defeated 3–12, despite two permanent members voting in the affirmative. Many interpreted the failure to flash the red light as tacit or de facto authorization. The difficulty with this is not just that it subverts the Charter and turns the principle of authorization on its head. As well, the veto clause would still come into play. Even if the vote in support of a 'red light' resolution was 14–1, the resolution would fail and the red light therefore could not be flashed, if that one solitary negative vote was that of a permanent member. Equally, when the vital interests of global or regional major powers are engaged, interventionary forces may go crashing through an entire forest of flashing red lights without paying any heed to them.

Alternatively, it may be argued that the intersection of international law and ethics creates a space where the precautionary principle can be borrowed from environmental ethics and law. Developed especially in Germany and France with regard to environmental law and the legal protection of health, it seeks to provide policy guidance in situations of inherent uncertainty. The equivalent of the prudential driving adage 'If in doubt, don't', the precautionary principle states that the absence of certainty must not delay the adoption of measures aimed at preventing the risk of serious and irreversible damage.[16] For if we wait until certainty (for example with respect to the scope, magnitude and gravity of impact, or causal links between anthropogenic activities and environmental degradation), then irreversible damage may already have been caused. Therefore, as per the precautionary principle, the legal responsibility to protect applies not only to those domestic public authorities who failed to take preventive measures against *known* risks and hazards, but also to those who did not take *precautionary* measures because of existing margins of doubt and uncertainty. Humanitarian atrocities, genocidal killings and ethnic cleansing occur against the backdrop of chaos, confusion and lack of real time reliable information. If we wait until clarity and certainty obtains, our task may become restitution and retribution, not protection. It should be protection and therefore, in the face of uncertainty, the default bias should be to avoid risk.

This is why it is important for the Security Council to deal promptly with any request for authority to intervene where there are allegations of large scale loss of human life or ethnic cleansing. The ICISS report recommends that the permanent five members of the Security Council should agree not to apply their veto power in matters where their vital state interests are not involved, so as not to obstruct the passage of resolutions authorizing military intervention for human protection purposes for which there is otherwise majority support. Action in selected cases outside a veto-paralysed Security Council framework is less defensible by those who refuse to accept any dilution of the veto power as a matter of general principle.[17]

If the Security Council rejects a proposal or fails to deal with it in a reasonable time, alternative options are: consideration of the matter by the General Assembly in Emergency Special Session under the 'Uniting for Peace' procedure; and action within area of jurisdiction by regional or sub-regional organizations, subject to their seeking subsequent authorization from the Security Council.

The Security Council should take into account in all its deliberations that, if it fails to discharge its responsibility to protect in conscience-shocking situations crying out for action, concerned states may not rule out other means to meet the gravity and urgency of that situation. This carries a double risk. Their actions may not be guided by the just cause and cautionary principles identified in the ICISS report and so their interventions may not be done well, with due authority, diligence and process. Alternatively, they may do it very well and the people of the world may conclude that their actions were necessary, just and proper, in which case the stature and credibility of the United Nations may suffer still further erosion.

## Conclusion

The Commission's report deals succinctly with the full range of issues involved in the debate. The fact that a dozen people of diverse background and varied starting positions were able to agree on a challenging, substantial and wide-ranging report encourages us to believe that an international consensus can indeed be forged around these ideas and principles. If and when the world is once again confronted by challenges on the scale of Rwanda, Kosovo and East Timor, we hope it will be better prepared to act with principled force. Too often in the past UN peace operations have fallen victim to coalitions of the unwilling, unable and un-likeminded. It is time to put collective might to the service of individual and international right.

How might this be done? What are the next steps? At a seminar in New York on 15 February 2002, organized by the International Peace Academy, most Security Council members seemed supportive of the main thrust of the Report. In May, Kofi Annan convened a Security Council retreat for discussing the policy and operational implications of the ICISS report. The Report itself also calls for a declaratory resolution by the General Assembly affirming the just cause threshold criteria that would trigger intervention and the four cautionary principles of right intention, last resort, proportionality and reasonable prospects.

If imitation be the sincerest form of flattery, it is interesting that Ambassador Jayantha Dhanapala, the UN Under-Secretary-General for Disarmament and a member of the Canberra Commission on the Elimination of Nuclear Weapons, recently proposed the creation of a new commission on the elimination of all weapons of mass destruction, drawing explicitly on the model of ICISS.[18]

# 6 In defence of the responsibility to protect[1]

I am pleased to have this opportunity, through the medium of a reply to two interesting and stimulating pieces by leading scholars in the field, to extend the debate on 'The Responsibility to Protect' even further. I do so as an ICISS Commissioner. But first some preliminary caveats. This rejoinder reflects my personal opinion and thinking and does not necessarily reflect the views of the United Nations University. Second, it does not even purport to speak in the name of ICISS: only the consensus Report of the Commission does that. Third, it has nevertheless benefited enormously from the debates and discussions with the other members of the Commission and from the extensive reading material collected by the research team as background material to assist the Commission's deliberations. Finally, but by no means least, our report seeks to speak to several audiences. Although the supplementary research volume is addressed mainly to the research community, the main report itself is addressed chiefly to the international policy community in general and to the UN-centred policy community in particular. As such it is at least as much a work of policy advocacy, if underpinned by serious scholarly research.

This chapter first sketches the background to the ICISS establishment and work, then looks at some specific observations by Professors Roberts and Warner and finally takes up the discussion with respect to some broader themes that they raise or resurrect.

## Background

The 1990s were a challenging decade for the international community with regard to conscience-shocking atrocities in many parts of the world. We generally failed to rise to the challenge and the price of our failure was paid by large numbers of innocent men, women and children. The terrorist attacks of 11 September 2001 shifted attention to the 'war on terrorism' and the international community has been preoccupied since then with the consequences and menacing new manifestations of that war. Nevertheless, as the co-chairs of ICISS noted in a subsequent article, 'Meanwhile, the debate about intervention for human protection purposes has not gone away. And it will not go away so long as human nature remains as fallible as it is and internal conflict and state failures stay as prevalent as they are.'[2]

The terrain on which the conceptual and policy contest over 'humanitarian intervention' has been fought is essentially normative. It takes the form of norm displacement, from the established norm of non-intervention to a claimed emerging new norm of 'humanitarian intervention'. The United Nations lies at the centre of this contest both metaphorically and literally. The UN Charter, more than any other single document in the world, encapsulates and articulates the agreed consensus on the prevailing norms that give structure and meaning to the foundations of world order. And the international community comes together physically, primarily within the hallowed halls of the United Nations. It is not surprising, therefore, that the UN should be the epicentre of the interplay between changing norms and shifting state practice.

Intervention for human protection purposes is based in the double belief that the sovereignty of a state has an accompanying responsibility on the part of that state; and that if the state defaults on the responsibility to protect its citizens, then the fallback responsibility to do so must be assumed and discharged by the international community.

## Adam Roberts

The key to the attempt to move the existing consensus forward is a change in the conceptual vocabulary, from the right and duty of 'humanitarian intervention' to the responsibility to protect. I am pleased that Professor Roberts acknowledges the advance that the new terminology represents. As it happens, I also share his scepticism as to whether we will succeed in displacing 'humanitarian intervention' from its established position of dominance in the discourse. But I believe we must try and that belief has been strengthened by the debate over Iraq during the past year. In effect we have seen the humanitarian community split into two camps: humanitarians for war and humanitarians against war. It is worth recalling that the NATO intervention in Kosovo was essentially an air campaign. If it is permissible to speak of 'humanitarian intervention', then by the same logic we should speak too of 'humanitarian bombing'. Yet most people recoil instinctively from that phrase, for they recognize it for a conceptual oxymoron. In principle 'humanitarian intervention' entails exactly the same internal inconsistency.

I remain puzzled with the statement that our report fails to point out that neither in Rwanda nor in Srebrenica was there a major problem regarding the legality of intervention. Just so: why create a controversy where there is none? On the substantive point, we do note that Rwanda was a failure of leadership by the UN and key member states (p. 73, para. 8.19). I agree wholeheartedly with Roberts that the Dutch soldiers failed to act in Srebrenica 'even in a situation where they had full legal authority to do so'. As noted above, this formed part of the backdrop against which ICISS was set up. We took our task to be to advance the debate rather than provide an elegant theoretical justification of what the Secretary-General had already said, to take Kofi Annan's challenge as our starting and not the end point.

The Commission was set up to get the international community out of the deep trenches into which the two opposing sides had dug themselves. Our mandate was to bridge the polemical divide and to come up with problem-solving formulations for the future. We adopted the position, which was surely right, that any attempt to examine the merits, law, legitimacy and political wisdom of past interventions would be backward-looking, possibly finger-pointing and certainly judgemental. In other words, we were not – and I for one am still not – convinced that such an exercise would be helpful to our task.

Nor, from the point of view of political advocacy and the desire to encourage a new consensus in the UN community, would it necessarily be helpful to face up explicitly 'to the fact that protection of vulnerable populations often requires a capacity and willingness to strike back . . . at the forces that threaten such populations . . . Such action may sometimes even require the defeat of a state's armed forces, or those of a non-state entity'. All this is indeed the unmistakable and unavoidable premise of outside interventions. The report does state clearly that 'the aim of the human protection operation is to enforce compliance' (p. 67, para. 7.51). It then becomes, for a report of this type, a matter of political judgement rather than academic rigor or logical clarity to decide how explicit to make certain things that are inherently sensitive in their politics (we would not have needed an international commission otherwise, surely?).

If defeat of a non-compliant state or regime is the only way to achieve the human protection goals, then so be it. But the primary motivation behind intervention – the cause rather than the necessary condition – must not be defeating an enemy state. The substance of the responsibility to protect is the provision of life-supporting protection and assistance to populations at risk. The goal of intervention for human protection purposes is not to wage war on a state in order to destroy it and eliminate its statehood, but to protect victims of atrocities inside the state, to embed the protection in reconstituted institutions after the intervention and then to withdraw all foreign troops. Thus military intervention for human protection purposes takes away the rights flowing from the status of sovereignty, but does not in itself challenge the status as such. It does supplant the rights of the state to *exercise* protective functions if the state has proven incapable or unwilling to do so with respect to genocidal killings, humanitarian atrocities and ethnic cleansing; or to suspend the right of the state to conduct itself free of external interference if such conduct is the cause of the above atrocities. The prevention of the exercise of sovereign rights under intervention for human protection purposes is always limited in time to a temporary period, until the capacity of the state itself to resume its protective functions can be restored and institutionalized. The scale, duration and intensity of the planned military intervention should therefore be the minimum necessary to secure the defined human protection objective.

Intervention for human protection purposes may also be limited in two further respects. It may be confined to a particular portion of the target state's territory rather than all of it, for example Kosovo and not all of Yugoslavia, where the abuses are actually occurring; or it may be limited with respect to a particular group that is the target of abuse, rather than apply to all citizens.

Professor Roberts faults our failure to mention the Helsinki Final Act of 1975. I agree with his assessment of the Helsinki process, but remain unconvinced that ICISS should have ventured down that path. Inducing change in totalitarian states with poor human rights records is a very laudable objective, but was not at the centre of our concerns in ICISS. There are many other things we could have written about and on some of these we might even have secured agreement within the Commission. But one of the great merits of this report, I think – thanks to the rigorous discipline imposed by the two co-chairs – was the tightness of the focus on the core objective to the exclusion of other debates, no matter how important or interesting, that were extraneous to our central task.

## Daniel Warner

According to Professor Warner, 'To intervene is to trespass, to go where one is not welcome and has no right to go.' Not so: doctors engage in surgical interventions all the time, mostly they are welcome to do so and their actions are with the consent of the patients on the operating table. Hence our repeated efforts to emphasize that we were talking mainly about coercive interventions against the wishes of the state. And, with respect, it is slightly more than mere trespass. Having thus defined intervention as unwelcome trespass, two paragraphs later Warner defines 'humanitarian intervention', '*when a government does not fulfil its obligations to its citizens*' (emphasis added), as 'substitution for the government'. I might accept this strange redefinition for failed state situations, but to conflate intervention into governmental substitution seems to me to stretch the meaning of words beyond the point of sustainability.

And in the next paragraph, Warner concludes that: 'The Commission blinked because it looked into an abyss.' Well actually, if you find yourself at an abyss, it may prove injurious to your health to blink, while it is quite a good idea to step back. To stay with the same metaphor, it is more accurate to say that with Rwanda, the Balkans, East Timor and Kofi Annan's challenge of 'humanitarian intervention', the international community found itself staring at the abyss. It stepped back and the Canadian government decided to set up ICISS to provide a roadmap to bring the international community back to a properly marked highway of international politics. Our report restates the highway code, identifies the safety markers for detours from the highway and clarifies that the job of highway patrols belongs properly to the United Nations.

Warner's most serious charge, to the extent that I can follow him, is that the Commission was guilty of a failure of imagination and nerve in not moving beyond the Westphalian world of sovereign states. Our mandate was to rescue the international community from the ideological trenches of 'state sovereignty' and 'humanitarian intervention'. As noted above, *The Responsibility to Protect* is not an exercise in academic daring, breaking down the barriers to knowledge and advancing their frontiers through bold intellectual thrusts. From the point of view of forging a new consensus in the international policy community, I cannot think of a more damaging conclusion than that sovereignty should be abandoned entirely. And this applies not just to the developing countries but also, even more forcefully, to the United States.

## Sovereignty

Given Professor Warner's comments, I can only agree with Professor Roberts that the obvious point about the continuing validity of the non-intervention norm needed restatement and gets it in our Report. It is the mirror to the doctrine of state sovereignty. The responsibility for protecting the lives and promoting the welfare of citizens lies first and foremost with the sovereign state. The international order is based on a system of sovereign states in the belief that this is the most efficient means of organizing the world in order to discharge the responsibility to the people of protecting their lives and livelihoods and promoting their wellbeing and freedoms. In most cases this is better done by strengthening state capacity and resilience: the best guarantee of human rights is a world of competent, responsible and legitimate sovereign states. Conversely, the human security of people is put in grave danger in conditions of fragile or failed states.

Westphalian sovereignty originated in the sixteenth–seventeenth centuries in the European search for a secular basis of state authority. It embodies the notion that in every system of government there must be some absolute power of final decision. The person or body exercising such decision must be legally competent to decide and be able to enforce the decision. The state's primary concern is with order.

Subsequently, sovereignty was redefined in terms of a social contract between citizens and rulers. Violations of the contract by the rulers voided the duty of the citizens to obey the commands of the sovereign. By the end of the nineteenth century a distinction was being drawn between legal sovereignty as vested in parliament and political sovereignty as vested in the electorate. In the twentieth century the trend was taken further with the notion of popular sovereignty.

The principle of state sovereignty has little to do with the merits and morality of governments in power. Rather, not unlike Churchill's aphorism on democracy, sovereignty is the least bad system of organizing international relations. And the United Nations is the chief agent of this system of states for exercising international authority in their name. A condition of any one state's sovereignty is a corresponding obligation to respect every other state's sovereignty. If that duty is violated, the victim state has the further right to defend its territorial integrity and political independence. UN membership was the final symbol of independent sovereign statehood and thus the seal of acceptance into the community of nations. The United Nations also became the principal international forum for collaborative action in the shared pursuit of the three goals of state building, nation building and economic development. The UN was therefore the main arena for the jealous protection, not the casual abrogation, of state sovereignty.

Yet even during the cold war state practice reflected the unwillingness of many countries to give up intervention as an instrument of policy. Communist leaders sometimes argued that relations within the socialist community could not be subject to a legal order reflecting capitalist class relations and that fraternal assistance to a fellow-socialist regime was not intervention. Others argued that counter-intervention, meant to assist victims of intervention, was lawful. Some justified armed incursions across borders on the principle of hot pursuit, while others claimed the right to pre-emptive self-defence against imminent or apprehended attack. 'Self-defence' was sometimes extended to include the right to launch punitive raids into neighbouring countries that had shown themselves unwilling or unable to stop their territory from being used as a launching pad for cross-border armed raids or terrorist attacks. Many interveners insisted that they had taken action only in response to requests from the governments of the countries. Few were prepared to rule out *a priori* the use of force in another country in order to rescue nationals who were trapped and threatened there.

The many examples of intervention in actual state practice throughout the twentieth century did not lead to an abandonment of the norm of non-intervention. Often the breaches provoked such fierce controversy and so much nationalistic passion that their net effect was to reinforce, not negate, the norm of non-intervention. The difficulty with justifying intervention is that the real world is characterized by moral ambiguity rather than clarity.

## 'Hankering after a general doctrine'

Professor Roberts writes that: 'The commission still seems to hanker after general doctrinal answers to the basic question of whether there is a right of humanitarian intervention and . . . it seeks a set of agreed standards by which interventions can be justified or evaluated.' In this connection, he notes that: 'Actual cases have a ghastly way of making a nonsense of even the most carefully crafted criteria: thus Chechnya (not mentioned at all in the main body of the report) might meet all the criteria one could devise justifying action, yet intervention would not follow.' I agree with the first part (the general caution), but with regard to the specific example, which has in fact come up in a number of seminars and discussions around the world, my answer is: there is no conceivable circumstance in which I can see the precautionary principle of 'reasonable prospects'[3] being satisfied with respect to international intervention in Chechnya.

I don't think anyone of the twelve Commissioners hankered after a general doctrinal answer. We all thought that political contingencies cannot be fully anticipated in all their glorious complexity and that, in the real world, policy choices would always be made on a case-by-case basis. With that in mind, we set out to identify those conscience-shocking situations where the case for international intervention was compelling and to enhance the prospects of such interventions. ('The most compelling task now is . . . to ensure that when the call goes out to the community of states for action, that call will be answered', p. 70, para. 8.7 of the report.) In turn, this meant that the circumstances had to be narrow, the bar for intervention high and the procedural and operational safeguards tight because the probability of international consensus is higher under conditions of due process, due authority and due diligence.

So yes, all of us would agree that 'actual crises do not present themselves tidily' and therefore I am puzzled as to why Professor Roberts should write of 'The trouble with this approach'. His chosen example, East Bengal in 1971, was not described as 'humanitarian intervention' by India at the time. Rather, the discourse of justification was still very much within the traditional vocabulary of self-defence, including 'demographic aggression' by 10 million refugees as noted by Roberts and threats to national and regional security and stability. But even more striking was the response of the UN membership in the Security Council and General Assembly debates between 5 and 21 December. Few accepted the claim of self-defence and none argued that India had a right (let alone duty) of 'humanitarian intervention' – not one.[4]

For the foreseeable future, there is only one country, namely the United States, with the capacity to project power around the globe, which it may, for political more than military reasons, seek to do in coalition with like-minded countries; and only one standing military defence organization with the capacity to undertake out-of-area operations, namely NATO. Questions of the lawfulness and legitimacy of overseas military action by individual or groups of states, which in practice means the US, NATO, or coalitions of the willing with them at the core, cannot be separated from the question of the authoritative determination of just cause and justified response: who, under what rules of evidence and procedure, can rightfully decide on what is to be done?

Much as smaller economies seek protection from the big economic powers in rules-based regimes such as the World Trade Organization or bilateral/regional free trade agreements that embed agreed codes of conduct and dispute settlement mechanisms, so the weak and vulnerable countries seek protection from the predatory instincts of the powerful – an abiding lesson of history, if ever there was one – in a rules-based world order that specifies both the proper conduct to be followed by all states and the mechanisms for reconciling differences between them. The United Nations lies at the centre and indeed symbolizes such an order. Those who would challenge and overthrow the existing order must therefore indicate what is their preferred alternative *system of rules, including dispute resolution*; simply rejecting an existing rule or norm, no matter how unsatisfactory, in order to overthrow an existing ruler, no matter how odious, is not enough.

Any one intervention does not simply violate the sovereignty of any given target state in any one instance; it also challenges the *principle* of a society of states resting on a system of well understood and habitually obeyed rules. The binding character of contracts does not rest on the reliance of one party to a contract on the word or signature of the other party. Rather, it rests on the institution of the contract itself. The same argument holds with respect to the UN Charter, which affirms and enshrines the principle of state sovereignty and the norm of non-intervention.

Much of the twentieth century advances in globalizing norms and international law has been progressive and beneficial. But their viability will be threatened if developing countries remain essentially norm-takers while Western countries act as the norm-setters, interpreters and enforcers.[5] For then norms will become the major transmission mechanism for embedding structural inequality in international law, instruments and regimes.

Reducing the entire debate simply to a question of UN authorization as a necessary condition for overseas military action is not good enough. If UN authorization is not a necessary condition, then either we accept the resulting international anarchy and the law of the jungle in world affairs, or we spell out the preferred alternative set of rules and the institutions and regimes in which they are embedded.

Logically, there are six alternatives:

1    Any one country can wage war against any other.
2    Any one coalition of states can wage war against another country or group.
3    Only NATO has such a right with respect to launching military action against a non-NATO country.
4    Only NATO has the right to determine if military intervention, whether by NATO *or any other coalition*, is justified against others outside the coalition.
5    A regional organization can take in-area military action against errant members of the organization (e.g. the Organization of African Unity against deviant OAU members, or NATO against deviant NATO members), if they have agreed in advance to such rules of the game for governing internal relations, or if they seek and get *ex post facto* authorization from the Security Council; but not against non-members in out-of-area operations.
6    Only the United Nations can legitimately authorize armed intervention.

The first and second are recipes for international anarchy. Indeed the challenge of 'humanitarian intervention'[6] arises from the increasingly clear recognition that we no longer cede the right to any one state to use massive force *within* its borders free of external scrutiny or criticism, whether it be Serbia in Kosovo, Indonesia in East Timor, India in Kashmir or Russia in Chechnya; claims for reversing the progressive restrictions on the right to inter-state armed violence will be met with even more scepticism. The third is a claim to unilateralism and exceptionalism that will never be conceded by the 'international community'. The fourth was unwittingly implicit in the argument that NATO's actions in Kosovo cannot be construed as having set a precedent. The assumption underlying the claim is both demonstrably false and almost breathtakingly arrogant in setting up NATO as the final arbiter of military intervention by itself *and* every other coalition. The fifth and sixth options pose the fewest difficulties, although the history of the Warsaw Pact (Hungary 1956, Czechoslovakia 1968) and that of the Organization of American States (OAS) should inject elements of caution even with respect to the fifth.

In Kosovo, the necessary condition for the specifically European institutional response to chaos in the European centre was the Security Council's own paralysis. The sufficient conditions were the precipitating factors of renewed Serb offensive, resistance to Western demands and rejection of the NATO ultimatum at Rambouillet. Although unauthorized, NATO action was collective and directed exclusively at averting or containing a humanitarian catastrophe. Nevertheless, the only just and lasting resolution of the challenge of military intervention for human protection purposes would be a new consensus proclaimed and embodied within the United Nations forum.

## The responsibility to protect and '9/11'

Professor Roberts' section on 'The Challenge of the Bush Doctrine' is, predictably and inevitably, among the most interesting in his review essay. There is little doubt that, as Roberts says, the two separate debates on intervention, focusing respectively on the ICISS report and on the Bush doctrine, have some common features. But to merge and confuse the two can only be to the detriment of both agendas. Consequently I, and I suspect most if not all of my ICISS colleagues, would be strongly averse to embedding the anti-terrorism campaign in the context of a broader discussion of intervention. Ill-considered rhetoric of pre-emptive strikes and of Iraq as an example of 'humanitarian intervention', risk draining support from our report rather than adding to the legitimacy of such enterprises. Unfortunately, in the real world of politics based on perceptions and emotive rhetoric, such loose talk may serve to complicate the task of mobilizing the requisite political will for those occasions where the responsibility to protect must be discharged by the international community.

When we convened a special ICISS meeting to discuss the implications of '9/11', none of us present needed persuading about the legitimacy of a military response – against the perpetrators of the atrocity and against regimes that harboured them – within the accepted understanding of individual and collective self-defence (us *against* them). But we also concluded that the campaign was conceptually and operationally distinct from intervention for human protection purposes (us *between* them: victims and perpetrators) – and I for one remain persuaded of the merits of that conclusion. The significant intrusions by the US administration into human rights instruments and practices, as well as the extension of the cover of the war on terrorism to Iraq, reinforce my scepticism about bringing the war on terrorism within the fold of the responsibility to protect.

Thus Richard Haass, director of the Policy Planning Unit of the US State Department, clearly picking up on our report, wrote recently of sovereignty as responsibility. In that context, he argued that when states fail to discharge their responsibility to fight terrorism, 'America will act – ideally with partners, but alone if necessary – to hold them accountable'.[7] To the extent that he restricts his comment to self-defence against cross-border terrorism, I have no problem with his statement. But if his statement is extended to military intervention for human protection purposes, I beg to differ.

After the events of 11 September 2001, the world has been preoccupied with the 'war on terrorism'. Yet the underlying factors that led to the creation of ICISS – the gap between the need for human protection, sometimes against people's own government, sometimes over the government's objections and at other times in situations where no functioning government exists, on the one hand; and the ability of outsiders to render effective and timely assistance by lawful means, on the other – have not gone away. It is our hope that the Report of ICISS will help the world to be better prepared, normatively, organizationally and operationally, to meet the challenge, wherever and whenever it arises again.

## From post-cold war to post-Westphalia?

In September 2002 Washington sought UN blessing for its military action against Iraq.[8] Its message to the UN was clear and crisp: we will wage war if we believe it to be necessary, with or without your approval; if you are not with us, you will become irrelevant. But over the next six months, instead of a pro forma test of UN relevance, the agenda steadily shifted to being a litmus test of US legitimacy. The issue transcends the insignificance of Saddam Hussein. It has metamorphosed into the question of what sort of world we wish to live in, who we wish to be ruled by and if we wish to live by rules and laws or by the force of arms.

The Europeans' rejection of the US call to war against Iraq and their insistence on the primacy of the Security Council as the sole validator of legitimate use of force in international affairs, drew sharp reminders from Washington (backed by the Australian government, among others), that the United States was merely following what NATO had done in Kosovo in 1999. On that occasion, the Europeans had all agreed to military enforcement outside the UN framework. To British Prime Minister Tony Blair, the Iraq war is as much based in values as was the Kosovo war. The European response to this seems to be yes, but: yes, the Kosovo war was outside the UN framework, but then we were faced with the reality of mass killings and ethnic cleansing at the time. By contrast, there is no imminent threat of large-scale killing in Iraq at the moment and so we can wait.

But if this is the European response then, to use the ICISS framework, it confuses the threshold principle of just cause (actual or imminent large-scale killing or ethnic expulsion) with the question of right authority. I should think that the United States is confronting France and Germany (and European public opinion?) with the logical conclusion of their policy vis-à-vis Kosovo in 1999.[9]

The US–UK policy on Iraq is a multiple assault on the foundations and rules of the existing state order as well as the transatlantic relationship. It seeks to replace self-defence and wars of necessity with preventive defence and wars of choice, the successful strategy of containment with the untried doctrine of pre-emption, deterrence with compellence, a multilateral system of global governance centred on the UN with a unilateral system of global dominance by the United States and leadership by consent-cum-persuasion to one by command and control; to abort the European search for a new world order based on the Kantian transition from barbarism to culture through liberal institutionalism and revert instead to the old world order that Europe discarded after several centuries of warfare, based on force of arms; and to supplant the Westphalian order of equal sovereign states with a post-Westphalian system of one pre-eminent if virtuous power. The most profound and long-lasting significance of 9/11 might thus be that it tipped us into a post-Westphalian world. US policy is full of contradictions within the Westphalian paradigm. How can the most prominent dissident in many global norms and regimes – from arms control to climate change and international criminal justice – claim to be the world's most powerful enforcer of global norms and regimes, including non-proliferation? How can the most vocal critic of the very notion of an international community anoint itself the international community's sheriff? How can London and Washington claim to enforce UN resolutions by denying the authority of the UN?

The answer lies in a conception of world order rooted outside the Westphalian framework of sovereign equality. This also explains why some of today's most potent threats come not from the conquering states within the Westphalian paradigm, but from failing states outside it. In effect Bush is saying that the gap between the fiction of legal equality and the reality of power preponderance has stretched beyond breaking point. Washington is no longer bound by such fiction. The United States will remain as fundamentally trustworthy, balanced and responsible a custodian of world order as before, but of a post-Westphalian order centred on the United States amidst a surrounding wasteland of vassal states; and, one might almost add – given the derogation of human rights norms and practices in the United States and with respect to captured prisoners and suspects, whether by US forces or after they are handed over to cooperating forces from other countries and whether US citizens or aliens – vassal subjects as well.

In this context of the multiple assault on the Westphalian system of states, the Responsibility to Protect might well offer safeguards rather than represent a fundamental threat to state sovereignty. Neither industrial nor developing countries are united and cohesive on the tension between intervention and sovereignty. There are differences between governments and civil society actors within countries; between continents and between countries within the same continent; and between civil society, political leaders and UN diplomats from the same country. Despite the variations, nevertheless, nowhere did we find an absolute and uncompromising rejection of intervention under all circumstances.[10] On balance, the desire to avoid another Rwanda (where the world stood by passively during genocide) was more powerful than the desire to avoid another Kosovo (where NATO intervened without UN authorization).

## Conclusion

We cannot be sanguine about the future. Calls for 'humanitarian intervention' could arise from any one or more of potential flashpoints; humanitarian carnage could be triggered by any combination of contingencies. We can take the attitude, like Mr Micawber, that she'll be right on the day – if anything can go right, it will – and repeat the tragedies of the 1990s. The price of a policy of denial will be paid by the victims, but also by our children tomorrow when they too are reduced to being passive and helpless spectators to atrocities, if not victims themselves.

ICISS was an independent commission – a fact that added greatly to its value, in my opinion. The Commissioners brought a variety of perspectives, backgrounds and experiences to bear in their reflections and deliberations on this vitally important topic. We were not united on every fine point of the debate. A clue to the key differences within the Commission is provided in the report itself. In their foreword, the co-chairs noted that:

> The Commissioners brought many different personal views to the table and the report on which we have agreed does not reflect in all respects the preferred views of any one of them. In particular, some of our members preferred a wider range of threshold criteria for military intervention than those proposed in our report and others a narrower range. Again, some Commissioners preferred more and others less, flexibility for military intervention outside the scope of Security Council approval.
>
> But the text on which we have found consensus does reflect the shared views of all Commissioners as to what is politically achievable in the world as we know it today . . . We share a belief that it is critical to move the international consensus forward and we know that we cannot begin to achieve that if we cannot find consensus among ourselves.
>
> (p. viii)

To the extent that our primary goal is to reposition the normative consensus, the Secretary-General is uniquely important to our task. In the 15 February 2002 seminar, to which Professor Roberts refers and in which I participated, Kofi Annan put the authority of his office behind the ICISS report. He described it as an 'extraordinary and eloquent report', 'a remarkable accomplishment' and the 'most comprehensive and carefully thought out response to date' to his challenge of humanitarian intervention. He said it takes away the last remaining excuses for the international community to sit back and do nothing when confronted with atrocities again. While there were doubts and hesitations about some of the nuances of the Commission's report and agreement that many serious hurdles were yet to be overcome, the consensus at the seminar was that if we are going to get any progress on this vexed and deeply divisive issue, then the Commission's report is the way to go. If critical governments can move beyond their reflexive hostility and suspicion of the very word 'intervention' itself, they are likely to find that *The Responsibility to Protect* contains all the safeguards they need and all that they are going to get, with respect to threshold causes, precautionary principles, lawful authorization and operational doctrine.

# 7   Collective security and the use of force

## Reflections on the report of the high-level panel on threats, challenges and change[1]

How can the United Nations be so restructured as to empower it to enforce resolutions against recalcitrant regimes such as Saddam Hussein's but not take any action against Israel?[2] Unless and until this is done, will Washington re-commit to the international organization? Conversely, if and when it is done, how many others will walk away from the world body? Can the United Nations square this particular circle of the circumstances in which it is right and wrong to use force across (and within) borders in today's world?

A wag is said to have remarked that 'The interesting thing about Richard Wagner's music is that it ain't as bad as it sounds'. The same might be said of the United Nations: it is not quite as bad as it is often made out to be. The United Nations is our collective instrument for organizing a volatile and dangerous world on a more predictable and orderly basis than would be possible without the existence of the international organization. Most people still look to the UN as humanity's best hope for a shared future, especially if it could somehow be reformed to reflect today's needs and realities.

The challenge posed by the magnitude 9 earthquake and the devastating tsunami of 26 December 2004 was a vivid illustration of the advantages of conceptualizing security within the inclusive framework of human security. The natural disaster caused catastrophic loss of life in many countries around the perimeter of the Indian Ocean. When we include the thousands of Westerners vacationing in the pleasure resorts, we realize just how many continents were united in the tragedy. Mother Nature did not discriminate between Muslim and Christian, Tamil and Sinhalese, poor and rich, native and foreigner. She claimed them all equally to her bosom in the sea to bring forcefully home the realization that we are indeed one human family. We inhabit the same planet earth and artificially constructed enmity and rivalry based on the competitive and exclusionary concept of national security can be irrelevant to securing citizens against the real big threats to their safety.

The general expectation was that the lead responsibility for organizing international rescue and relief operations belonged properly to the United Nations as the symbol and representative of the international community. Thus even when nominated to the select core group of four aid coordinators, India demurred, saying that the UN should lead. In this the government was backed by a leading Indian newspaper,[3] and the opinion was echoed in several other major newspapers around the region and the world.[4] Many of the countries present at the donor summit in Jakarta on 6 January, including most of the afflicted countries, urged the UN to take the leading role. President Susilo Bambang Yudhoyono of Indonesia, the worst hit nation, said that: 'We must ensure that we benefit from the experience of the United Nations in establishing and managing special emergency funds and relief efforts.'[5] US Secretary of State Colin Powell confirmed that the four-nation core group to coordinate tsunami relief (Australia, India, Japan and the United States) would be disbanded and folded into broader UN operations. A number of UN agencies swung immediately into action as soon as the world awoke to the magnitude of the disaster: the office for the coordination of humanitarian affairs, the children's fund (UNICEF), the World Food Programme (WFP), the World Health Organization (WHO), etc. The Secretary-General cancelled his annual holiday, returned to his desk in New York, joined the crisis summit meeting in Jakarta and flew on to Sri Lanka. Press reports described him as wrought by what he had seen: nothing on this scale had happened during the UN's sixty-year lifespan.

The Iraq war roiled the UN-centred world of international diplomacy as few other issues have since the creation of the organization in 1945. At the heart of the dispute was not the nature of the Saddam Hussein regime, on which there was and can be no disagreement, but rather the nature and exercise of American power. Borrowing popular language, while the United States may be from Mars, the United Nations proved to be from Venus. Progress towards international civilization requires that US power be harnessed to UN authority, so that force is put to the service of law. By their bitter separation over Iraq, the United States and the UN provoked a legitimacy crisis about each other: of American power and UN authority. The certainty of moral clarity put the Bush administration on a course that seriously eroded its moral authority in the exercise of world power. The lack of a sense of moral clarity – values that it espouses and principles in defence of which it is prepared to stand up and be counted – diminished the UN's moral authority.

There was also the larger question of the changing nature of threats in the modern world, the inadequacy of existing norms and laws in being able to address such threats and thus the need for new 'rules of the game' to replace them. The United Nations is the arena for collective action, not a forum where nations who are unable to do anything individually should get together to decide that nothing can be done collectively. The urgent task is to devise an institutional framework that can marry prudent anticipatory self-defence against imminent threats to the centuries-old dream of a world where force is put to the service of law that protects the innocent without shielding the criminals.

The fragility of post-war Iraq confirmed that it is easier to wage war without UN blessing than it is to win the peace – but victory in war is pointless without a resulting secure peace. Speaking to the General Assembly on 23 September 2003, Secretary-General Kofi Annan noted that, 'We have come to a fork in the road . . . a moment no less decisive than 1945 itself, when the United Nations was founded.'[6] In a number of key meetings during and after World War II, world leaders drew up rules to govern international behaviour and established a network of institutions, centred on the UN, to work together for the common good. Both the rules and institutions – the system of global governance with the United Nations as the core – are under serious challenge. On the one hand, Annan noted, the Iraq war could set a precedent for the 'proliferation of the unilateral and lawless use of force'. On the other hand, he asked, to what extent might states be resorting to unilateral instruments because of a loss of faith in 'the adequacy and effectiveness of the rules and instruments' at their disposal?

## Context

Established to provide predictability and order in a world in constant flux, the organization – a bridge between power and principles, between state-based realism and universal idealism – is at once the symbol of humanity's collective aspirations for a better life in a safer world for all, a forum for negotiating the terms of converting the collective aspirations into a common programme of action and the principal international instrument for the realization of the aspirations and the implementation of the plans. The United Nations has to operate today in a global environment that is vastly more challenging, complex and demanding than the world of 1945.

The basis of world order has come under increasing strain in recent years due to seven major disconnects. The first is the gap between the inflated expectations of what the United Nations can accomplish and the modest resources given to it. A second is the growing disconnect between the threats to peace and security and the obstacles to economic development, lying increasingly within states rather than in relations among them. A third and related disconnect is the persistence of policy authority and the requisite resources for tackling problems being vested in states, while the source and scope of the problems are increasingly global and require the globalization of the process of policy-making. A fourth is the greater recognition given to individuals as both subjects and objects of international relations, reflecting an increasingly internationalized human conscience. A fifth is the growing gravity of threats rooted in non-state actors, including but not limited to terrorists. A sixth is the growing salience of weapons of mass destruction that in their reach and destructiveness challenge the basis of the territorial state. And the seventh is the strategic disconnect between the distribution of military, political and economic power in the real world and the distribution of decision-making authority in the artificially constructed world of intergovernmental organizations. The most acute manifestation of this is the growing disparity between the soft as well as hard power of the United States and that of all others and the challenge that this poses to the Westphalian fiction of sovereign states equal in status, capacity, power and legitimacy.

In other words, the crisis over Iraq was as much a symptom of underlying seismic shifts in world politics as a cause of further diminished UN authority. It was doubly damaging. In the countries that waged war on Saddam Hussein, the UN was bitterly attacked for failing to give international blessing to the effort to end over a decade's defiance of world will by a particularly brutal regime. In the many more countries that opposed the war, the UN was seen as having betrayed its most fundamental of all mandates: to stop wars of aggression, particularly by major powers. Not everyone in the UN Secretariat in New York realizes that the more serious threat to the UN's viability may come not from the United States, but from developing countries who have become disillusioned with the organization as the forum for legitimizing American dominance. That is, if the UN becomes for the rest of the world what the old Warsaw Pact was for all the former Soviet satellites, it is a threat to the autonomy and security of most member states, not the collective instrument for protecting them through strength in unity.

In order to try to re-establish or forge a new consensus on the norms and laws governing the use of force in world affairs in relation to contemporary threats, Kofi Annan brought together a group of sixteen distinguished experts to probe the nature and gravity of today's threats and recommend collective solutions to them through a reformed United Nations. The composition of the panel was initially ridiculed for its average age (around seventy) when the task was to look to the future: 'Alzheimer's commission', 'relics trying to reform a relic' and 'a cross between nostalgia and déjà vu' were among the (unattributed) choice descriptions.[7] The choice of an American as research director (and a US-based Canadian as his deputy) further underlined the lack of sensitivity within the UN secretariat to the widely-held perception around the world that the UN is unduly deferential to its host country, constantly exposed to US-centric worldviews and analyses by the dominant US media, prone to pre-emptive appeasement of US concerns and sensitivities and insuffi-ciently attentive to developing-country views and aspirations.[8] The Research Director and Deputy can also be expected to play some role in the international scholarly discourse on the report following its publication and to achieve some career gains; both represent lost opportunities for developing countries. In retrospect, it might have been better to have had joint research directors, with one each from a Western and developing country.

## Conceptual and normative advances

In the event the panel's report has confounded the most sceptical and exceeded the expectations of most UN observers, even while it falls short of the boldness of vision and action demanded by the most keen. The report is both comprehensive and coherent, presenting a total of 101 recommendations in furtherance of the conviction that 'The maintenance of world peace and security depends importantly on there being a common global understanding, and acceptance, of when the application of force is both legal and legitimate'.[9]

The overarching themes are our shared vulnerability and the primacy of the rule of law embedded in universal institutions and procedures that are efficient, effective and equitable. The central thesis, and hence the title of the report, is that no country can afford to deal with today's threats alone and no threat can be dealt with effectively unless other threats are addressed at the same time. For example, the worldwide economic consequences of the terrorist attacks of 11 September 2001 included an additional ten million people being pushed below the poverty line (p. 19, para. 18). Or the failure of a poor or fragile state to contain an emerging mass infectious disease can have a devastating impact on the life and security of the citizens of the most affluent and powerful state. And terrorism feeds on grievances rooted in poverty, foreign occupation, lack of democracy and human rights and weak and corruptible state structures.

The report's four major conceptual–cum–normative advancements are the inter-connectedness of today's threats; legitimacy criteria for the use of military force; an agreed definition of terrorism; and the need to extend normative constraints to non-state actors. Its most important institutional recommendations concern the reform of the Security Council, with alternative models testifying to the inability to reach agreement within the panel.

The report identifies the major threats as war and violence among and within states; the use and proliferation of weapons of mass destruction; terrorism; transnational organized crime; and poverty, infectious disease and environmental degradation. The threats can come from state and non-state actors and endanger human as well as national security. Collective security is necessary because today's threats cannot be contained within national boundaries, because they are interconnected and because they have to be addressed simultaneously at all levels. This is all very well, but does not address the real challenge of how to institute and operationalize a workable collective security *system*. Both the League and the UN experience confirm that there are inherent difficulties with the concept of organizing a system of collective security against unknown and unidentifiable aggressors in advance and that the enthusiasm for the level of preparedness and sacrifices necessary fades as memories of exceptionally grave crises dim.

According to the panel, the primary challenge to the international community is to ensure that imminent threats do not materialize and distant threats do not become imminent. This requires early, decisive and collective action against all the threats before they can cause the worst devastation. Such a prophylactic approach must emphasize development as a structural prevention approach while including the possibility of preventive military action. The panel endorses UN-authorized preventive action, but not unilateral preventive action.

The panel makes the important point that because the use of force is legal does not mean that it is thereby also ethical and wise. Instead it proposes five criteria of legitimacy: seriousness of threat, proper purpose, last resort, proportional means and balance of consequences (pp. 57–8, para. 207). These borrow from the report of the ICISS, *The Responsibility to Protect*.[10] With respect to internal conflicts, the panel explicitly endorses the ICISS argument that 'the issue is not the "right to intervene" of any State, but the "responsibility to protect" of *every* State' (p. 56, para. 201, emphasis in original). The mutual vulnerability and 'multiplier effects' of threats help to explain why sovereignty today has to include the state's responsibility to protect its own people and obligations to the wider international community alongside the privileges of sovereignty. Hence too the need to enhance state capacity in order to enable it to exercise sovereignty responsibly.[11]

The legitimacy criteria will simultaneously make the Security Council more responsive to outbreaks of humanitarian atrocities than hitherto and make it more difficult for individual states or ad hoc 'coalitions of the willing' to appropriate the language of humanitarianism for geopolitical and unilateral interventions. But can any criteria overcome the problem of competing ideologies and divided interests?

No amount of articulation and clarification of agreed criteria can compensate for their selective application. Much of the recent selectivity has come in the context of the so-called war on terror. The section on terrorism (pp. 45–9) achieves a good balance between immediate threats and root causes, between short term tactics and comprehensive strategies, between assistance and sanctions and between local, national, regional and global efforts. This is buttressed by three significant strengths. First, it proposes a clear yet simple definition of terrorism: 'any action . . . that is intended to cause death or serious bodily harm to civilians or non-combatants, when the purpose of such an act, by its nature or context, is to intimidate a population, or to compel a Government or an international organization to do or to abstain from doing any act' (p. 49, para. 164.d). Second, it affirms that 'terrorism is never an acceptable tactic, even for the most defensible of causes' and therefore 'must be condemned clearly and unequivocally by all' (p. 48, paras 157, 161). And third, recalling that existing normative instruments with regard to the use of force by states are well developed and robust, the panel calls for a similar degree of normative strength concerning the use of force by non-state actors (p. 48, para. 159). Many NGOs should take heed of this call for a balance between state and non-state actors in the normative architecture of international peace and security.

That said, the panel failed to grapple with the core of the American sense of growing disenchantment with the UN, namely that the Westphalian order may have passed its use-by date. All states are *not* equal in status, capacity, legitimacy and morality. On most objective criteria, there is the United States and there are the rest. The fact that some 'legitimate' governments (meaning recognized as such) are engaged in criminal activities indicates the troubling degree to which the very word has been corrupted. Why should a concert of democracies willingly submit its actions to the restraining discipline of the judgement of self-serving regimes? It seems intuitively plausible to posit that the structure of global governance, including international organizations, must bear some relationship to the underlying distribution of power (the final disconnect in the list of seven identified above). Is the weight of anomalies (positive ones such as the single European project as well as negative ones such as most of those discussed in this chapter) now too heavy for the Westphalian fiction to be sustainable for much longer?

On Iraq, Washington did not help its case for war against Saddam Hussein by issuing a confused mix of motives and explanations. In the resulting 'noise' of diplomatic traffic, answers were not forthcoming to two crucial questions: Why Iraq and why now? Any single answer to the first – such as known/suspected links to terrorism or to weapons of mass destruction – would always complicate attempts to answer the second, since people could instantly counter with more compelling cases of the same pathology.

For instance, with respect to nuclear weapons, while evidence of such remained elusive in Iraq, North Korea did almost everything but actually conduct a nuclear test. The glib conclusion drawn by the antiwar lobby, therefore, was that Washington's inconsistent response to the simultaneous crises showed two things: that Iraq did not possess usable nuclear weapons and North Korea does not have oil. Yet, glibness aside, Washington could have constructed a powerful case for its action on Iraq precisely by linking the two crises. To the extent that we cannot be certain that North Korea has not already crossed the nuclear threshold, what options are available to the international community for dealing with Pyongyang without causing grave damage to ourselves? The UN Security Council seems barely able to table the North Korean threat for discussion and resolution. Similarly, it would have been impossible to defang Saddam of nuclear weapons the day after he acquired and used them; the UN is incapable of doing so the day before; hence the American determination to do so instead.

The reality of contemporary threats – a virtual nuclear-weapons capability that can exist inside non-proliferation regimes and be crossed at too short a notice for international organizations to be able to react defensively in time, and non-state actors who are outside the jurisdiction and control of multilateral agreements whose signatories are states – means that significant gaps exist in the legal and institutional framework to combat them. If international institutions cannot cope with today's real threats, states will try to do so themselves, either unilaterally or in company with like-minded allies. Pre-emption is not permitted under the UN Charter as it is not considered within the acknowledged right of self-defence. But if pre-emption is strategically necessary and morally justified (why should an American president or an Australian prime minister wait for another mass murder and be prohibited from taking prophylactic action?) but not legally permitted, then the existing framework of laws and rules – not the anticipatory military action – is defective.

## Institutional restructuring

The report has some useful comments on how to streamline, strengthen and revitalize the roles and functions of the General Assembly, the Economic and Social Council and the Secretary-General. It also calls sensibly for the deletion of the enemy clauses that cause unnecessary resentment, for example in Japan;

the formal disbanding of the Trusteeship Council; and the abolition of the Military Staff Committee through appropriate Charter amendments (p. 77, paras 298–300). But the most critical section is the one dealing with the Security Council (pp. 66–9). The call for reforming the Security Council is justified by the need for greater credibility, legitimacy, representation, effectiveness and enhanced capacity and willingness to act in defence of the common peace. As well as geographical balance, membership criteria should include contributions to the regular budget, voluntary contributions to UN activities and agencies, and troop and other personnel contributions to UN peace operations. Those who contribute the most should have a commensurate say in making decisions; those who make the decisions should contribute commensurately.

The panel notes that a decision on Security Council enlargement 'is now a necessity' (p. 67, para. 250). The urgency for reform now indeed is extreme and the report of the high-level panel plus the dynamics of the international political environment have created a window of opportunity that, once closed, may not open again for some considerable time. The Council cannot realistically be expected to honour its responsibility to protect without major reform of its structure and procedures. Hence the importance of seizing the moment and closing a deal.

Unable to agree between them, the panel outlines two models (pp. 67–8). Both would see an expansion of the Council from fifteen to twenty-four members, six each from Africa, Asia and the Pacific, Europe and the Americas. Under Model A, there would be three additional elected and six additional permanent members (in practice, these would be Brazil, Germany, India, Japan and two of Egypt, Nigeria and South Africa). Under Model B, there would be one additional two-year elected member and eight additional members elected to renewable four-year terms, two from each region.

Neither model is radical, revolutionary or new. The essential elements of both have been discussed for many years. One could argue that the panel shied away from the courage of its convictions and as a result neither model is entirely free of flaws. 'Although the United Nations gave birth to the notion of human security, it proved poorly equipped to provide it' (p. 18, para. 13). A major reason for this is the dominance of the UN system by states. Yet the report is itself state-centric in its approach to Security Council reform. The regions of the world are divided and grouped according to numbers of states. Yet India by itself has more people than all of Africa with fifty-three countries, as well as the Americas (in the revised grouping) with thirty-five states. To ignore population as a criterion of representation seems as odd as to insist on operationalizing it mathematically to the exclusion of all other criteria.

There is a larger point relating to the extraordinary neglect and marginal-ization of Asia. Asians contribute close to half the total number of UN peacekeepers and one quarter of the UN's regular and peacekeeping budget. They have also absorbed around one-quarter of total UN peacekeeping deaths. But there is not a single Asian in the senior ranks of the DPKO and overall they comprise a mere 17 per cent of senior UN staff. Of the fifty-nine high-level representatives of the Secretary-General, Asia had just seven. (And, of the fifty-nine, there was only one Indian compared to three Norwegians and four Canadians.) This for a continent that accounts for around 60 per cent of the world's population, contains some of the world's oldest civilizations and is not short of experienced and sophisticated persons well versed in diplomatic discourse. It is worth recalling that Asians tend to be high, even over, achievers. Their under-achievement in the UN system is at best a curiosity that needs investigation and explanation, at worst a scandal and an indictment of the Asia group at the UN in New York. Making a public fuss is alien to the Asian way. But in the context of a culture of self-serving and self-advancing arguments at the United Nations, the result is a failure by Asian governmental representatives to promote the interests of their people in the UN system. They should be more assertive in proposing professionally competent Asian names for suitable senior posts and then lobbying for them. And the UN should learn to limit, if not reject, post-retirement nominees.

The panel acknowledges the veto as being 'anachronistic' but sees 'no practical way of changing the existing members' veto powers'. Accordingly it recommends neither the expansion of the veto to new permanent members under Model A, nor its elimination for the existing five permanent members (P5), although it does recommend a curtailment of the veto's use (p. 68, para. 256). If the veto is a genuine obstacle to the effective functioning of the Security Council, it should be abandoned. The panel should perhaps have so recommended and let the permanent members bear the weight of international opprobrium for rejecting the recommendation in defence of narrow self-interest. It seems illogical in any case to have a further differentiation within permanent members under Model A, those with and without veto. Of course, the aspiring new members may well in the end agree to this as the price of gaining permanent membership.

The most flawed, albeit good-intentioned, suggestion may well be Model B. Sadly, in the real world of bitter regional rivalries and enmity, this could prove a pernicious formula for exacerbating existing tensions and conflicts in most regions. Just imagine India, Indonesia, Japan and Pakistan in Asia – or Argentina, Brazil and Mexico in Latin America, or even Egypt, Nigeria and South Africa in Africa – forever fighting it out for two additional 'second-class' (with non-renewable, two-year terms being the third class) seats on the Security Council. The United Nations should manage and ease regional tensions, not provide additional opportunities for exacerbating and inflaming them.

Opposition to Security Council reform comes from three groups: those with a vested interest in the status quo, especially the P5; the regional rivals of each of the leading candidate countries; and a large group who would see their status diminished still further with the growth of permanent members from five to eleven. All three groups have found it expedient to adopt the tactic of divide-and-rule, convincing the leading contenders to compete with one another. Only very recently have Brazil, Germany, India and Japan awakened to the realization that either they will all become permanent members in one major round of reforms, or none of them will. The four countries acting together can constitute a powerful bloc in world affairs. Will the immovable object of Security Council reform prove stronger than the irresistible force of these four exerting their full clout in the world of international diplomacy? It seems likely that the report will 'out' the opponents, forcing them into the open, and by doing so provide opportunities to the reformers to develop strategies for overcoming the obstacles.

There are four further institutional recommendations. First, to enhance coordination of the UN's primary mandate, the panel recommends the creation of a second Deputy Secretary-General post for peace and security (pp. 37, 75, paras 98, 293). While the intention is to strengthen the senior management, there will be the risk of eroding the authority of the Secretary-General by taking away some of the substantive responsibility and leaving him with more ornamental functions. Second, the panel recommends the establishment of a new Peacebuilding Commission in order to identify countries sliding towards state collapse and institute measures to halt the slide, and to plan for and assist in the transition from war and conflict to peace and post-conflict peacebuilding (pp. 69–70, paras 261–9). Third, in order to reverse growing cynicism about the hypocrisy of existing institutions and practices and noting that states have begun to seek membership of the Human Rights Commission not to strengthen human rights but to shield their own actions from Commission scrutiny, the panel recommends that it become universal in membership (pp. 74–5, paras 282–90). But will this solve the problem of human rights violator regimes acting in a bloc to shield themselves and their abusive peers from international scrutiny? The more sensible recommendation might have been to strengthen, not enlarge, the commission, by laying down benchmarks for election such as ratification of all UN human rights treaties, cooperation with UN investigations, willingness to discuss country-specific allegations of abuse and so on.

And fourth, potentially most importantly yet to date least noted, the panel foreshadows the transformation of the G20 group of finance ministers into a leaders' (heads of government) group that would embrace 80 per cent of the world's population and 90 per cent of its economic activity (p. 73, para. 281).[12]

At a time when so much world attention and international angst seems focused on the subject of weapons of mass destruction, the panel failed to grasp the opportunity to upgrade the UN's Department of Disarmament Affairs from a poor relation (in human and financial resources) to one of the major departments in the UN Secretariat.

## Other considerations

Reflecting the dominance of practitioners and the absence of ideas people, the high-level panel argues that the UN 'was never intended to be a utopian exercise', but 'a collective security system that worked' (p. 13). For someone from the world of ideas, this is difficult to accept. I would argue that the United Nations lies at the intersection of realism and idealism. On the one hand, it will be fatally incapacitated if it ignores the world of realpolitik, of power and wealth maximizing states, in which it operates. On the other hand, it will be fatally compromised if it abandons its sense of moral mission and international solidarity based on a common humanity, for Utopia is fundamental to its identity.

One of the most interesting sections of the report is the first one that maps out the world of 2005 in comparison to that of 1945. It makes the point that without the UN, the past sixty years would most likely have been a far bloodier place. There are striking charts and figures, although some are open to contrary interpretations. Thus poverty is strongly associated with civil war (Figure 2, p. 20). But just what is the direction of causality: does civil conflict cause and/or perpetuate poverty (because capital, necessary for poverty alleviation, is extremely risk-averse and seeks a stable investment climate), or the other way round?

The report is full of recitations and reiterations of good and worthy efforts, for example a timetable to reach the agreed goal of 0.7 per cent of GNP as official development assistance, further development of renewable energy sources, moving from crude and blunt to smart and targeted sanctions, reducing the gap between the promise and performance of the Kyoto Protocol, and involving civil society, the private sector and regional organizations. To be a devil's advocate with respect to just one of these worthy goals: is there a *single* example of a state succeeding in achieving the goal of development as a result mainly of foreign aid? There is at least an intellectual case to be made that foreign aid is a misnomer, in that more often it reflects the geopolitical and commercial interests of the donor than the recipient; that it provides cover to donor countries for production and trade policies that impose significant harm on many developing countries, such as agricultural subsidies, import tariffs and quotas and labour market rigidities; and that it provides an alibi for many developing countries' self-inflicted failures of policy instruments and frameworks.

The report does not always shy away from topics contested by the most powerful states. Thus it recommends that the Security Council should stand ready to refer cases to the International Criminal Court (p. 35, para. 90) and it encourages all countries to join the controversial Proliferation Security Initiative to interdict illicit trade in nuclear components (p. 43, para. 132). The second will please Washington.

The report joins much of the disarmament community in warning that 'We are approaching a point at which the erosion of the non-proliferation regime could become irreversible and result in a cascade of proliferation' (p. 39, para. 111). But, in contrast to the section on terrorism, it does not make with suffi-cient force and clarity the link between the possession of nuclear weapons by some and the attractiveness of the nuclear option to others: the logics of nuclear non-proliferation and disarmament are essentially the same. There is an asymmetry of calls for disarmament in voluntary, graduated steps towards eventual total abolition that are exempt from international verification regimes and compliance mechanisms, and legally binding, verifiable and in principle internationally enforceable non-proliferation obligations. This is best illustrated by the conceptual fudge in asking Middle Eastern and South Asian countries to ratify the Comprehensive Test Ban Treaty and negotiate regional nuclear-weapon-free zones (p. 41, para. 124). Should India, Pakistan and Israel do so as nuclear-weapons-states? If so, does this not formalize their nuclear status outside the NPT and also, why not make the same call to the other five nuclear powers? If not, then why call for rollbacks by just three and not all eight nuclear powers?

## Conclusion

When Secretary-General Kofi Annan presented the report to the UN General Assembly on 8 December 2004, he received a prolonged standing ovation – a very rare occurrence. This had nothing to do with the merits or attractiveness of the report, but was rather a reaction to the crass calls from some American lawmakers and commentators for Annan to resign because of the totally unrelated oil-for-food scandal before an impartial committee had completed its investigations and submitted its report.[13] Whether the goodwill will last and neutralize for the long term the earlier perceptions of disproportionate attentiveness to Washington by the highest echelons of the UN Secretariat remains to be seen. Annan intends to devote the sixtieth anniversary year of the United Nations, and the balance of his remaining tenure until the end of 2006, to implementing as much of the reform agenda as can be agreed on by the international community. The agenda will be set by his formal response to the panel's report, expected to be presented around March 2005. The major debate and evidence of international opinion will come in the annual session of the General Assembly starting in September 2005. One of the more interesting things to watch for will be whether the differences of opinion, based on competing interests, helps to break the pattern of voting by consensus in some of the key groups in UN politics. If so, this 'reform' might in itself be of lasting benefit to the UN, for the insistence on consensus has produced the politics of the lowest common denominator, allowing the most recalcitrant of a group like the Non-aligned Movement to hold any progress to ransom. Too often have too many member states refused to let majority group interests come in the way of the principle of an artificially preserved consensus. Just as a chain is only as strong as the weakest link, so the rate of progress of any group that believes in decisions by consensus is only as fast as the slowest of the group.

The United Nations is the embodiment of the international community and the custodian of world conscience. It is also an international bureaucracy with many failings and flaws; and a forum often used and abused by governments – who control it, not the other way round – for finger pointing, not problem solving. Too often has the UN been shown to be proof against occasions of the larger kind, demonstrating a failure to tackle urgent collective action problems due to institutionalized inability, incapacity or unwillingness.

But more than these attributes of bureaucratic rigidity, institutional timidity and intergovernmental trench warfare, the United Nations is the one body that houses the divided fragments of humanity. It is an idea, a symbol of an 'imagined community' of strangers. It exists to bring about a world where fear is changed to hope, want gives way to dignity and apprehensions are turned into aspirations.

# 8 The responsibility to protect and prosecute

## The parallel erosion of sovereignty and impunity[1]

*Ramesh Thakur and Vesselin Popovski*

The multilateral system of global governance centred on the United Nations is in danger of falling apart. In that case, the problem of international anarchy will intensify. Yet in part the system is starting to unravel because of the spread of anarchy within the sovereign jurisdiction of member states of the international organization, some of whom have abused the attribute of state sovereignty underpinning the contemporary world order as a licence to kill with impunity. Some others lack the essential attributes of sovereignty that would enable them to protect the lives and safety of their citizens against a range of armed predatory groups. Revulsion at the murder of large numbers of civilians in a range of atrocity crimes – the drowning of the ceremony of innocence – has led to a softening of public and governmental support for the norms and institutions that shield the perpetrators of atrocity crimes from international criminal accountability. The failure to act can indeed be interpreted as the best lacking the courage of their conviction while the worst engage in mass murder with passionate intensity. 'Mobilizing political will' is a more prosaic way of saying that the best need to rediscover and act on their convictions.

Discussion and analyses of the protection of civilians and the prosecution of perpetrators have hitherto proceeded along separate lines. It is our contention that the international protection and prosecution agendas are two sides of the same coin. The Second World War gave birth to the UN Charter and the Nuremberg Charter. The first was forward-looking, aiming to ensure peace and security, economic cooperation and respect for human rights. The second was backward-looking, aiming to punish those who started the war and committed horrific crimes against humanity. The defence lawyers in Nuremberg argued that the international law is concerned with the actions of sovereign states, not of individuals and therefore the defendants should not be liable for international crimes. The judges rejected this defence and in a landmark advance from the ancient state-centric tradition, they made individuals directly accountable in international law. But if individuals are bound by and can be prosecuted under international law, then it must logically follow that individuals must equally be protected by international law. The idea of international individual accountability twinned with an increasingly robust international human rights norm. The recognition of individuals as subjects of international duties logically led to the recognition of individuals as beneficiaries of international rights. The individualization of the responsibility of the perpetrators has been paralleled with the individualization of the protection of the victims.

This dual process of individualization of rights and duties in international law was rapidly codified in the 1948 Genocide Convention, the four 1949 Geneva Conventions and the 1977 Additional Protocols which helped to develop international humanitarian law. In 1948 the Universal Declaration of Human Rights was adopted, followed by two UN Covenants on political and civil; and on economic, social and cultural rights. These two branches of law – international humanitarian law and human rights law – have a central feature in common: both deal with the protection of victims. Yet they are also different: international humanitarian law applies in time of armed conflict, human rights law in time of peace. International humanitarian law is a contract among states and regulates how to fight wars; human rights law is a contract between states and citizens and regulates how to live in peace. International humanitarian law protects the civilians and soldiers of the enemy; human rights law protects the state's own civilians. In international humanitarian law states (prosecutors) sue individuals; in human rights law individuals sue states.

In sum, the problem is the atrocities committed against innocent civilians. The interrelated twin tasks are to protect the victims and punish the perpetrators. Both require substantial derogations of sovereignty, the first with respect to the norm of non-intervention and the second with respect to sovereign impunity up to the level of heads of government and state. At the same time, both require sensitive judgement calls: the use of external military force to protect civilians inside sovereign jurisdiction must first satisfy legitimacy criteria rooted largely in just war theory, while the prosecution of alleged atrocity criminals must be balanced against the consequences for the prospects and process of peace, the need for post-conflict reconciliation and the fragility of international as well as domestic institutions.

This chapter begins with an outline of the background factors that have helped to put the twin issue on the policy agenda of international affairs. We will then describe the main elements of the responsibility to protect and institutions of international criminal justice respectively. In the third section, we will examine the dilemmas and choices that have to be made with regard to whether, when and how to implement the double agenda. Finally, we will point out how the principles underpinning the operational agendas of protection and punishment are remarkably similar.

## Background: a changed world from 1945 to 2005

The end of the Second World War and the establishment of the United Nations in 1945 and the formal adoption of the responsibility to protect norm at the summit of world leaders held at the United Nations in 2005 mark convenient chronological bookends for us. During this period, the key changes relevant to our analysis include the changing nature of armed conflict that has put civilians on the frontline of conflict-related casualties; the rise of a powerful human rights movement and the parallel growth of international humanitarian law, leading to the emergence of a humanitarian community dedicated to championing the cause of civilian protection; the emergence of a robust civil society that is transnational rather than sovereignty-bound; the rise of human security as an alternative paradigm to national security; and globalization, which (1) has shrunk distances; brought images of human suffering into our living rooms and on our breakfast tables in graphic detail and real time while simultaneously expanding our capacity to respond meaningfully, thereby increasing the calls to do so; and (2) made total state control of border crossings by people, goods, finance, information, disease, drugs and so on physically impossible, thereby severely curtailing the exercise of sovereignty in practice.

## Changing nature and locale of armed conflict

The number of armed conflicts rose steadily until the end of the cold war, peaked in the early 1990s and has declined since then. The nature of armed conflict itself has changed,[2] with most being internal rather than inter-state. Today we have more wars and more UN peace operations in Africa than the rest of the world combined. Often, wars of national liberation leading to the creation of new countries were followed by wars of national debilitation as the new states faced internal threats to their authority, legitimacy and territorial integrity from secessionist movements.

Non-combatants are now on the frontline of modern battles and civilians comprise up to 90 per cent of conflict-related casualties. The UN is an organization dedicated to the territorial integrity, political independence and national sovereignty of its member states and the maintenance of international peace and security on that basis. But the overwhelming majority of today's armed conflicts are intra- and not inter-state. With the changed nature of war, the United Nations confronts a major difficulty: how to reconcile its foundational principle of member states' sovereignty with the primary mandate to maintain international peace and security and the equally compelling mission to promote the interests and welfare of 'We the peoples of the United Nations'. Secretary-General Kofi Annan discussed the dilemma in the conceptual language of two sovereignties, vesting respectively in the state and in the people.[3]

Thus the need to help and protect civilians at risk of death and displacement caused by armed conflict is now paramount. Diplomats, international and non-governmental organizations (NGOs) alike will be judged on how well they discharge or dishonour their international responsibility to protect. The agenda of the Security Council, the World Bank, inter- and non-governmental humanitarian actors, international criminal justice institutions and international civil society converge on this point.

So too does that of UN peace operations. This was not the case with classical peacekeeping.[4] Traditional peacekeeping aimed to contain and stabilize volatile regions and interstate conflicts until such time as negotiations produced last peace agreements. The newer 'complex humanitarian emergencies' produ multiple crises all at once: collapsed state structures; humanitarian tragedies caused by starvation, disease or genocide; large-scale fighting and slaughter between rival ethnic or bandit groups; horrific human rights atrocities; and the inter-mingling of criminal elements and child soldiers with irregular forces. A high-level international panel, chaired by former Algerian foreign minister Lakhdar Brahimi and charged with realigning peace operations with current challenges and realities, concluded that 'when the United Nations does send its forces to uphold the peace, they must be prepared to confront the lingering forces of war and violence with the ability and determination to defeat them'. For in the final analysis, 'no amount of good intentions can substitute for the funda-mental ability to project credible force if complex peacekeeping, in particular, is to succeed'.[5] Mandates and the resources to match them, have to be guided by pragmatic, realistic analysis and thinking. The UN Secretariat 'must not apply best-case planning assumptions to situations where the local actors have historically exhibited worst-case behaviour'.[6]

Nor should the need for impartial peacekeeping translate automatically into moral equivalence among the conflict parties on the ground: in some cases local parties consist not of moral equals but aggressors and victims. Political neutrality has too often degenerated into military timidity, the abdication of the duty to protect civilians and an operational failure to confront openly those who challenge peacekeeping missions in the field. Impartiality should not translate into complicity with evil. The Charter sets out the principles that the UN must defend and the values that it must uphold.[7] The reluctance to distinguish victim from aggressor implies a degree of moral equivalency between the two and damages the institution of UN peacekeeping.

### Human rights

The multiplication of internal conflicts was accompanied by a worsening of the abuses of the human rights of millions of people. International concern with human rights prior to the Second World War dwelt on the laws of warfare, slavery and protection of minorities. In addition to the 1948 Universal Declaration of Human Rights, the UN has adopted scores of other legal instruments on human rights.

Human rights advocacy rests on 'the moral imagination to feel the pain of others' as if it were one's own, treats others as 'rights-bearing equals', not 'dependents in tutelage', and can be viewed as 'a juridical articulation of duty by those in zones of safety toward those in zones of danger'.[8] The origins of the Universal Declaration in the experiences of European civilization are important, not for the reason that most critics cite, but its opposite. It is less an expression of European triumphalism and imperial self-confidence than a guilt-ridden Christendom's renunciation of its ugly recent record; less an assertion of the superiority of European human nature than revulsion at the recent history of European savagery; not an effort to universalize Western values but to ban the dark side of Western vices such as racial and religious bigotry.[9] Far from cross-cultural divisions, the loss of a son killed by government thugs unites mothers of all religions and nationalities in shared pain, grief and anger. The challenge is how best to interpret and apply universal values with due sensitivity to local contexts and sensibilities.

The tensions crippling the efficacy, credibility and legitimacy of the formal human rights machinery reflect domestic and international politics at their most raw. Human rights can be violated most cruelly, pervasively and systematically by governments. Efforts to monitor and enforce human rights therefore take the form chiefly of claims by citizens against their own governments. But the multilateral system is fundamentally intergovernmental, and so the different governments have a common interest in limiting the scope and enforceability of international investigative agencies. At the same time, we see human rights manipulated in international relations to demonize adversary regimes in efforts, not always unsuccessful, to wrap commercial and geopolitical calculations in the flag of universal values.

While the International Court of Justice deals with justice among states, the increasing attention and sensitivity to human rights abuses and humanitarian atrocities raise questions of individual criminal accountability in a world of sovereign states. The international community has responded to barbarism by drafting and adopting international legal instruments that ban it.[10]

On the occasion of Raphael Lemkin's birth centenary, Kofi Annan recalled that to describe an old crime, Lemkin had coined the new word 'genocide' in 1943, two years before the world became familiar with Auschwitz, Belsen and Dachau; almost single-handedly drafted an international multilateral treaty declaring genocide an international crime; and then turned to the United Nations[11] in its earliest days and implored member states to adopt it.[12] The Genocide Convention, adopted by the General Assembly on 9 December 1948, was a milestone in defining genocide as a crime against humanity and thus a matter of universal criminal jurisdiction.

### Human security

'Human security' has its roots partly in the human rights tradition that regards the state as the chief threat to its own citizens and partly in the development agenda that looks to the state as the chief agent of change for the better. The rise of the human security paradigm puts the individual at the centre of the debate, analysis and policy.[13] He or she is paramount and the state is a collective instrument to protect human life and promote human welfare. The fundamental components of human security – the security of people against threats to personal safety and life – can be put at risk by external aggression, but also by factors within a country, including 'security' forces, acid rain, forest fires, rising sea levels, floods, earthquakes and tsunamis.

The reformulation of national security into human security is simple, yet has profound consequences for how we see the world, how we organize our political affairs, how we make choices in public and foreign policy and how we relate to fellow human beings from many different countries and cultures. It has a twofold relevance to our present argument. First, it directs our attention to the reality that the discourse of national security is often (ab)used to justify state atrocities against its own citizens, whereas human security is resistant to being conflated into regime security. And second, it is the conceptual root of the sense of international solidarity that impels us to protect victims of atrocities and punish their tormentors.

## Civil society

Although it takes governments to convert emerging norms (for example international criminal accountability) into binding law through multilateral conventions and treaties, for example the Rome Statute establishing the International Criminal Court (ICC), many civil society organizations seek to shape the evolution and adoption of norms and lobby for their adoption in formal agreements. There has been an exponential growth in the number of civil society actors. The net result of expanding global citizen action has been to extend the theory and deepen the practice of grassroots democracy without borders. Civil society activism across borders, issue-specific coalitions among complementary groups from around the world and engagement with like-minded governments and intergovernmental organizations have been distinguishing features of the work of NGOs and important explanations for their success. They bridge the 'disconnect between the political geography of the state on the one side and the new geography of economic and social relations on the other'.[14]

Society has become too complex for citizens' demands to be satisfied solely by governments at national, regional and global levels. Instead civil society organizations play increasingly active roles in shaping norms, laws and policies. This provides additional levers to people and governments to improve the effectiveness and enhance the legitimacy of public policy at all levels of governance, while at the same time posing challenges of representation, accountability and legitimacy both to governments and back to the civil society actors.

## Globalization

Transnational civil society activism is but one symptom of a globalizing world. Globalization releases many productive forces that can help to uplift millions from poverty, deprivation and degradation. But it can also unleash destructive forces – 'uncivil society' – such as flows of arms, terrorism, disease, prostitution, drug and people smuggling, etc. that are neither controllable nor solvable by individual governments.

There has also been a certain globalization of the process of policy-making that remains incomplete. The major problems and challenges are increasingly global in their scope and impact and require concerted global solutions. But the policy authority for tackling all problems remains vested in states, who also retain the monopoly over the coercive capacity to mobilize the necessary resources. This particular disconnect explains the often fitful, hesitant and inadequate efforts in addressing many of today's major challenges.

## The erosion of sovereignty

Modern international society is built around sovereign statehood as its bedrock organizing principle. The combined effect of the broad trends identified above is to pose significant conceptual and policy challenges to the notion of state sovereignty. The juridical equality of states can exist alongside extreme disparities of size, wealth, power and status. Nevertheless, sovereignty is the foundational principle on which contemporary world order rests, dating from the 1648 Peace of Westphalia and affirmed by the ICJ and expressed in UN Charter Article 2(1).

The United Nations is the chief agent of the system of states for exercising international authority in their name. UN membership has typically been the final symbol of sovereign statehood for freshly independent countries and their seal of acceptance into the international community of states. Article 2(7) of the UN Charter prohibits the organization from intervening in 'matters that are essentially within the domestic jurisdiction' of any member state.

Yet by signing the Charter a country accepts collective obligations and international scrutiny. The restrictions of Article 2(7) can be set aside when the Security Council decides to act under the collective enforcement Chapter VII. The scope of what constitutes threats and breaches has steadily widened to include such matters as HIV/AIDS, terrorism and atrocities. In any case, Article 2(7) concerns matters 'essentially' within domestic jurisdiction. This implies that the issue is subject to judgement, which may differ from one competent authority to another and may evolve over time in response to altered perceptions of the threats to international peace and security. Moreover, as shown in Somalia, the collapse of state authority means that there is no functioning government to fulfil an essential condition of sovereignty, on the one hand and the violence, instability and disorder can spill over from that failed state to others, on the other. The Security Council thus dealt with Somalia under the coercive clauses of Chapter VII rather than the consensual Chapter VI. Applying this argument more broadly, some analysts have questioned just how many of today's states would meet the strict requirements of sovereign statehood, describing many as 'quasi-states'.[15] And finally, the norm of non-intervention has softened as that of human rights has hardened.

## The responsibility to protect

The twin protection–prosecution agenda lies at the crossroads of the above trends that between them have heightened real-time awareness of depredations and atrocities, increased pressures to respond effectively, expanded the toolkit to do so and fenced in the exercise of both internal and external sovereignty with innumerable threads of global norms and treaties. The United Nations is the forum of choice for debating and deciding on collective action requiring the use of military force. It also has been the principal forum for the progressive advancement of the human rights agenda in its totality, including group-based social, economic and cultural rights as well as individual civil and political rights.

## Sovereignty as responsibility

Sovereignty, far from being absolute, has thus generally been considered to be contingent. The more significant change of recent times is that it has been reconceived as being instrumental. Its validation rests not in a mystical reification of the state, but in its utility as a tool for the state serving the interests of the citizens. Internal forms and precepts of governance must conform to international norms and standards of state conduct. That is, sovereignty must be exercised with due responsibility. This crucial normative shift was articulated by Francis M. Deng, the Special Representative of the Secretary-General for Internally Displaced Persons.[16]

Another challenge came with the adoption of new standards of conduct for states in the protection and advancement of international human rights. Over time, the chief threats to international security have come from violent eruptions of crises within states, including civil wars, while the goals of promoting human rights and democratic governance, protecting civilian victims of humanitarian atrocities and punishing governmental perpetrators of mass crimes have become more important.

The Charter contains an inherent tension between the principles of state sovereignty and human rights, which explains the controversy over humanitarian intervention. Individuals became subjects of international law as bearers of duties and holders of rights under a growing corpus of human rights and international humanitarian law treaties and conventions – especially the Charter, the Universal Declaration of Human Rights and the two covenants, the four Geneva Conventions plus the two prohibiting torture and genocide. The cluster of norms inhibiting, if not prohibiting, humanitarian intervention includes, alongside the norm of non-intervention, state sovereignty, domestic jurisdiction, pacific settlement of disputes, non-use of force and, in the case of UN-authorized use of force, impartiality.

In the first four decades, usually state sovereignty was privileged over human rights. The balance tilted in the 1990s. In a number of cases, the Security Council endorsed the use of force with the primary goal of humanitarian protection and assistance: the establishment of no-fly zones in Northern Iraq to protect the Kurdish minority, the proclamation (no matter how ineffectually) of UN safe areas in Bosnia, the delivery of humanitarian relief in Somalia, the restoration of the democratically elected government of Haiti and the deployment of the multinational Kosovo Force (KFOR) in Kosovo after the 1999 war.[17]

There was a second change. From 1945 to the end of the cold war in 1989–90, the preservation of peace was privileged over the protection of human rights. The Charter talks of both but provides concrete instruments for the maintenance of the former. The proliferation of complex humanitarian emergencies and the inappropriateness of the classical tenets of UN peacekeeping for dealing with them highlighted the inherent tension between the neutrality of traditional peacekeeping and the partial consequences of peace enforcement.

*The Responsibility to Protect*, the report of the Canadian-sponsored ICISS, sought to change the conceptual language, pin the responsibility on state authorities at the national and the Security Council at the international level and ensure that interventions, when they do take place, are done properly.[18] It adapted sovereignty as responsibility and proceeded to replace the familiar 'humanitarian intervention' with 'the responsibility to protect'. Based on state practice, Security Council precedent, established and emerging norms and evolving customary international law, ICISS held that the proscription against intervention is not absolute.

While the state whose people are directly affected has the default responsibility to protect, a residual responsibility also resides with the broader international community of states. This is activated when a particular state either is unwilling or unable to fulfil its responsibility to protect; or is itself the perpetrator of crimes or atrocities; or where populations living outside a particular state are directly threatened by actions taking place there. The fallback responsibility requires that in some circumstances action must be taken by external parties to support populations that are in jeopardy or under serious threat.

The Secretary-General's High Level Panel on UN reforms reaffirmed the importance of changing the terminology from the deeply divisive 'humanitarian intervention' to 'the responsibility to protect' if the international community is going to forge a new consensus. In the event, the 'responsibility to protect' was one of the few substantive items to survive the negotiations at the 2005 World Summit.[19]

## International criminal justice

### International criminal court

The 128-article Rome Statute of the ICC was adopted at the conclusion of the UN Diplomatic Conference held from 15 June to 17 July 1998. It marked the culmination of a decade-long process initiated by the General Assembly in 1989 when it requested the International Law Commission to study the subject of the establishment of an ICC. The final vote was 120 in favour and 7 against (among them China and the United States, two permanent members of the Security Council) with 21 abstentions (including India, representing one-sixth of humanity). Participants included representatives from 160 countries plus 33 observers from intergovernmental organizations and 236 observers from NGOs. The ICC Statute received its sixtieth ratification in April 2002 and came into effect in July 2002. On 22 April 2003 Luis Moreno Ocampo of Argentina, who helped to put his country's former military rulers on trial, was elected as its first prosecutor. By 1 January 2007, 139 countries had signed and 104 had ratified the Rome Statute.

The way to apprehend and punish the perpetrators of conscience-shocking crimes on a mass scale is through an international legal framework that establishes the notion of 'universal jurisdiction',[20] where jurisdiction in respect of such crimes depends not on the place where they are committed, but on the nature of the crime itself. If they are truly 'crimes against humanity', they can be prosecuted before the courts of any country. The Geneva Conventions of 1949 established the category of war crimes called 'grave breaches', which could be prosecuted in the courts of all countries that have ratified the conventions.

The UN Charter was never meant to be a tyrant's charter of impunity or his constitutional instrument of choice for self-protection. The world has moved on from the restrictive culture of sovereign impunity of previous centuries to an enlightened culture of international accountability more suited to the modern sensibility. Nuremberg and Tokyo were instances of victors' justice.[21] Yet by historical standards, both tribunals were remarkable for giving defeated leaders the opportunity to defend their actions in a court of law instead of being dispatched for summary execution. The ad hoc tribunals of the 1990s are important milestones in efforts to fill institutional gaps in the original central mission of the UN, viz. to control group violence. They have been neither unqualified successes nor total failures. While they have helped to bring hope and justice to some victims, combat the impunity of some perpetrators and greatly enrich the jurisprudence of international criminal and humanitarian law, they have been expensive, time-consuming and contributed little to sustainable national capacities for justice administration.

The international criminal tribunals have been ad hoc and ex post facto, set up to try limited numbers of individuals for specific activities, in specific situations and specific regions. As such, they suffer from particularism. An international criminal court with universal jurisdiction has been the missing link in the system of international criminal justice.[22] The International Court of Justice handles cases between states, but not between individuals. Without an international criminal court that holds individuals responsible for their actions where governments fail, or are not able to do so, acts of genocide and egregious violations of human rights often go unpunished. Since 1945, there have been many instances of crimes against humanity and war crimes for which no individuals have been held accountable.

The ICC's permanence, institutionalized identity and universal jurisdiction will enable an escape from the tyranny of the episodic and attenuate perceptions of politically motivated investigations and selective justice. Only universal liability can address the 'drift to universalism'[23] from the Nuremberg and Tokyo to the

Yugoslavia and Rwanda tribunals, along with such other way-stations as the detention of Pinochet in Britain. Permanence also helps to cumulate and build on precedents. The ICC will be an efficient and cost-effective alternative to ad hoc tribunals with respect to money, time and energy and may also provide sensible alternatives to dubious sanctions and unilateral military retaliation.

The establishment of the ICC as a permanent and universal international criminal court marks one of the most significant advances in international law. Yet the reluctance to join the ICC by three permanent members of the Security Council – China, Russia and the United States – and also by other populous countries such as India, Indonesia, Pakistan and others was testimony to a significant division of opinion in the international community. In the battle over the ICC, reasonable US demands were listened to and accommodated. But gradually the conviction grew that objections were being raised and arguments were being framed to fit a predetermined policy of opposing the very idea of a credible and independent ICC with universal jurisdiction. Cherif Bassiouni, chair of the Rome Statute's drafting committee, wrote later that most delegations concluded that 'it would be better to stop giving in to the United States; they believed the United States would never be satisfied with the concessions it got and ultimately would never sign the Treaty for completely unrelated domestic political reasons'.[24]

Nevertheless, there are two respects in which the US fears about the ICC may be well founded: the rule-of-law standards and the integration of criminal justice within an overarching framework of democratic governance.

For a trial to be authentic, the possibility of acquittal must be as much an inbuilt requirement as the possibility of conviction. The US criminal justice system goes about the farthest in the world in protecting the rights of the arrested and accused. International criminal law, it has been argued, shifted the focus from the defence to the prosecution.[25] The International Criminal Tribunal for former Yugoslavia (ICTY) 'does not always respect the rights of the criminal defendant in ways consistent with international human rights norms or national constitutions'.[26] The UN has to ensure that any process of trial and prosecution is credible, meets international standards on the independence and impartiality of prosecutors and judges, and respects the rights of victims as well as defendants.[27]

Second, the ICC is not embedded in a broader system of democratic policy making, there is no political check on it and therefore its authority to overturn policy established by national democracies is questionable. In a national system, the office of the prosecutor functions within a well-established structure of state governance, while the ICC 'is not established as part of a centralized system of international governance that can govern the entire international community'.[28] The ICC may experience legitimacy problems 'insofar as it provides for jurisdiction over non-party nationals, displaces the state as the conduit of democratic representation and provides no alternative mechanism for democratic governance'.[29]

Christine Chinkin quotes from one of the international criminal cases, referring to the Bosnian Muslim women victims of war-related sexual violence, that consent could not be freely given when the women had nowhere to go and no place to hide.[30] We will perhaps have made our transition from barbarism to culture when the burden of that haunting phrase is transferred from the victim to the perpetrators and would-be perpetrators.

## Balancing competing claims

Neither the protection nor the prosecution agenda is absolute, to be privileged in every instance over all competing claims. Even when there is agreement that military intervention may sometimes be necessary and unavoidable in order to protect innocent people from life-threatening danger by interposing an outside force between actual and apprehended victims and perpetrators, key questions remain about agency, lawfulness and legitimacy. ICISS argued that the UN is the principal institution for building, consolidating and using the authority of the international community. Because of this, it is especially important that every effort be made to encourage the Security Council to exercise – and not abdicate – its responsibilities.

The ethic of conviction would impose obligations to prosecute people for their past criminal misdeeds to the full extent of the law. The ethic of responsibility imposes the countervailing requirement to judge the wisdom of alternative courses of action with respect to their consequences for social harmony in the future. International criminal justice takes away from domestic authorities the options of alternative modes of healing and restitution with a view to reconciliation that puts the traumas of the past firmly in the past.[31] The legal clarity of judicial verdicts sits uncomfortably with the nuanced morality of confronting *and overcoming*, through a mix of justice and high politics, a jointly troubled past. Truth commissions provide a halfway house between victors' or foreigners' justice and collective amnesia. Truth commissions take a victim-centred approach, help to establish a historical record and contribute to memorialising defining epochs in a nation's history.

Another problem lies in the contradictory logics of peace and justice. Peace is forward-looking, problem-solving and integrative, requiring reconciliation between past enemies within an all-inclusive community. Justice is backward-looking, finger-pointing and retributive, requiring acknowledgement and atonement, if not trial and punishment, of the perpetrators of past crimes.

In both tasks – protection of victims and prosecution of perpetrators – the application of international mechanisms comes second, only after the domestic mechanisms are either exhausted or powerless. While the ad hoc international criminal tribunals have primacy over the operation of domestic court systems,[32] the ICC has been constructed to give primacy to domestic systems and become operative only in the event of domestic unwillingness or incapacity. Article 17 of the Rome Statute stipulates that the jurisdiction of the ICC is to be activated only when states are 'unwilling or unable genuinely to investigate or prosecute'.

Similarly, the 'responsibility to protect' concept expects and requests states first to protect their populations and triggers international intervention only after governments are either weak and unable, or unwilling (complicit in crimes) to do so. This prevalence of domestic over international jurisdiction presents the UN and other assistance agencies with a very important mission – how to build capacities and empower states to deal with both tasks – protection of victims and prosecution of perpetrators.

One final red flag that also relates to both the agendas. Governments of the United States, Britain, Australia, France etc. find it beyond their imagination to conceive of circumstances in which their countries might be the targets of military intervention by 'the international community'. Consequently they are unable to empathize with the concerns of developing countries who do fear being the targets of international intervention by tomorrow's moral majority. There is a simple enough solution to this and even UN-authorized interventions will generate North–South friction until such time as the solution is adopted. This is the vexed issue of Security Council reform with respect to composition, procedures and accountability. On composition, it needs a better representation of contemporary power realities, continents and developing countries in both permanent and elected categories. On procedures, it needs to be far more open, transparent and democratic. On accountability, it must be made far more answerable to the General Assembly and also brought within the jurisdictional oversight of the World Court. Absent these reforms, all military interventions will be considered to be in the interests of the rich and powerful minority targeted at the poor and weak majority.

Similarly, international criminal justice will remain permanently suspect as victors' justice until such time as some of the major Western leaders and commanding generals are also put on trial, convicted and sentenced.[33]

## Conclusion

The differences in the international protection and punishment agendas apply, *mutatis mutandis*, to the domestic law enforcement organs. Every state needs police and army to protect the population and laws and courts to punish the criminals. The police and army are part of the executive branch of the government, empowered accordingly and authorized to act expediently. The prosecution and judges are part of a separate judicial system, fully independent in their deliberations and decisions from the government.

That said, the specific mechanisms for protection of people and prosecution of perpetrators should not be overestimated. The ICTY has no police force to search mountains and arrest suspects. When the ad hoc tribunals were established by the Security Council, the language in the resolutions – that they will be instrumental in 'the maintenance of international peace and security' – raised unnecessarily ambitious expectations. The tribunals can play only a limited and very specific part in the long and difficult process of peacebuilding. Being adversarial by nature, they are not best in reconciling people. Trauma and tensions in the societies can and should be addressed by other less confrontational forums, such as truth commissions, reconciliation and rebuilding initiatives, public apologies etc. One has to remember that the victims (survivors and relatives) of crimes – although they certainly deserve all possible sympathy – are not the only rights-holders. The logic of retribution through criminal justice need to be tempered with the logic of restoration and reconciliation of the societies.

Second, the protection of innocent civilians and the prosecution of perpetrators of atrocities should never be divided into ethnic or religious lines. Victims of all sides need equal protection and perpetrators from all sides – for example Serbs, Croats, Bosnian Muslims or Albanians – need to face the same penalties. One problem with the legitimacy of the ICTY was the initial heavy imbalance between the high number of prosecuted Serbs and the low number of prosecuted persons from the other ethnic groups, not to mention the total lack of prosecution of any of the possible war crimes committed by NATO during the bombing in 1999.

The changed nature of armed conflict demands the enforcement of two tasks: the apprehension and punishment of the evildoers; and the protection of the innocent. The two tasks aim at the same final objective – the reduction and elimination of violent conflicts. But they require different techniques and instruments. The prosecution of perpetrators necessitates a permanent court. The protection of civilian people needs a permanent army. The first has already been established – the ICC. The second – UN Emergency Peace Service (UNEPS) is under discussion,[34] with some regional capacities already developed within the African Union (AU) and the European Union (EU).

Such permanent bodies – the ICC and the UNEPS – are essential foundations to materialize the joint responsibility to protect and prosecute, nevertheless, the differences between the two tasks should not be confused. The protection of the innocent needs to be expedient, whereas the prosecution of perpetrators needs to be slow and deliberate, taking into consideration due process and fairness. 'Quick justice' *à la* Saddam Hussein's trial and execution is an oxymoron. Conversely, a slow and tardy response to atrocities (as in Darfur) is no response. The protection of innocents demands strong political engagement. Heads of states and governments need to get to their phones as soon as possible, discuss options, make decisions and give clear and firm orders to their generals. On the opposite side, they should not give orders to the prosecutors or judges – criminal accountability has to be apolitical, independent, based on strict legality and not influenced by external agents.

# 9 R2P

## From idea to norm – and action?[1]

*Ramesh Thakur and Thomas G. Weiss*

The most fundamental human right is to life itself – indeed, what could be more fundamental to a working system of global governance, however defined and however rudimentary? As Pope Benedict XVI put it in his address to the United Nations General Assembly in New York in April 2008: 'Recognition of the unity of the human family and attention to the innate dignity of every man and woman, today find renewed emphasis in the principle of the responsibility to protect . . . this principle has to invoke the idea of the person as image of the Creator.'[2] But establishing a universal standard to protect life under the most extreme threats represents a normative challenge because outsiders wishing to protect or assist affected populations confront the harsh reality of the non-intervention principle enshrined in UN Charter Article 2(7).

Possibly the most dramatic normative development of our time – comparable to the Nuremberg trials and the 1948 Convention on Genocide in the immediate aftermath of the Second World War – relates to the use of military force to protect human beings. The publication of *Global R2P* reflects the fact that no longer is it necessary to finesse the tensions between sovereignty and human rights in the Charter; they can now be confronted. Sovereignty no longer implies the licence to kill.

No idea has moved faster in the international normative arena than the 'responsibility to protect' (R2P), the title of the 2001 report from the ICISS.[3] Over time, domestic and international jurisdictions are blurring, which became most evident with the willingness – sometimes authorized by the United Nations, sometimes by regional organizations – to shelve sacrosanct sovereignty by using military force for human protection purposes in the 1990s.

Created from the ashes of the Second World War with the allies determined to prevent a repeat of Adolf Hitler's abominations, the United Nations for most of its existence has focused far more on external aggression than internal mass killings. Yet Nazi Germany was guilty of both. Unlike aggression against other countries, the systematic and large-scale extermination of Jews was a new horror. In this new century, the world organization is at long last elevating the doctrine of preventing mass atrocities against people to the same level of collective responsibility as preventing and repelling armed aggression against states.

Traditional warfare is the use of force by rival armies of enemy states fighting over a clash of interests: us against them. Collective security rests on the use of force by the international community of states to defeat or punish an aggressor: all against one. Traditional peacekeeping involves the insertion of neutral and lightly armed third-party soldiers as a physical buffer between enemy combatants who have agreed to a ceasefire. Peace-enforcement accepted the use of force by better armed – but still neutral – international soldiers against spoilers.

R2P is a more sophisticated and politically a far more broadly acceptable reformulation of the more familiar 'humanitarian intervention'. It differs from all these in that it refers to the use of military force by outsiders for the protection of victims of mass atrocities. R2P redefines sovereignty as responsibility; locates the responsibility in the first instance with the state; but it argues that if the state is unwilling or unable to honour the responsibility, or itself turns perpetrator of atrocities against its people, then the residual responsibility to protect the victims of atrocity crimes shifts to the international community of states, acting ideally through the Security Council.

R2P has a decided UN flavour. Its roots are to be found in statements by former Secretary-General Kofi Annan; the norm gives pride of place to the UN if the international community of states is to honour its international responsibility to protect; and, if the norm is to be the basis of a new international consensus, this can only come about in the UN forum.

The purpose of this chapter is to 'contextualize' R2P within current efforts to understand the web of 'global governance' that constitutes the few elements of international society and order that Hedley Bull so assiduously pursued in the face of 'international anarchy'.[4] How, in short, do we build an international system that responds to threats such as mass murder and mass ethnic cleansing in the absence of a central authority?

We define 'governance' as the sum of laws, norms, policies and institutions that define, constitute and mediate relations between citizens, society, market and the state – the wielders and objects of the exercise of public power. 'Global governance' – which can be good, bad, or indifferent – refers to collective problem-solving arrangements. These may be visible but quite informal (e.g. practices or guidelines) or temporary units (e.g. coalitions). But they may also be far more formal, taking the shape of rules (laws, norms, codes of behaviour) as well as constituted institutions and practices (formal and informal) to manage collective affairs by a variety of actors (state authorities, intergovernmental organizations, civil society organizations and private sector entities).

Global government would imply an international system with at least some of the capacities of national governments – notably the power to control or repel threats, to raise revenues, allocate expenditures, redistribute incomes and require compliance from citizens as well as ensure their rights. We clearly do not have anything resembling that. Global governance implies systems with imperfections and limitations – in a phrase, international cooperation where there is no global government, only states mostly pursuing their own national or regional interests. That we do have.

This chapter begins with truth in packaging – Ramesh Thakur was an ICISS commissioner and Thomas G. Weiss was its research director. We present the story of the journey of R2P from an idea to a global norm now in drastic need of implementing action. The United Nations is a vital part of the story of contemporary global governance and the astonishingly rapid journey of R2P from an idea to the centre of the international normative, policy and institutional arenas provides us with a powerful and persuasive way to analyse contemporary international organization. When Secretary-General Kofi Annan issued his famous 'challenge of humanitarian intervention' in September 1999, he provoked such a furious backlash from so many countries that some wondered about his future in the UN. Yet a mere six years later, the norm was endorsed by the world leaders gathered at the UN. Annan called it one of his 'most precious of all' achievements.[5]

We begin by outlining the origins of the R2P idea and then describe the background factors in the 1990s that paved the way for the advancement of this norm. Next, we describe the main actors in the story: the norm entrepreneurs, champions and brokers, followed by an account of the process by which the ICISS arrived at its landmark report on R2P. This is followed by a description of the sustained engagement with the R2P agenda from 2001, when the ICISS report was published, to its adoption at the 2005 World Summit. We end with a sketch of the tasks and challenges that lie ahead to move R2P from a norm to a template for policy and action.

## Roots and origins of the R2P idea

From one point of view, the idea of sovereignty as responsibility is not all that new or fresh. Rather, it has a long evolutionary pedigree. 'The principle of "responsibility to protect" was considered by the ancient *ius gentium* as the foundation of every action taken by those in government with regard to the governed', Pope Benedict XVI told UN diplomats. While the responsibility to protect 'has only recently been defined, . . . it was always present implicitly at the origins of the United Nations, and is now increasingly characteristic of its activity'.[6] The ICISS report consolidated a number of disparate trends and borrowed language first developed by Francis M. Deng – currently the Special Representative of the Secretary-General for Prevention of Genocide and at the time the special representative on internally displaced persons (IDPs) – and Roberta Cohen to help address the problem of IDPs.[7] Rather than create a new norm, ICISS registered and dramatized a norm shift already underway and found language to make it more palatable to nay-sayers.

The importance of sovereignty as the key organizing principle of the modern world order needed and received a strong affirmation in the ICISS report. It took pains to emphasize that a cohesive and peaceful international system is more likely to be achieved through the cooperation of effective and legitimate states, confident of their place in the world, than in an environment of fragile, collapsed, fragmenting or generally chaotic states. Sovereignty provides order, stability and predictability in international relations and not merely a pretext for abuse.

As such, it implies a dual responsibility: externally – to respect the sovereignty of other states and internally, to respect the dignity and basic rights of all the people within the state.

This is a less radical departure from established precept and practice than it appears. The authority of the state is nowhere regarded as absolute. Internally, it is shared among different levels of governmental authorities, from the local through the provincial to the national. And it is distributed among different sectors of authorities, such as the legislature, executive, judiciary and bureaucracy.

As it happens, one of the best examples is India,[8] a powerful country that expresses strong opposition to 'humanitarian intervention'. The fundamental rights in the Indian constitution guarantee the dignity and worth of individuals essentially against the state and empower the judiciary to monitor and enforce state compliance. That is, the state is responsible and can be held *accountable for acts of commission* that violate citizens' rights.

At the same time, several of India's independence leaders also believed that liberty is an empty abstraction to the hungry; freedom is meaningful only with economic security. In the light of India's poverty, 'economic rights' (for example, the right to an adequate means of livelihood) could not realistically be enshrined as a basic right enforceable in the courts; but they were enshrined as ideals. The constitution accordingly incorporated them as directive principles, describing them as 'fundamental in the governance of the country and it shall be the duty of the state to apply these principles in making laws'. Some of these are in the nature of socioeconomic rights, except that they cannot be enforced through the courts. When critics and political opponents criticize the government for failure to honour the directive principles, in essence they are arguing for holding the state *responsible for acts of omission*.

Internationally too, sovereignty is understood as embracing responsibility – in human rights covenants, UN efforts and state practice itself. There is no transfer or dilution of the *status* of state sovereignty. But there is a necessary change in the *exercise* of sovereignty: from sovereignty as control to sovereignty as responsibility in both internal functions and external duties.

The normative advances of the responsibility to protect can in no small measure be traced back to early efforts by the Brookings Project on Internal Displacement to give concrete meaning to the mandate of the representative of the Secretary-General for internally displaced persons. Although the ICISS never formally acknowledged the parentage of the idea, Lloyd Axworthy – who as Canadian foreign minister launched the commission – has written: 'The first time I heard the notion of "responsibility to protect" was when Deng visited me in Ottawa and argued for a clear commitment by the international community to deal with the IDP issue.'[9]

In his work on behalf of IDPs, Deng introduced into the literature on internal displacement a concept that had been developed by him, William Zartman and other scholars in their work on governance in Africa.[10] Deng's eventual colleague and project co-director at the Brookings Institution, Roberta Cohen, emphasized the international dimensions of protection. 'Sovereignty,' she wrote in 1991, 'carries with it a responsibility on the part of governments to protect their citizens.'[11] Deng explained its origins in work begun in the late 1980s to see how the end of the cold war changed the way that conflict and conflict resolution were perceived in Africa. It was a way of squaring the circle, to reconcile the seemingly clashing principles of state sovereignty and non-intervention, on the one hand, with the need to halt the worst kinds of abuse of human rights, on the other hand and even to intervene militarily in the most egregious of cases.

This conceptualization to address the phenomenon of internal displacement then gained momentum with Annan's articulation of 'two sovereignties' in the late 1990s and the formulation of the responsibility to protect in 2001. As a result, the characteristics of a sovereign – territory, authority, population, independence – spelled out in the 1934 Montevideo Convention on the Rights and Duties of States have been complemented by another: a modicum of respect for human rights. State sovereignty is considerably less sacrosanct today than in 1945. When a state is manifestly incapable or unwilling to do so and peaceful means fail, the resort to international judicial pursuit, sanctions and even outside military force remains a possibility. The threshold for non-consensual intervention is high – not merely substantial human rights abuses but genocide or ethnic cleansing – but the fact that it remains a policy option represents significant new middle ground in international relations.

While a number of the world's most abusive governments would disagree, nonetheless a normative consensus is emerging in international society about a state's responsibilities and accountabilities both to domestic and international constituencies. Abusers that are major powers (e.g. China and Russia) or resource-rich (e.g. Saudi Arabia) are of course able to exercise their sovereignty with little fear of forceful outside intervention; but nonetheless it is becoming increasingly difficult for states to claim the prerogatives of sovereignty unless they meet internationally agreed responsibilities, which include protecting the human rights of and providing life-sustaining assistance to, all those within its jurisdiction. Failure to meet obligations legitimizes at least high-decibel levels of criticism and intrusion and, when the politics are right, even outside intervention by the United Nations and the community of responsible states, or a coalition of them, against a member of their club that misbehaves egregiously.

## Background factors

Going to war was an acknowledged attribute of state sovereignty and war itself was an accepted institution of the Westphalian system with distinctive rules, etiquette, norms and stable patterns of practices to govern armed conflicts.[12] In that quasi-Hobbesian world barely removed from the state of nature, the main protection against aggression was countervailing power, which increased both the cost of victory and the risk of failure. Since 1945, the UN has spawned a corpus of law to stigmatize aggression and create a robust norm against it.

The world organization exists to check the predatory instincts of the powerful towards the weak – one of the most enduring but not endearing lessons of history, whether in domestic jurisdictions inside state borders or in international relations. Now there are significant restrictions on the authority of states to use force either domestically or internationally.

A further challenge to the Westphalian order came with individuals becoming subjects of international law as bearers of duties and holders of rights under a growing corpus of human rights and international humanitarian law treaties and conventions: the Charter, Universal Declaration of Human Rights and the two covenants, the Geneva Conventions and Additional Protocols and the two convention prohibiting torture and genocide and so on.

With weapons of mass destruction (WMDs) and with nuclear weapons in particular, doctrines and strategies of use and deployment emphasized mass casualties among civilians as the main, intended target. Even with conventional weapons, the emphasis has shifted from main battle tanks and bombers to small arms as the weapon of choice in contemporary armed conflicts. Moreover, non-combatants dying from conflict-related starvation and disease now vastly outnumber troops killed directly in warfare, by a ratio of up to 9:1. The 'maintenance of international peace and security', for which primary responsibility is vested in the Security Council, in practice translates today into the protection of civilians.

The proliferation of complex humanitarian emergencies after the end of the cold war and the inappropriateness of the classical tenets of UN peacekeeping for dealing with them,[13] highlighted the inherent tension between the neutrality and impartiality of traditional peacekeeping and the partial consequences of peace enforcement. The Brahimi Report confronted the dilemma squarely and concluded that political neutrality has often degenerated into military timidity and the abdication of the duty to protect civilians. While striving to remain impartial, the UN should soften its principle of neutrality between belligerents in favour of 'adherence to the principles of the Charter and to the objectives of [the] mandate'.[14]

There is yet another key background factor behind the rise of R2P, namely the softening of sovereignty in so many of its empirical dimensions. It has become commonplace to note that under the impact of globalization, political, social, commercial-economic, environmental and technological influences cross borders without passports. The total range of cross-border flows and activities has increased while the proportion subject to control and regulation by governments has diminished. National frontiers are becoming less relevant in determining the flow of ideas, information, goods, services, capital, labour and technology. The speed of modern communications makes borders increasingly permeable, while the volume of cross-border flows threatens to overwhelm the capacity of states to manage them.

Moreover, the proliferation of states has led to the creation and recognition of many states that are weak, fragile, disrupted, collapsed or failed. For example, just as East Timor has become a de facto protectorate of Australia, so the security (internal and external) and economic viability of Kosovo is underwritten ultimately by Europe; meanwhile, Somalia continues to hobble along as a state without any of the traditional attributes.

## 'Humanitarian Intervention' in the 1990s

The cumulative effect of these changes poses significant conceptual, policy and operational challenges to the notion and exercise of state sovereignty. ICISS responded to a series of military–civilian interactions in humanitarian crises,[15] in which the background factors culminated and intersected; and it confronted directly the divergent reactions – or rather, the non-reactions – by the Security Council to Rwanda and Kosovo. In 1994, intervention was too little and too late to halt or even slow the murder of what may have been as many as 800,000 people in the Great Lakes region of Africa. In 1999, the formidable NATO finessed the council and waged war for the first time in Kosovo. But many observers saw the seventy-eight-day bombing effort as being too much, too late, too little (in ruling out the use of ground troops) and too counterproductive, perhaps creating as much human suffering among IDPs and refugees as it relieved. In both cases, the Security Council failed to act expeditiously and authorize the use of deadly force to protect vulnerable populations. In both cases, many – but not all – human rights advocates and humanitarian agencies supported the military protection of civilians whose lives were threatened, thereby exposing the glaring normative gap for collective action more clearly than in the past.

If the UN was going to be relevant, it had to engineer a basis for international involvement in the ugly civil wars that produced such conscience-shocking suffering. The earlier debate about whether humanitarian disasters qualified as 'threats to international peace and security' had resolved itself because so many humanitarian crises had been the object of Security Council action for precisely these reasons.

Our point of departure in reviewing the thrust of the ICISS should be made clear at the outset: the lack of reaction in Rwanda represents a far more serious threat to international order and justice than the Security Council's paralysis in Kosovo. Past or potential victims undoubtedly would agree with this judgment. For instance, the most thorough survey to date of victims in war zones suggests that there is too little rather than too much humanitarian intervention. Fully two-thirds of civilians under siege who were interviewed in twelve war-torn societies by the International Committee of the Red Cross want more intervention and only 10 per cent want none.[16] In addition, a 2005 mapping exercise of operational contexts for humanitarian agencies finds that recipients 'are more concerned about *what* is provided than about *who* provides it'.[17]

## Actors

Norms neither arise nor are converted into laws and regimes by some mysterious process. They require identifiable agents. The crucial actors promoting and shepherding R2P through the maze of UN politics can be broken down into norm entrepreneurs, champions and brokers.

As a *norm entrepreneur*, the UN Secretary-General is a unique international actor with distinctive characteristics and bases of authority and influence, but also with limitations.[18] There were several moral pleas in 1999 from the future Nobel laureate, Kofi Annan. And if we fast forward to his speech in New York in March 2004 to commemorate the tenth anniversary of the Rwanda genocide, he regretted that he could and should have done more.[19] He was driven similarly by his experience of being in charge of peacekeeping at the time of the Srebrenica massacre in 1995.

As Annan graphically told a 1998 audience at Ditchley Park, 'state frontiers ... should no longer be seen as a watertight protection for war criminals or mass murderers'.[20] He argued that human rights concerns transcended claims of sovereignty, a theme that he put forward more delicately a year later at the Millennium Summit.[21] The reaction was loud, bitter and predictable, especially from China, Russia and much of the Third World. 'Intervention' – for whatever reasons, even humanitarian – remains taboo.[22] The chorus of complaints in the General Assembly after Annan's remarks in September 1999 had a remarkably similar tenor to negative reactions in the Commission on Human Rights about many aspects of Deng's mandate as representative of the Secretary-General. Diplomats are often out of touch with opinion in developing countries around the world, which tended to be much more nuanced.[23]

It helped also that Annan, the only UN insider to have held the organization's top job, had an unmatched grasp of the politics of the organization. He explained the utility to the UN of outside intellectual energies:

> There are certain issues that are better done outside and there are certain issues that can only be done inside ... But take a look at the intervention issue. I couldn't have done it inside. It would have been very divisive. And the member states were very uncomfortable because, as an organization, sovereignty is our bedrock and bible – here is someone coming with ideas which are almost challenging it. So I had to sow the seed and let them digest it but take the study outside and then bring in the results for them to look at it. I find that when you are dealing with issues where the member states are divided and have very strong views and very strong regional views, if you do the work inside the discussions become so acrimonious that however good a document is, sometimes you have problems ... But if you bring it from outside ... they accept it.[24]

R2P's state *champion* from start to finish was Canada, a country strongly committed to UN-centred multilateralism, with a history of close engagement with the world organization, political credibility in both North and South and a proud tradition of successful global initiatives. Foreign Minister Lloyd Axworthy initiated the establishment of the commission in response to Annan's challenge in fall 1999. He was still the minister when the commission was assembled but retired from politics not long after. The commission's work continued under his successors, John Manley and Bill Graham, as foreign minister. When Paul Martin succeeded Jean Chrétien as prime minister, again there was no break in the continuity, helped by a change in leadership not in government. There were also several other like-minded countries such as Norway and Switzerland, as well as major foundations such as Macarthur and other actors such as the ICRC, which worked closely with ICISS in supportive advocacy.

The *norm broker* was the ICISS. Its mandate was to build a broader understanding of the tension between intervention and state sovereignty and to find common ground for military intervention to support humanitarian objectives. Humanitarian imperatives and principles of sovereignty are recon-ciled through 'the responsibility to protect', a paraphrase of 'sovereignty as responsibility', with some conceptual and enormous political consequences.

## ICISS process

The background factors and the range of actors engaged with the issue over the past decade go a long way towards explaining the movement of sovereignty as responsibility from the fringes to the mainstream of international relations in general and UN diplomacy in particular. The Canadian government's initiative in September 2000 followed Annan's poignant rhetorical question: 'If humanitarian intervention is, indeed, an unacceptable assault on sovereignty, how should we respond to a Rwanda, to a Srebrenica – to gross and systematic violations of human rights that offend every precept of our common human-ity?'[25] Given the supposedly wide disparity of views across the North–South divide – industrialized countries more enthusiastic in principle, developing countries more wary about providing a rationale for outside intervention – ICISS was co-chaired by persons from each camp (Mohamed Sahnoun and Gareth Evans) and its commissioners were also evenly divided. But sovereignty as responsibility is not really a North-versus-South issue other than at a misleadingly superficial level, even though that is how, like so many other international issues, it is usually parsed. The extensive ICISS outreach and consultations offered evidence of how differences across and within regions – Africa, Asia and Latin America – and between governments and civil society within countries are varied and subtle.

Ten consultations in both the Northern and Southern Hemispheres sought the views of governments, scholars, intergovernmental and non-governmental humanitarian actors and journalists.[26] The cacophony cannot be summarized except to say that what was most notable, in historical perspective, is that nowhere did *anyone* argue that intervention to sustain humanitarian objectives is *never* justifiable.[27] After the genocide in Rwanda, very few policymakers, pundits or practitioners exclude protective intervention as a last resort that is necessary under some tragic contingency.

## From the report to the world summit, filling the policy gap

The ICISS final report was published with exceptionally bad timing in December 2001, very shortly after the terrorist attacks of September 11. Understandably, the world's attention was preoccupied with the consequences of and responses to that horrific event. The invasion of Iraq and the ouster of Saddam Hussein by a US-led coalition acting without UN authorization had a doubly damaging effect. First, as tensions mounted over 2002 and early 2003, few had the time to focus on R2P. Second, as the WMD justification for the war fell apart and claims of close links between Saddam's regime and al-Qaeda also proved spurious, the coalition of the willing – Australia, Britain and the United States as the three main belligerent states – began retroactively to use the language of humanitarian intervention and R2P as the main plank of justification for their actions in Iraq.

Some of the ICISS commissioners argued strenuously in the public debate that Iraq would not have met the R2P test for intervention.[28] Co-chair Gareth Evans, Commissioner Ramesh Thakur and Research Director Thomas Weiss spoke and wrote extensively in the years following the publication of the report to multiple audiences: policy (intergovernmental and government officials), scholarly and civil society.[29] The Canadian government organized an extensive series of consultations with governments, regional organizations and civil society forums, typically using the two co-chairs, as well as Thakur and Weiss (and some other ICISS members within their regions) to help promote the report. As the message resonated, many civil society organizations began advocacy and dissemination work on their own as well. And of course Kofi Annan remained fully engaged with the issue.

The Secretary-General's High-level Panel on Threats, Challenges and Change, which included ICISS co-chair Gareth Evans, reaffirmed the importance of the terminology change from the deeply divisive 'humanitarian intervention' to 'the responsibility to protect'.[30] It proposed five criteria of legitimacy: seriousness of threat, proper purpose, last resort, proportional means and balance of consequences.[31] In a significant breakthrough for the growing acceptance of the new norm, China's official paper on UN reforms, published on 7 June 2005, noted that 'Each state shoulders the primary responsibility to protect its own population . . . . When a massive humanitarian crisis occurs, it is the legitimate concern of the international community to ease and defuse the crisis'. It went on to list the conditions and safeguards, including Security Council authorization, which form the core of the responsibility to protect.[32] In the meantime, in the United States, the Gingrich-Mitchell task force too endorsed the responsibility to protect, including the calls for the norm to be affirmed by the Security Council and the General Assembly.[33]

In his own report before the World Summit, Annan made an explicit reference to ICISS and R2P as well as to the HLP, endorsed the legitimacy criteria and urged the Security Council to adopt a resolution 'setting out these principles and expressing its intention to be guided by them' when authorizing the use of force. This would 'add transparency to its deliberations and make its decisions more likely to be respected, by both Governments and world public opinion'.[34]

The *World Summit Outcome Document* (2005) makes clear the need for international intervention when countries fail to shield their citizens from, or more likely actively sponsor, mass-atrocity crimes.[35] Some of the harshest supportive critics see the emphasis on the state and the requirement for a Security Council decision as constituting 'R2P lite' and others the actual language in paragraphs 138–9 as being wordier and woollier than the ICISS version.[36] We do not disagree, but nonetheless we see the document as a step forward in a long process.

## R2P as normative advancement

The most significant achievement of R2P is to fill a crucial normative gap. The clearest way to gauge the impact of this emerging norm is to situate the rapid evolution of attitudes and awareness. The political brouhaha over 'humanitarian intervention' provided the basis for compromise in the work by ICISS whose final report opens with words that could have come directly from Deng and Cohen's pen or word-processor:

> State sovereignty implies responsibility and the primary responsibility for the protection of its people lies with the state itself. Where a population is suffering serious harm, as a result of internal war, insurgency, repression or state failure and the state in question is unwilling or unable to halt or avert it, the principle of non-intervention yields to the international responsibility to protect.[37]

These developments are not, of course, without critics among states as well as analysts. A host of the usual suspects in the Third World (e.g. Algeria, Malaysia, Egypt, India, Cuba, the Sudan and Venezuela) along with China and Russia oftentimes, but not always, are among the loudest critics. India, Algeria and Russia together account for what may be 1.5 million IDPs and are clearly uneasy with any publicity about the plight of those people.[38] They are joined by analytical critics ranging from those who fear it will become an instrument of abuse by the most powerful to others who worry that it will give the powerful an excuse to avoid international action. Thus, Mohammed Ayoob sees it as conjuring up 'images of colonial domination under the guise of nineteenth-century "standard of civilization" doctrine';[39] David Rieff questions whether 'it has actually kept a single jackboot out of a single human face';[40] and for Alex Bellamy the language itself has been 'abused by states keen to avoid assuming any responsibility for saving some of the world's most vulnerable people'.[41] And of course Washington drags its feet because it categorically refuses to have its military committed by others. Moreover, scepticism emanates from practitioners such as the Calcutta Research Group's Paula Banarjee who judges that sovereignty as responsibility 'is of little importance as the government defines both sovereignty and responsibility . . . [and] often sovereignty means powerlessness of marginal groups and responsibility is only to the so-called majority'.[42]

We are more sanguine about the potential consequences of having filled this normative gap as well as about the necessity for outside intervention and its beneficial impact. Even if the sun seems to have set for the moment,[43] it could prove the prelude to a new dawn. The sea change in mainstream normative views since the beginning of the 1990s contrasts even more sharply with the experience of the 1970s.[44] Three interventions with very substantial humanitarian pay-offs were not even partially framed or justified by the interveners in such terms. At that time, the notion of using outside military force when a sovereign state acted irresponsibly towards its citizens simply was too far from the mainstream of acceptable international relations. International order was firmly grounded in the inviolability of sovereignty and therefore states were more attuned to their own unique political interests than to humanitarian imperatives. Specifically, India's invasion of East Pakistan in 1971, Tanzania's of Uganda and Vietnam's of Cambodia later in the decade, were unilateral efforts geared to regime change; and they all were explicitly justified as self-defence. In retrospect, all three are frequently cited as evidence of an emerging right to humanitarian intervention. Yet, none was approved by the Security Council – and Vietnam's was actually condemned.

Clearly the international normative climate is dramatically different and in great measure along the lines recommended first by Deng and Cohen, later by the Secretary-General and finally by the more visible ICISS. On some occasions, the fundamental rights of civilians assume relatively more weight than the prerogatives of states to act with impunity and hide behind the façade of sovereignty. UN authorization of military intervention is not of course an option against major powers as international tolerance for Russian and Chinese atrocities in Chechnya and Xinjiang aptly demonstrates. However, the good should not be an enemy of the best. Some action, even if inconsistent, is better than none.

The relationship between sovereignty and intervention is thus increasingly viewed as complementary rather than contradictory. Sovereignty is conceived as a conditional right dependent upon respect for a minimum standard of human rights and upon each state's honouring its obligation to protect its citizens. If states are manifestly unwilling or unable to do so, the responsibility to protect them should be borne by the international community of states.

The sea change also reflected the Security Council's framing of issues, for instance its emphasis on vulnerable groups – including resolution 1261 that condemns the targeting of children, resolution 1265 on the protection of civilians in armed conflict, resolution 1325 that specifically addresses the impact of war on women and resolution 1400 that extends the UN mission in Sierra Leone mainly on the basis of IDPs. Former *New York Times* columnist Anthony Lewis is on target when he characterizes the ICISS's framing of issues as 'the international state of the mind'.[45]

None of this normative development took place in a vacuum. By redefining sovereignty as responsibility, the report addressed the demand-side of intervention, especially Rwanda. It would have been difficult for the ICISS to refine the interpretation of sovereignty had the egregious non-decision by the international community of states not led to hundreds of thousands of deaths. The ICISS is part of the expansion of actors so central to global governance, the 'Third United Nations',[46] which directly influences the other two components of the world organization, states and the secretariat. Their definitions and views have helped fill normative gaps, both at the UN and elsewhere.

## International criminal pursuit, filling the institutional gap

We have witnessed what amount to revolutionary advances in the criminalization of domestic and international violence by armed groups and their individual leaders.[47] Having petitioned the League of Nations to outlaw 'acts of barbarism and vandalism' in his youth, as a Jew in occupied Poland Raphael Lemkin fought in the underground resistance and in late 1944 published one of the most fateful works of political thought of the last century: *Axis Rule in Occupied Europe: Laws of Occupation, Analysis of Government, Proposals for Redress*.[48] On his birth centenary, Annan reminded his audience that 'article VI of the Convention, which binds the Parties to try persons charged with genocide before a national or international tribunal, has for all practical purposes remained a dead letter'.[49] But recent developments give hope: the crime of genocide was included in the statutes of the International Criminal Tribunals for Rwanda (ICTR),[50] the former Yugoslavia (ICTY),[51] and the International Criminal Court (ICC).[52]

The landscape of international criminal justice has changed dramatically in an astonishingly short period of time.[53] In 1990, tyrants could have been reasonably confident of the guarantee of sovereign impunity for their atrocities. Today there is of course no guarantee of prosecution and accountability, but not a single brutish ruler can be totally confident of escaping international justice. The certainty of impunity is gone as the international criminal pursuit of serving presidents – Slobodan Milosevic, Charles Taylor and Omar Hassan al-Bashir – along with Radovan Karadzic, the self-styled head of Serb Republic, aptly demonstrates. The United Nations has been at the centre of this great normative, policy and institutional advance.

## Tasks ahead, helping to fill the compliance gap

R2P is a call to action on prevention, intervention and post-conflict reconstruction – not the opening lines of a Socratic dialogue by diplomats. There is always a danger with radical advances that commitments at grand summits will suffer many a slip after the champagne flutes are stored. R2P is not just a slogan and failure to act will make a mockery of the noble sentiments. The implementation and compliance gap, in short, is especially distasteful when mass murder and ethnic cleansing are the result of sitting on the sidelines.

The 2005 *World Summit Outcome Document* notwithstanding, some national diplomats insist that the heads of state and government rejected R2P in 2005.[54] The first danger thus is that of rollback: a shamefaced edging back from the agreed norm of 2005, a form of buyer's remorse. The need exists for continued advocacy and activism by civil society and concerned governments to remain steadfast and hold all governments' feet to the fire of individual and collective responsibility to protect at-risk populations. When Gareth Evans gave a lecture in August 2007 in Colombo about R2P and what it meant for Sri Lanka, he unleashed a storm of hostility that the 'so-called' R2P norm 'is nothing but a licence for the white man to intervene in the affairs of dark sovereign countries, whenever the white man thinks it fit to do so'. Rather flatteringly, his 2007 visit to the island armed with R2P was compared to the coming of Christopher Columbus in 1492 and Vasco da Gama in 1498 armed with the Bible and the sword.[55] One newspaper reported on 'crackpot ideas' like R2P that have been 'dismissed in academic and political circles as the latest "neo-imperialist" tactic of the big powers to intervene in the affairs of small nations'.[56]

Many regimes that fear the searchlight of international attention being shone on their misdeeds will try to chip away at the norm until only a façade remains. The advocates of R2P cannot allow them to succeed. Better that the serially abusive regimes live with this fear of international intervention than that their people fear being visited by death and disappearance squads. Of course, they could remove the cause of such fear by working, by themselves or in concert with international friends, to remove the causes and prevent a crisis from arising.

A second, opposite danger of rollback lies with the aggressive humanitarian warriors who gave 'humanitarian intervention' such a bad name in the first place. Iraq is the best example of why the authors and promoters of R2P fear 'friends' as much as opponents.[57] Developing countries' histories and their people's collective memories are full of past examples of trauma and suffering rooted in the white man's burden. The weight of that historical baggage is simply too strong to sustain the continued use of the language of humanitarian intervention.

The attachment of some analysts to that language is puzzling and problematic. It is puzzling, because the ICISS report argued explicitly and forcefully about the shortcomings of this terminology and the merits of a deliberate shift to the conceptual vocabulary of R2P. Many commentators simply ignore that, as if the argument has not been made. If they disagree with the report, they should confront the issue and explain why. The problematic element arises from the politics of the discourse. The ICISS report offered and the High-level Panel's and Secretary-General Kofi Annan's reports preferred, the R2P formulation as less confrontational and polarizing, more likely to lead to a consensus across the bitter North–South divide. 'Humanitarian intervention' approaches the topic explicitly from the Western interveners' perspective and isolates and privileges 'intervention'. R2P is victim-centred and surrounds intervention with prevention before and rebuilding afterwards.

History proves that sovereignty and the norm of non-intervention not-withstanding, regional and global powers have intervened, repeatedly, in the affairs of weaker states.[58] After the end of the cold war, the Security Council experienced a spurt of enforcement activity within civil wars to provide international relief and assistance to victims of large-scale atrocities from perpetrator or failing states.[59] From Liberia and the Balkans to Somalia, Kosovo and East Timor, conscience-shocking humanitarian catastrophes were explicitly recognized as threats to international peace and security requiring and justifying forcible responses. When the Security Council was unable to act due to lack of enforcement capacity, it subcontracted the military operation to UN-authorized coalitions. And if it proved unwilling to act, sometimes groups of countries forged 'coalitions of the willing' to act anyway even without Security Council authorization.

R2P offers developing countries better protection through agreed and negotiated-in-advance rules and roadmaps for when outside intervention is justified and how it may be done under UN authority rather than unilaterally. It will thus lead to the 'Gulliverization' of the use of force by major global and regional powers, tying it with numerous threads of global norms and rules. Absent R2P, they have relatively more freedom, not less, to do what they want. R2P is rooted in human solidarity, not in exceptionalism of the virtuous West against the evil rest.

Another danger from over-enthusiastic supporters is misuse of the concept in non-R2P contexts. A group of retired NATO generals including an ICISS commissioner, for example, used it to justify the first use of nuclear weapons to prevent nuclear proliferation.[60] Others have used the label to refer to action to halt the spread of HIV/AIDS or to protect indigenous populations from climate change.

An admittedly tougher case arose in May 2008. Contradicting official sources, independent observers estimated that the death toll from Burma's deadly Cyclone Nargis could surpass 100,000. The numbers displaced, homeless and in desperate need of immediate humanitarian relief were as high as 1.5 million. Infuriatingly, the generals running – 'ruining' is more accurate – the country refused to open their borders to supplies of aid piling up around Burma. Bizarrely but predictably, they attached higher priority to going ahead with a sham referendum calculated to give their rule a veneer of legitimacy.[61]

Against this backdrop, French Foreign Minister Bernard Kouchner publicly suggested that the Security Council should invoke R2P. However, his views were sharply challenged by a number of senior UN officials, several Western ambassadors and most developing countries, including all the Asian countries that count in the region and in the UN.

In the end, R2P was not officially invoked; but it is not necessary for the Security Council to actually table a resolution to have an impact. It is plausible, but not verifiable at this juncture, that the 'bad cop' Kouchner made it possible for the 'good cops' of the Association of Southeast Asian Nations (ASEAN), the UN Secretary-General and humanitarians to be more effective than they might otherwise have been. In any event, the worst predictions for the aftermath of Cyclone Nargis proved overblown. On this occasion, at least, it was probably preferable not to go to the mat and reintroduce the North–South polarization over 'humanitarian intervention' that ICISS worked so hard to overcome with the R2P formula.

The urgent task was to provide humanitarian relief and reconstruction; military intervention would not have helped and might have imperilled the delivery of such assistance. It would have also set off another war when our goal should be to end those already being fought and stop the threat of new ones erupting. And it would have jeopardized the chances of creating international consensus and generating the political will to take military action when mass killings break out again in some corner of the world, as will assuredly happen.

As the Burmese conundrum shows, to date our responses have typically been ad hoc and reactive, rather than consolidated, comprehensive and systematic. We need a 'paradigm shift' from a culture of reaction to one of prevention and rebuilding. Millions lost their lives during the Holocaust and in Cambodia, Rwanda, Srebrenica and Darfur. After each we said 'never again' and then looked back each next time, with varying degrees of incomprehension, horror, anger and shame, asking ourselves how we could possibly have let it all happen again.

At the same time, opponents have a point in cautioning about the moral hazard that would result from over-enthusiastic recourse to international intervention. It can create perverse incentives for rebels and dissidents to provoke state retaliation to armed challenges. This was recognized by Kofi Annan just one year after his 'challenge of humanitarian intervention'.[62] This too needs further research.

So too does the question of whether groups who constitute a minority in one country and are targeted for killings or ethnic cleansing based on their group identity, are owed any responsibility by their kin state: China vis-à-vis overseas Chinese, say in Indonesia, or India vis-à-vis ethnic Indians in Fiji or Tamil Hindus in Sri Lanka, or Russia vis-à-vis Russians in the Baltic states, or Albania vis-à-vis Albanians around the Balkans, or the West vis-à-vis the whites in Zimbabwe.

Yet another item on the research agenda would be to examine past cases of iconic examples of horrific atrocities and genocidal killings in twentieth-century history, including the Holocaust, Bangladesh, Cambodia, Rwanda and the Balkans. The goal would be to identify when and how R2P could have been invoked to legitimize international intervention and prevent or halt the atrocities. The advantage of such research is that these are all cases on which today there is agreement about the shameful failures of outsiders to take effective action in time. The research should help build a 'case load' of R2P-type situations as a guide to future deliberations, evidence-based analyses and robust action.

The Third UN continues advocating on this issue. For example, a sub-unit within the World Federalist Movement's office in New York has been engaged in support of R2P for several years. Recognizing that the global endorsement of the norm in 2005 was but the prelude to translating it into timely action to prevent crises and stop atrocities, the Global Centre for R2P, based at The CUNY Graduate Center's Ralph Bunche Institute, was launched in February 2008 at the United Nations.[63]

The Global Center will work to make this doctrine a reality in collaboration with associated centres worldwide. Secretary-General Ban Ki-moon has welcomed the Global Center's establishment as 'an effective advocate in the struggle to prevent the world's most heinous mass crimes'. Supported by Australia, Belgium, Britain, Canada, France, the Netherlands, Norway, Rwanda and other foundations and private donors, it will generate research, conduct high-level advocacy and facilitate activities of those working to advance the R2P agenda.

## Conclusion

The R2P norm has become accepted with a surprising rapidity. When post-election violence broke out in Kenya in early 2008, Francis Deng urged the authorities to meet their responsibility to protect the civilian population;[64] and Archbishop Emeritus Desmond Tutu interpreted the African and global reaction to the Kenyan violence as 'action on a fundamental principle – the Responsibility to Protect'.[65] The United Nations has played a key role in different ways and phases of the process, from initial articulation of the notion by an individual UN official, to the Secretary-General openly challenging member states to replace the clearly broken consensus on the use of force in order to stop atrocities inside sovereign borders, the creation of an international commission in response, its recommendations directed in turn back at the UN policy community and the endorsement of the norm by a summit of world leaders. Moreover, it is a good illustration of how the three United Nations worked in tandem.

If we return to our definition of global governance, R2P is about the changing conceptions of the appropriate relations between citizens and states in an interdependent and globalizing world: the norms, laws and practices that constitute those relations and the variety of civil society, governmental and intergovernmental actors engaged in efforts to redefine and reconstitute the norms, laws and practices. Most of these efforts posit the United Nations as the central reference point, whether to emphasize or deny its indispensability. ICISS itself was careful to embed R2P within the context of evolving Security Council practices and customary international law. Based on state practice, council precedents, established and emerging norms and evolving customary international law, the ICISS held that the proscription against intervention is not absolute.

As a universal organization, the United Nations is an ideal forum to seek consensus about normative approaches that govern global problems and would work best with a worldwide application of a norm. The host of problems ranging from reducing acid rain to impeding money laundering to halting pandemics clearly provide instances for which universal norms and approaches are required and emerging. At the same time, the UN is a maddening forum because dissent by powerful states or even coalitions of less powerful ones means either no action, or agreement only on a lowest common denominator. As we mentioned at the outset, watching Darfur's slow-motion genocide or the Burmese junta's ongoing abuses exacerbated in the aftermath of Cyclone Nargis illustrate the difficulty of giving operational meaning to the norm of the responsibility to protect. Normative progress is evident towards halting conscience-shocking murder and ethnic cleansing, but we still are unable to utter 'never again'.

# 10 The responsibility to protect and the North–South divide[1]

We had 'a teachable moment' on 17 July 2009 when Sergeant James Crowley arrested Harvard Professor Henry Louis Gates in Boston. The incident showed how it is possible for both sides in a disputed sequence of events to be part right and wrong at the same time. Intelligent and reasonable people who share a common experience can yet interpret events differently and draw contradictory conclusions, for we view events through the prism of our respective collective and individual historical narratives and life experiences. It is risky to ascribe patterns of behaviour to groups based on assumptions of monolithic identity. Many whites were critical of Crowley's behaviour and acknowledged the reality of racially segregated justice in the US legal system and law enforcement practices. Several blacks criticized Gates for having overreacted against an officer doing his duty. Despite these individual variations, it remains possible to generalize at the group level. Proportionately, far more blacks and Hispanics than whites empathized and sympathized with Gates, for they come out of the same historical narrative and collective consciousness.[2]

Similarly, in world politics, at a certain level of analysis, it is possible to argue that in general, compared to the industrialized Western countries, developing countries are more suspicious of claims to a right of humanitarian intervention, more interested in justice among rather than within nations,[3] more concerned about the root causes of terrorism such as poverty, illiteracy and territorial grievances, more interested in economic development than worried about nuclear proliferation, and more committed to the defence of national sovereignty than the promotion of human rights.[4]

The fact that there are individual differences within developing countries and among Westerners neither negates nor invalidates the generalization. To the extent that developing country viewpoints rarely get an airing, let alone a respectful hearing, in Western mainstream media, Western publics and governments typically have a seriously distorted understanding of many international issues. Responding to the agenda-setting discourse by Obama on 18 March 2008 on race and politics in modern America, Nicholas Kristof noted that 'the Obama campaign has led many white Americans to listen in for the first time to some of the black conversation – and they are thunderstruck'.[5] To those from or with knowledge of the worldview of developing countries, a similar chasm exists between the industrialized Western and the developing countries, the so-called global North and South: except that the North is yet to listen in to the Southern conversation. At the thirteenth African Union summit of heads of government/state in July 2009, for example, Africa's leaders agreed to denounce the International Criminal Court (ICC) and refuse to arrest and extradite Sudan's President Omar al-Bashir to the ICC. Some of the leaders said that it was a signal to the West not to impose its ways on Africa.[6]

Part of the reason for the contrasting North–South worldviews is the changing nature of armed conflict.[7] For most Westerners 'war' has become a remote abstraction far removed from their daily experience. Not so for many developing countries, especially in Africa. Today's wars are mostly fought in poor countries with small arms and light weapons between weak government forces and ill-trained rebels. Disease and malnutrition resulting from warfare kill far more people today than missiles, bombs and bullets. The majority of armed conflicts involve challenges to national integration or to the government's authority. Westerners are incapable of comprehending the framework within which their developing country counterparts must cope with such challenges; most developing country leaders can empathize with one another on this point. While to Western minds intervening to stop the bloodletting is restoring order around the periphery, to developing countries international intervention is a direct threat to territorial integrity.

The Non-aligned Movement – with more than one hundred members, the most representative group of countries outside the United Nations itself – three times rejected 'the so-called "right of humanitarian intervention"' after the Kosovo war in 1999 and the subsequent statements from UN Secretary-General Kofi Annan.[8] Yet a mere decade later, in an interview with *Time* magazine, Liberia's President Ellen Johnson Sirleaf said: 'Look at how we have gone from ... non-interference in our internal affairs to respect for the principle of the responsibility to protect.'[9]

The chapter begins with a survey of views and opinions across the major developing regions in 2001 during the ICISS outreach exercise,[10] describes the evolution and consolidation of the norm between 2001 and 2009, discusses some challenging test cases, and concludes with an analysis of the 2009 General Assembly debate on responsibility to protect (R2P).

## The divisiveness of 'humanitarian intervention'

> General Bonaparte, following the footsteps of Alexander would have entered India not as a devastating conqueror ... but as a liberator. He would have expelled the English forever ... and ... restored independence, peace, and happiness .... All the Princes in India were longing for French intervention.[11]

As the above quote shows, the practice of intervention, and the belief that this is in the best interests of the natives who will warmly welcome and benefit from it, has a long but not distinguished lineage. The privileging of some crises that are securitized over others that are not reflects the interests and perspectives of the powerful and the rich at the expense of the weak and the poor. In Europe, centralizing states sought to bring order to their societies by claiming a monopoly on the legitimate use of force. Developing countries fear that in some sections of the West today, the view has gained ground that anyone *but* the legitimate authorities can use force.

Their emotional attachment to sovereignty is rooted in the history of Europe's encounter with Arabs, Africans and Asians. Only the use of strong and forceful language can convey the depth of passion behind developing countries' input of historical trauma on the subject:

> 'They' (the European colonisers) came to liberate 'us' (the colonized natives) from our local tyrants and stayed to rule as benevolent despots. In the name of enlightenment, they defiled our lands, plundered our resources and expanded their empires. Some, like the Belgians in the Congo, left only ruin, devastation and chaos whose dark shadows continue to blight. Others, like the British in India, left behind ideas, ideals and structures of good governance and the infrastructure of economic development alongside memories of national humiliation. Should they be surprised that their fine talk of humanitarian intervention translates in our consciousness into efforts to resurrect and perpetuate rule by foreigners? That we look for the ugly reality of geostrategic and commercial calculations camouflaged in lofty rhetoric? Should we be mute accomplices when they substitute their mythology of humanitarian intervention for our narratives of colonial oppression? Do they think we do not remember or do not care, or is it simply that they themselves do not care?[12]

But the commitment to sovereignty is also functional. Sovereignty is the bedrock principle of the modern international system of states that anchors order and stability. Rather than seeking to undermine sovereignty, the international community should strive to strengthen the institutions of state and make them legitimate and empowering of people and respectful and protective of their rights.[13]

### Asia

The Asia consultations were enriched by the many examples from within that formed the historical backdrop to the more abstract discussion, from Bangladesh and Cambodia in the 1970s to Sri Lanka and the Maldives in the 1980s and East Timor in the 1990s. The consultations were notable also for the sympathetic reception to the reformulation of 'humanitarian intervention' into R2P, with the responsibilities to prevent and rebuild as integral components of it.

On balance, 'the idea of humanitarian intervention has received a generally hostile response in Asia'. The reformulation of 'humanitarian intervention' as the 'responsibility to protect . . . does not entirely succeed in separating the humanitarian imperative from the political and geopolitical constraints of a UN system that will remain dominated by the P5'.[14] In the roundtable discussions in New Delhi and Beijing in June 2001, it was argued that humanitarianism is good, interventionism is bad, and 'humanitarian intervention' is 'tantamount to marrying evil to good'.[15] In such a shotgun marriage, far from humanitarianism burnishing meddlesome interventions, it will itself be tainted by interventionism.

The doctrine of humanitarian intervention, it was claimed, has no basis in the UN Charter, which recognizes only self-defence and the maintenance and restoration of international peace and security as legitimate grounds for the use of force. Its use for moral reasons is dangerous and counter-productive. On the one hand it can encourage warring parties inside a country to be rigid and irresponsible in the hope of internationalizing the conflict.[16] On the other hand it can facilitate interventions by those exploiting the cloak of legality for their own purposes. Far from ending or ameliorating the effects of large-scale killings, both unintended effects can prolong and aggravate the crisis. There is also an inherent conceptual incoherence. The individualistic conception of human rights in Western discourse is somehow mystically transformed into collective rights (the protection of groups of people) at the same time as the collective rights of the entire nation are still denied legitimacy. Moreover, the inconsistent practice, double standards and sporadic nature of Western powers' interest in human rights protection, from the Middle East, Africa, Latin America and Asia to Europe, shows that noble principles are convenient cloaks for hegemonic interests.

With respect to the agency for lawful authorization, there was consensus around the world on the central role of the UN. For China as one of the five permanent members, self-interest restricts this to the paramount role of the Security Council. Elsewhere, and especially in New Delhi, there was one additional argument made with some emphasis. If the Security Council was going to be making decisions on interventions as an evolutionary adaptation of the Charter, then the question of reforming its structure and procedures becomes vitally important. Otherwise, more frequent interventions launched by an unreconstructed Security Council would erode the global legitimacy of the UN rather than imbue the interventions with international legitimacy.

There was also general agreement that interventions cannot become the pretext for imposing external political preferences with regard to regimes and political and economic systems. Consequently, even though sovereignty may be violated, the cases justifying such action must be tightly restricted to such heinous crimes as genocide and mass murders, it must always be the option of last resort, it must be temporary, intervening forces must withdraw as soon as possible, their actions while inside the target country must be guided by considerations of political impartiality and neutrality between the domestic political contenders as well as strict fidelity to international humanitarian law, and, above all, they must respect and ensure the territorial integrity of the target state.[17]

In the three years following the publication of the ICISS report, frequent and intensive interactions with analysts and officials from Asia–Pacific showed that there was a reluctance to accept the principal conclusions of R2P based on an instinctive resistance to the very word 'intervention' by the majority who had not read the ICISS report.[18] Conversely, among those who had read it, there was surprising sympathy for its main thrusts and recommendations, with the sense that R2P was needed but ahead of its time.[19]

### Middle East

The double standards criticism was raised most forcefully in the Middle East with regard to the Palestinians. Mohammed Ayoob has articulated the argument forcefully: 'Israel's continued occupation and the continuing armed assault against the Palestinians is already a breach of international security that makes it obligatory for the Security Council to intervene under Chapter VII of the charter.'[20] Ambassador Omran el-Shafie of the Egyptian Council for Foreign Affairs expressed the dominant Arab belief that the Palestinians' exercise of the right to self-determination had been met with 'excessive and disproportionate force'. Yet he also acknowledged that internal armed conflicts can compel the government to use excessive force and it was difficult to establish the conditions under which this could justify international intervention.[21] Others noted that the results of Western intervention had not always been beneficial and sometimes had aggravated the crises and created fresh problems. Most supported the involvement of regional and civil society organizations in close coordination with the UN.[22]

### Africa

Article 4(h) of the Constitutive Act of the Africa Union, adopted in 2000, explicitly spells out the principle of intervention: the 'right of the Union to intervene in a Member State' with respect to the commission of 'war crimes, genocide and crimes against humanity'.[23] One analyst calls this a shift from 'humanitarian' to 'statutory' intervention wherein African states 'have them-selves accepted sovereignty not as a shield but as a responsibility'.[24]

There are many possible explanations for the greater willingness of Africans to accept intervention. Their greatest fear is state failure leading to humanitarian crises, where the sensitivity to intervention is less. Asia and Latin America have been more successful in state consolidation and for them the trigger to intervention is more likely to be alleged human rights violations, which is far more contentious. Sovereignty is elusive in the African context of tensions and polarization between state and society. Many weak African states lack empirical sovereignty, being subject instead to warlords, robber barons, gun and drug runners, etc. In effect sovereignty has been 'alienated' from society and become restricted to an international relational dimension (the negative conception of non-interference rather than the positive one of enabling attributes and assets).[25]

Far too many regimes had used the shield of sovereignty for their abusive records, treating African people as objects and not actors. In response, civil society groups had concluded that, in the midst of massive atrocities and egregious abuses, sovereignty should be subordinate to international concerns and humanitarian assistance. But they too were uncomfortable with the association of the term 'humanitarian' with 'war' and appreciated the shift from 'humanitarian intervention' to the 'responsibility to protect' with preventive and post-conflict peacebuilding as integral components.[26] They also wanted to ensure that interventions result from the explicit authority of a mandated multilateral organization and to link them to a political strategy that facilitated engagement with the country subject to intervention.

### Latin America

Latin America has been a frequent target of intervention by its powerful northern neighbour. The continent also has had its share of rogue regimes (often backed by Washington) that brutalized their own people. The dual experience has shaped its response to the tension between sovereignty and intervention.[27]

Chile's Foreign Minister Maria Soledad Alvear acknowledged that 'humanitarian intervention' is one of the most controversial and hotly disputed topics on the international agenda that highlights 'a disturbing vacuum in our collective humanitarian system' in coping effectively with massacres and other tragedies. The fundamental ethical premise must be that human beings are united by solidarity across borders. Sovereignty is rooted in painful historical encounters and many have understandable fears that generalizing a supposed right to intervention could be abused by the great powers to launch unilateral interventions. The tension must be approached and resolved with sensitivity and caution. For Chile, the UN Charter 'constitutes the only possible legal framework . . . governing humanitarian intervention'. In turn this ties the topic to UN practice, the role of the Security Council and the use of the veto. At the same time, she added, 'we must remember that our interests do not always coincide with those of the permanent members, and that international law and United Nations practice are not frozen in time'.[28]

Others noted that geography and history ensure that in Latin America, 'the contrast between [US] hard power and [UN] legitimacy is viewed in even more vivid colours than in other regions of the globe'.[29] The UN reflected and depended on the interests of member states, was not organized to make quick decisions and needs innovations to permit a global oversight system. Participants agreed that the Security Council is the most acceptable institution for authorizing intervention, but disagreed on what was permissible when circumstances called for intervention but the Council failed to act.

## From 2001 to 2009

*The Responsibility to Protect* was published in late 2001. The agenda was kept alive by the UN Secretary-General's High-Level Panel in 2004,[30] followed by

Kofi Annan's own report in 2005[31] before endorsement of R2P by government leaders meeting at the UN's world summit in autumn 2005.[32]

Drawing on Special Adviser Edward Luck's wide-ranging consultations, in January 2009 Annan's successor Ban Ki-moon published his report on implementing R2P, which fleshes out in greater and clearer detail many of the original ICISS ideas.[33] It notes explicitly that all peoples inside a state's territorial jurisdiction, not just citizens but also immigrants, foreign students and visitors, must be protected by a state (para. 11.1). It clarifies and elaborates that because force is the last resort does not mean we have to go through a sequential or graduated set of responses before responding robustly to an urgent crisis (para. 50). Building on the 2005 outcome document, the report is effective in packaging R2P in the language of three pillars: the state's own responsibility to protect all peoples on its territory, international assistance to help build a state's capacity to deliver on its responsibility, and the international responsibility to protect. But it overdid the metaphor by insisting that the 'edifice' of R2P will tilt, totter and collapse unless all three pillars are of equal height and strength (para. 12). The most important element – the weightiest pillar – is the state's own responsibility and the most critical is the international community's response to fresh outbreaks of mass atrocity crimes.

The report did not retreat from the necessity for outside military action in some circumstances but it diluted the central defining feature of R2P.[34] Its added value was that it crystallized an emerging new norm of using international force to prevent and halt mass killings by reconceptualizing sovereignty as responsibility. The use of force by the UN against a state's consent will always be controversial and contested. That is no reason to hand over control of the pace, direction and substance of the agenda of our shared, solemn responsibility to the R2P sceptics. How do we build *international* capacity and will to protect at-risk populations when state authorities are complicit either through incapacity or, more culpably, direct complicity?

In the meantime, it is in the field with actual test cases where the rubber has already hit the road insofar as the norm–implementation gap is concerned. Some actual test cases are worth discussing for highlighting North–South divisions over R2P and for their potential to build a case load of R2P-type situations as a guide to future deliberations, evidence-based analyses and robust action.[35]

### Iraq 2003

The worst act of domestic criminal behaviour by a government is large-scale killings of its own people; among the worst acts of international criminal behaviour, attack and invasion of another country. The international history of the twentieth century was in part the story of a twin-track approach to tame both internal and external impulses to armed criminality by states. Together these attempted to translate an increasingly internationalized human conscience and a growing sense of international community into a new normative architecture of world order. Saddam Hussein's record of brutality was a taunting reminder of the distance yet to be traversed before we reach the first goal of eradicating domestic state criminality; his ouster and capture by unilateral force of arms was a daunting setback to the effort to outlaw and criminalize wars of choice as an instrument of state policy in international affairs.

After the failure to find any weapons of mass destruction in defeated and occupied Iraq, and with the inability to produce any evidence linking Saddam Hussein to al Qaeda or the terrorist attacks of 11 September 2001, the belligerent countries retreated into the discourse of 'humanitarian intervention' dressed up in the language of R2P to justify the Iraq war.[36] This could have proved fatal to the prospects of the R2P norm dissemination, particularly in the developing countries. The clear evidence of dissent among many Western countries prevented it from becoming a global North–South issue. With time and patience the argument by the originators and advocates of R2P carried the day that, in the absence of an agreed new consensus on the international use of force, the Iraq war showed how easy it is to manipulate the debate to favour the war option.

Far from meeting the test of having engaged in conflict prevention in Iraq prior to initiating hostilities, Britain and the United States were the most insistent in keeping in place the comprehensive UN sanctions that caused large-scale deaths, inflicted considerable human misery on Iraqi civilians and negated any efforts at development. The basics cause of this was Saddam Hussein's refusal to comply fully with UN demands, but the price of his intransigence was exacted from his people.

On the legitimacy criteria of R2P, as set out in the 2001 ICISS report and reformulated in the 2004 Report of the UN High-Level Panel, protective intervention would have been an acceptable option in Iraq in the late 1980s. The major difficulty, of course, was that Saddam was the West's 'useful idiot' at that time, supported politically and assisted materially as a bulwark against the revolutionary regime in Iran. R2P does not envision retroactive validation more than a decade after atrocities are committed.

The primary purpose of an intervention must be to halt or avert human suffering, if necessary by defeating a non-compliant state or regime. There was and remains confusion about the mix of President George W. Bush's motives for war: personal (revenge for Saddam's failed attempt to assassinate George Bush Senior, the unfinished agenda from Gulf War I for the many policymakers from that era who were part of the US administration in 2003), oil, geopolitical and military-technological (using Iraq as the testing ground for the revolutionary new doctrine of strategic pre-emption). But there is consensus that the humanitarian motive was adduced after the fact with the failure to find any WMD in Iraq or establish credible links of Saddam to Osama bin Laden or 9/11.

Just as there was no clear answer to 'Why Iraq?', there was no answer to 'Why now?'. Military intervention can only be justified when every non-military option for the prevention or peaceful resolution of the crisis has been explored, with reasonable grounds for believing that lesser measures would not have succeeded. The verdict on Iraq became clear surprisingly quickly: all alternative options had not been exhausted; UN inspectors under Hans Blix should have been given more time to complete their task.[37]

The requirement that the scale, duration and intensity of the planned military intervention should be the minimum necessary to secure the defined human protection objective is difficult to assess in the case of Iraq, since human protection was not the primary objective. It does seem that the main war was conducted with military efficiency, civilians were not the chief target and indeed the coalition tried to minimize civilian casualties as best they could in an insecure and highly volatile environment. But while this was true of the major combat phase at the start, civilians increasingly bore the brunt of the cross-fire between the belligerents in the post-war insurgency phase.

The Iraq war cannot be judged to have met the criterion of a reasonable chance of success in halting or averting the suffering to justify the intervention, with the consequences of action not likely to be worse than the consequences of inaction. On the contrary, the continuing brutal instability and the rise of Iraq as the hotbed of terrorist activity as a *result* of the war was predicted by many analysts.

The criterion of right authority was clearly *violated*. Had it been given, UN authorization would have conferred the veneer of legality on the war but made the organization complicit in an illegitimate war against a sovereign member state. This suggests that while UN authorization may be a necessary condition for legality, it is not a sufficient condition.

### Myanmar 2008: feel good, do more harm

In Burma's deadly Cyclone Nargis, principles, politics and practicality converged in counselling caution in invoking R2P. There is no morally significant difference between large numbers of people being killed by soldiers firing into crowds or the government blocking help being delivered to victims of natural disasters. Conceptually, the shift from the crime of mass killings by acts of commission such as shooting people and acts of omission such as preventing them from getting food and medical attention is a difference of degree, not kind. Legally, the four categories where R2P applies are genocide, war crimes, ethnic cleansing and crimes against humanity. The original ICISS report had explicitly included 'overwhelming natural or environmental catastrophes' causing significant loss of life as triggering R2P if the state was unable or unwilling to cope, or rebuffed assistance (para. 4.20). This was dropped by 2005. But 'crimes against humanity' was included and could arguably apply to the Burmese generals' actions in blocking outside aid.

Politically, however, we cannot ignore the significance of the exclusion of natural and environmental disasters in 2005. Clearly, the normative consensus on the new global norm did not extend beyond the acts of commission of atrocity crimes by delinquent governments. To attempt to reintroduce it by the back door would strengthen suspicion of Western motivations and reinforce cynicism of Western tactics. The UN must base its decisions on the collectively expressed will of its member states, not on that of an independent commission or individual member states. This is why John Holmes, the UN's under-secretary-general for humanitarian affairs and a former British ambassador to France, described French Foreign Minister Bernard Kouchner's call for the application of R2P as unnecessarily confrontational. The British cabinet minister for international development Douglas Alexander rejected it as 'incendiary'.[38] Britain's UN ambassador, John Sawers, said R2P did not apply to natural disasters.[39]

Practically, there is no humanitarian crisis so grave that it cannot be made worse by military intervention.[40] The generals are in effective control of Burma. The only way to get aid quickly to where it was most needed was with the cooperation of the authorities. If they refused, the notion of fighting one's way through to the victims is ludicrous. The militarily overstretched Western powers had neither the capacity nor the will to start another war in the jungles of Southeast Asia. If foreign soldiers are involved, it does not take long for a war of liberation or humanitarian assistance to morph into a war of foreign occupation in the eyes of the local populace.

If the invocation of R2P does not help in the immediate emergency, may indeed cause even more determined opposition and intensify the backlash against R2P, then the painfully forged consensus on the R2P norm will fracture without any material help being provided to the displaced and distressed. That is, help will be less forthcoming to the next group of victims of large-scale killings. The correct equation thus is that invoking R2P in Burma would have endangered lives elsewhere tomorrow without saving any and possibly even delaying help for the Nargis victims today. Feeling good about one's own moral superiority by accusing others of privileging a norm over saving lives is a peculiar form of self-indulgence that perpetuates the killing fields without alleviating anyone's suffering.

Diplomatic pressure was better exerted on the basis of humanitarian principles enshrined in a number of UN General Assembly resolutions than on the coercive language of military intervention for which no one had the stomach and few had the capacity. These include the Guiding Principles for Humanitarian Assistance of Resolution 46/182 in 1991, the 2005 world summit outcome document, Resolution A/RES/61/134 of December 2006, and Resolution A/RES/62/93 of December 2007. These recognize and reaffirm the norm of state sovereignty and the principle of state consent but also call on the afflicted states to facilitate the work of humanitarian actors providing relief and assistance and provide safe and unhindered access to humanitarian personnel. In the end, Secretary-General Ban's use of the bully pulpit, good offices and personal on-the-spot diplomacy did make a difference in helping many in distress through relaxing some curbs on international relief efforts.

### South Ossetia 2009: cartographic lines of statehood versus bloodlines of nationhood

The map lines that delineate statehood can become blurred by the bloodlines of nationhood.[41] This happened with the conflict between Russia and Georgia over South Ossetia in 2008 and is of particular concern to many developing countries whose borders reflect the convenience of administrative boundaries of former colonial powers rather than territorial demarcations of different ethnonational groups. Inter-ethnic conflict and genocide have demonstrated the dangers of failing to protect people targeted by their fellow citizens. How can kinship ties across borders strengthen greater trans-border pan-national identity without challenging territorially defined national security? The general international opinion around the world in 2008 was that Russia invoked R2P to camouflage highly traditional geopolitical calculations in launching military action against Georgia in defence of its interests in South Ossetia.[42] Unilateral intervention by a 'kin state' can lead to conflict within and between states. This presents a dilemma: while the world cannot stand by when minority rights are being trampled, the protection of national minorities should not be used as an excuse to violate state sovereignty. How can R2P be applied to the protection of persons belonging to national minorities? Whose responsibility is it to protect such persons? A sensible answer might come from the formula that France uses to describe its relationship with Quebec in Canada: *ni ingérence ni indifférence* (neither interference/intervention nor indifference).

The question of protecting members of the kin group in neighbouring or distant locations outside the territorial borders is conceptually linked also to the question of protecting one's citizens who come under attack overseas. With increased volumes of international travel, growing numbers of people risk being caught in foreign zones of danger. Can a state be said to have a duty to protect its nationals abroad? If a state has the responsibility to protect citizens and foreigners alike on its territory, does it not also have the correlative duty to protect its individual citizens caught in danger on foreign soil when mass atrocities – that would shock the international community's conscience and activate the international responsibility to protect – are not involved but the host government is unwilling or unable to protect them, or is itself the source of harm to them?

### Gaza 2008–9

It is not helpful to seek remedy in R2P when better or more appropriate tools and instruments are available for dealing with the crisis to hand. A good example of this occurred in December 2008–January 2009, when Israel launched a massive offensive in Hamas-ruled Gaza, putatively in response to rocket attacks from Gaza against civilian targets in Israel. There were issues of international and UN Charter law involved: the well-established rights to self defence against armed attack and to resist foreign occupation, the validity of these justifications for the resort to violence by Israel and Palestinians, and the limits to the exercise of these rights. There were issues of international humanitarian law: regardless of whether the use of force itself is lawful or not, the conduct of hostilities is still governed by the Geneva laws with respect to proportionality, necessity and distinction between combatants and civilians. There were charges and counter-charges of possible war crimes. Amidst all this, the invocation of R2P did not seem to be the most pressing or relevant contribution.

At the same time, Gaza raised the question of occupying powers' responsibility to protect all peoples living under their jurisdiction. The Goldstone Report marshalled evidence of wrongdoing by both Hamas and Israel during the Gaza war and called on both Palestinian and Israeli authorities to conduct good-faith investigations in conformity with international standards.[43] It called on the Security Council to monitor these and, if credible inquiries were not carried out within six months, to refer them to the ICC.[44] Both recommendations are in line with what European and US governments advocate regularly elsewhere. Failure to follow them in the Gaza context will undermine the broader international legal principles and also the West's 'ability to press for justice in places such as Kenya, the Congo and Darfur'.[45]

### Sri Lanka 2009

In May 2009 there was fresh debate over the relevance and applicability of R2P to Sri Lanka in the closing stages of the government's successful military campaign against the Liberation Tigers of Tamil Eelam (LTTE). Sri Lanka was waging a military offensive against a guerrilla army that had fought a brutal war against the legitimate state for twenty-six years, killed up to 80,000 people, and assassinated an Indian prime minister as well as a Sri Lankan president. The Tigers were among the most ruthless terrorist organizations and designated as such by more than thirty countries. They pioneered the use of women suicide bombers, invented the explosive suicide belt, killed many civilians including Tamils, recruited child soldiers and often raised funds from the Tamil diaspora through extortion. Post-conflict recovery and progress was not possible until they had been decisively defeated on the battlefield.

Yet, even if true, this did not obscure the humanitarian tragedy of large-scale civilian deaths and shelling of civilian targets such as schools and hospitals in the shrinking area still held by the Tigers as government troops closed in. Around 7,000 civilians died in 2009 alone. To what extent did R2P apply to the Tigers, the government and the international community for evacuating – by land, sea and air – the civilians caught in the crossfire?

R2P places the responsibility first and foremost on the state itself. Given the Tigers' nature and record, it was not unreasonable for the government to build the capacity and demonstrate the determination to defeat the Tigers as part of its responsibility to protect. R2P proponents cannot advocate the international use of force against government troops engaged in atrocities against civilians, but not permit governments to use military force to protect their people from atrocities perpetrated by terrorists. Ceasefires are not neutral in their impact on the warring sides. The Tigers used previous pauses to rest, recover, regroup, recruit, rearm and return to terrorism. Had the Tigers been amenable to letting civilians caught in the crossfire escape, outsiders could legitimately have asked for another pause or ceasefire in order to help evacuate them. Another means for avoiding a bloodbath was for the Tigers to surrender. Another twenty-five years of war would have killed many more civilians. There is also the moral hazard of validating the tactic of taking civilians hostage as human shields.

These considerations help to explain the outcome of the Human Rights Council deliberations.[46] Western countries tabled a censorious resolution calling for unfettered access to 270,000 civilians detained in government-run camps and an investigation of alleged war crimes by both sides. China, Cuba, Egypt and India were among twenty-nine developing countries who supported a Sri Lanka-sponsored resolution describing the conflict as a domestic matter that did not warrant 'outside interference', praising the defeat of the Tigers, condemning the rebels for using civilians as human shields and accepting the government's argument that aid groups should be given access to the detainees only 'as may be appropriate'. While Colombo was jubilant, Western diplomats and human rights officials were said to be shocked by the outcome at the end of the acrimonious two-day special session, saying it called into question the whole purpose of the Human Rights Council.

Where R2P does apply to the government is in its preventive and rebuilding components. As for war crimes or crimes against humanity that may have been committed by both sides during the civil war,[47] as in Gaza, these need to be investigated credibly by national or, failing that, international accountability mechanisms.

## The July 2009 General Assembly debate

The General Assembly debate on R2P on 23, 24 and 28 July 2009 was addressed by ninety-four speakers, almost two-thirds of them from Africa, Asia and Latin America. Almost all reaffirmed the 2005 consensus,[48] expressed opposition to any effort to reopen it and insisted that its scope be restricted to the four crimes of genocide, crimes against humanity, war crimes, and ethnic cleansing. Most supported the Secretary-General's three pillar strategy based on the 2005 document. There was near-unanimity in accepting state and international responsibility to prevent atrocities through building state capacity and will and providing international assistance (pillars one and two) and in grounding these fundamental obligations in the UN Charter, human rights treaties and international humanitarian law. Most affirmed that should other measures not be adequate, timely and decisive coercive action, including the use of force, is warranted to save lives. Only a few speakers rejected the use of force in any circumstance and only Cuba, Nicaragua, Sudan and Venezuela sought to roll back the 2005 consensus. Several expressed reservations about selectivity and double standards in the implementation of R2P and criticism of past Security

Council failures to act, with some urging voluntary self-restraint in the use of the veto when faced with atrocity crimes. Even so, it is hard to describe the debate as anything other than a resounding success for the R2P principle, and for advocates and victims working to prevent atrocity crimes by all means necessary within the Charter regime that governs international relations.

The debate was called for by General Assembly president Father Miguel D'Escoto Brockmann of Nicaragua, who in his background note described R2P as 'redecorated colonialism'.[49] He warned of the risk of R2P being misused 'to justify arbitrary and selective interventions against the weakest states'; of lack of enforceable accountability on the abusers of R2P; and of double standards in its application.[50] Ed Luck emphasized that R2P seeks to 'discourage unilateralism, military adventurism and an over-dependence on military responses to humanitarian need'.[51]

Professor Jean Bricmont of Belgium, insisting that 'The protection of the weak always depends on limitations of the power of the strong', argued that R2P would in effect relax those limitations.[52] US Professor Noam Chomsky argued that 'virtually every use of force in international affairs has been justified in terms of R2P', 'the cousin of humanitarian intervention'.[53] It fell to ICISS co-chair Gareth Evans to place R2P in context and rebut mischaracterizations.[54] The fourth speaker was Ngugi wa Thiong'o, a Kenyan writer, who welcomed the development of R2P in response to crises like the Rwanda genocide.[55]

In the debate that followed,[56] several speakers from developing countries emphasized the need to stick closely to the 2005 Outcome Document. In this they had been foreshadowed by China's Ambassador Liu Zhenmin in a Security Council debate on 4 December 2006, when he warned that the Outcome Document was 'a very cautious representation of the responsibility to protect populations from genocide, war crimes, ethnic cleansing and crimes against humanity . . . it is not appropriate to expand, wilfully to interpret or even abuse this concept'.[57] Yet that is precisely what was suggested in 2008 in the context of Cyclone Nargis and then again by the London-based One World Trust.[58] Ban is surely right in warning that 'it would be counterproductive, and possibly even destructive, to try to revisit the negotiations that led to the provisions of paragraphs 138 and 139 of the Summit Outcome'.[59]

Several speakers talked of the need for a proper balance of responsibilities between the General Assembly and the Security Council in developing and implementing the new norm. Some pointed to a linkage between R2P and the agenda of international criminal prosecution. Yet several kept coming back to the core of the R2P norm: that in extremis, something has to be done to avoid a shameful repeat of Rwanda-type inaction. Thus Ghana's delegate noted that R2P attempted to strike a balance between non-interference and non-indifference. In a marked change from its strong opposition to R2P in 2001, even India's Ambassador Hardeep Singh Puri emphasized that 'A State's responsibility to protect its citizens was among the foremost of its responsibilities'.[60] The pro-R2P interventions by the delegates of East Timor and Rwanda were especially poignant.[61]

## Conclusion

In the construction of the normative architecture of world order after the end of the cold war, developing countries have been ringside observers, not members of the project design or implementation team. It seems reasonable to conclude that they were reassured by the refusal of most countries to broaden the 2005 crimes to cover natural disasters in Myanmar in 2008 and the broad support of Sri Lanka's right to defend the state against a violent secession by terrorist means in 2009. Had these cases gone in the opposite direction, the tenor and outcome of the July 2009 General Assembly debate might well have been quite different.

That said, it is also important that leaders of the global South examine their own policies and strategies critically. If the impetus for action in international affairs usually appears to come from the North, this is partly due to a failure of leadership from the South. Instead of forever opposing, complaining and finding themselves on the losing side anyway, developing countries should learn how to master the so-called 'New Diplomacy' and become norm entrepreneurs. Otherwise in practice they risk simply being dismissed as the international 'nattering nawabs of negativism'.

Our ability and tools to act beyond our borders have increased tremendously and thereby increased demands and expectations 'to do something'. Consider an analogy from health policy. Rapid advances in medical technology have greatly expanded the range, accuracy and number of medical interventions. With enhanced capacity and increased tools have come more choices that have to be made, often involving philosophical, ethical, political and legal dilemmas. The idea of simply standing by and letting nature take its course has become less and less acceptable. Parents can be charged in court for criminal negligence for refusing to seek timely medical help for ailing children.

Similarly, the real choice in world politics today is no longer between intervention and non-intervention, but between different modes of intervention: ad hoc or rules-based, unilateral or multilateral, and consensual or deeply divisive. The question is not whether interventions should be forbidden under all circumstances, but whether the powerful should respect procedural safeguards if interventions are to be justified. To interveners, R2P offers the prospect of more effective results. To potential targets of intervention, R2P offers the option and comfort of a rules-based system, instead of one based solely on might.

It would be far better to embed international intervention within the constraining discipline of the principles and caution underlying R2P than to risk the inherently more volatile nature of unilateral interventions. In the absence of an agreed new set of rules, there will be nothing to stop the powerful from intervening 'anywhere and everywhere'. This is why in the General Assembly debate in July 2009, speaker after speaker, from the global North and South, described the 2005 Outcome Document's endorsement of R2P as historic because it spoke to the fundamental purposes of the United Nations and responds to a fundamental and critical challenge of the twenty-first century.

Moreover, every time a state protests that R2P is not applicable to it, that critics have misunderstood the facts or not taken due account of the context, it acknowledges and reinforces the global norm even while questioning its applicability in the specific case to hand. Similarly, much as imitation is the sincerest form of flattery, Russia's invocation of the R2P norm in its 2008 invasion of Georgia was a tribute to the moral power of R2P.[62]

All too often, supporters are trapped into providing ammunition to the critics by their failure to pay attention to politics. Yet Steve Stedman, who had headed the High-level Panel's secretariat and was then appointed senior adviser to Annan at the rank of Assistant Secretary-General, subsequently described R2P as 'a new norm . . . to legalize humanitarian intervention'.[63] The powerful sense of grievance and resentment at the historical baggage of 'humanitarian intervention' is missed by too many Western academics. At the end of the day, R2P is mainly about protecting at-risk populations largely in developing countries. These are the states that will face external involvement in their internal affairs, with the risk of military intervention at the end of the spectrum of modes of international engagement. Because they will be the primary victims and potential beneficiaries, the conversation on R2P should be principally among their governments, scholars and civil society representatives.

The debate is also wrongly framed on substance. In the real world, we know there will be more atrocities, victims and perpetrators – and interventions. They were common before R2P and are not guaranteed with R2P. Navi Pillay, the South African UN High Commissioner for Human Rights, urged that 'We should all undertake an honest assessment of our ability to save lives in extraordinary situations' like Rwanda and former Yugoslavia.[64] It was good to have the likes of Rwanda, Sierra Leone, Bosnia-Herzegovina, East Timor, Indonesia, Nigeria, South Africa, India and Japan speak in support of R2P.

By the same token, however, Westerners need to recognize and accommodate developing country sensitivities. The crisis over 'humanitarian intervention' arose because too many developing countries concluded that, intoxicated by its triumph in the cold war, a newly aggressive West was trying to ram its values, priorities and agenda down their throats. Even today, differences within both camps notwithstanding, the global North/South divide is the most significant point of contention for 'the international community'.[65] With regard to the use of force, for example, advocates of the right to non-UN authorized humanitarian intervention in essence insisted that the internal use of force by the rest would be held to international scrutiny, but the international use of force by the West could be free of UN scrutiny. For developing countries, the United Nations was a key instrument for protection of vulnerable nations from predatory major powers; for many Westerners, it was acting to thwart forceful action to forestall or stop the killing of vulnerable people.

In the meantime, there actually has been an example of a successful road testing of R2P. According to Kofi Annan, 'I saw the crisis in the R2P prism with a Kenyan government unable to contain the situation or protect its people . . . . I knew that if the international community did not intervene, things would go hopelessly wrong. The problem is when we say "intervention", people think military, when in fact that's a last resort. Kenya is a successful example of R2P at work'.[66]

R2P is much more fundamentally about building state capacity than undermining state sovereignty. The scope for military intervention under its provenance is narrow and tight. The instruments for implementing its prevention and reconstruction responsibilities on a broad front are plentiful. When post-election violence broke out in Kenya in December 2007–January 2008, Francis Deng urged the authorities to meet their responsibility to protect the civilian population.[67] Archbishop Emeritus Desmond Tutu interpreted the African and global reaction to the Kenyan violence as 'action on a fundamental principle – the Responsibility to Protect'.[68] Called in to mediate, Annan too saw the crisis in R2P terms. His successful mediation to produce a power-sharing deal is our only positive R2P marker to date.

The 2005 Outcome Document formulation of R2P meets the minimum requirement of the call to action of classical humanitarian intervention while protecting the bottom line interests of the weaker developing countries and thereby assuaging their legitimate concerns. It navigates the treacherous shoals between the Scylla of callous indifference to the plight of victims and the Charybdis of self-righteous interference in others' internal affairs. As argued by ICISS co-chair Mohamed Sahnoun, in many ways R2P is a distinctly African contribution to global human rights.[69] Similarly, India's constitution imposes R2P-type responsibility on governments in its chapters on fundamental rights and directive principles of state policy.[70] Contrary to what many developing country governments might claim, it is rooted as firmly in their own indigenous values and traditions than in abstract notions of sovereignty derived from European thought and practice. Many traditional Asian cultures stress the symbiotic link between duties owed by kings to subjects and loyalty of citizens to sovereigns, a point made by civil society representatives who accordingly conclude that, far from abridging, R2P *enhances* sovereignty.[71]

The General Assembly debate showed how easy it is to mistake the volubility of the few for broad agreement among the many. Support for R2P in the global South may not, yet, be very deep, but it is broad. Stephen Krasner famously described sovereignty as organized hypocrisy.[72] For 350 years, from the Treaty of Westphalia in 1648 to 1998, sovereignty functioned as institutionalized indifference. In the final analysis, R2P is our normative instrument of choice to convert a shocked international conscience into timely and decisive collective action.

# 11 R2P and the protection of civilians in armed conflict

> If the protection of civilians is the standard by which UN peacekeeping is measured in the public eye, then the UN – and the international community more broadly – still does not have the correct configuration of resources, structures, or will in place to predictably and consistently meet such a standard.[1]

Given the changing nature and victims of armed conflict, the need for clarity, consistency and reliability in the use of armed force for civilian protection lies at the heart of the UN's credibility in the maintenance of peace and security. If we take a victim-centred instead of a Security Council-centric approach, the key criterion of success and effectiveness of a UN peace operation – or, for that matter, of non-UN counterinsurgency operations as in Iraq and Afghanistan – is the ability to protect civilians caught in the crossfire of conflict. Far too often have too many innocents been caught in the trap of an ever-widening definition of 'legitimate targets' for killing, maiming and rape by ill-disciplined soldiers and non-state combatants. In response, too many states have capitulated much too easily to the temptation to stretch the rule of proportionality and blur the civilian-combatant distinction. 'As a result', Norway's Foreign Minister Jonas Gahr Støre notes, 'the protection of civilians is weakened, human rights are violated and international humanitarian law is being undermined'.[2] Those trying to do something about it are putting their lives on the line in growing numbers. In 2008, 260 humanitarian workers were killed, kidnapped or wounded – the worst casualty toll in twelve years and higher than among UN peacekeeping soldiers.[3]

As argued in Chapter 8, the changed nature of armed conflict demands the implementation of two tasks: the apprehension and punishment of the evildoers; and the protection of the innocent. Both aim at the same final objective – the reduction and elimination of violent conflicts. But they require different techniques and instruments. The prosecution of perpetrators necessitates a criminal justice system. The protection of civilian people needs a readily deployable pool of military troops. Both are facilitated by a smooth, efficient, reliable, reciprocal and mutually trusted interface between military, civilian and criminal justice components of a whole-of-intervention protection agenda: the subject of this chapter. They require active and close collaboration among governmental, intergovernmental and non-governmental actors; among local, national, regional and global actors; and among military, police, civilian and humanitarian actors. They also denote a connected agenda from preventing conflict to managing it, muting it and resolving it through governance institutions. Consequently, unlike set-piece battles between armies of enemy states where war-fighting can be isolated from diplomacy and judged on its own results (victory, stalemate or defeat on the battlefield), the success of military missions for protection of civilians is woven more seamlessly into the civilian components of the integrated agenda. This too calls for an appreciation of the complementary roles at the civil–military interface.

The argument proceeds in seven parts. I will begin by mapping the changing security landscape in general since 1945, then spend some time on the changes in peacekeeping in particular. The responsibility to protect (R2P) is discussed in its three components of prevention, intervention and rebuilding.[4] In the last two sections I examine regional peacekeeping and then focus on Afghanistan as a specific illustration of many of the arguments.

## The changed security landscape since 1945

During the period since 1945, the key changes relevant to the present analysis include:

- the changing nature of armed conflict that has put civilians on the frontline of conflict-related casualties;
- the rise of a powerful human rights movement and the parallel growth of international humanitarian law (IHL), leading to the emergence of a humanitarian community dedicated to championing the cause of civilian protection;
- the emergence of a robust civil society that is transnational rather than sovereignty-bound;
- the rise of human security as an alternative paradigm to national security; and
- globalization, which has shrunk distances; brought images of human suffering into our living rooms and on our breakfast tables in graphic detail and real time while simultaneously expanding our capacity to respond meaningfully, thereby increasing the calls to do so; and made total state control of border crossings by people, goods, finance, information, disease, drugs and so on physically impossible, thereby severely curtailing the exercise of sovereignty.

The cumulative effect of these changes is to qualify both the theory and the practice of state sovereignty. In addition, significant changes in the nature, weapons, parties and locales of inter-group armed conflict have shifted the burden of harm more and more on civilians through direct killings, death by disease, rape as an instrument of warfare and ethnic cleansing, and displacement. The policy implication for all international actors – governmental, intergovernmental and non-governmental; humanitarian, peacekeeping and developmental – working in conflict and post-conflict zones is that their performance will be judged importantly on the criterion of protecting civilians from deadly harm.

The law of the Charter governs *when* force may be used; IHL governs *how* force may be used. While the International Court of Justice deals with disputes among states, the increasing attention and sensitivity to human rights abuses and humanitarian atrocities raise questions of individual criminal accountability in a world of sovereign states. The international community has responded to barbarism by drafting and adopting international legal instruments that ban it.[5] The Genocide Convention, adopted by the General Assembly on 9 December 1948, was a milestone in defining genocide as a crime against humanity and thus a matter of universal criminal jurisdiction.

In his landmark report in March 2005 setting the terms of the global debate on UN reforms, Secretary-General Kofi Annan for the first time elevated human rights to co-equal status and importance alongside security and development. He argued that security cannot be achieved in the midst of persistent and severe poverty, development is not possible in conditions of insecurity, neither security nor development is achievable and sustainable without ensuring the human rights of citizens, and the attainment of all three requires multilateral cooperation.[6]

The human rights movement grew as an effort to curb arbitrary excesses by states against the liberties and rights of their citizens. International humanitarian law emerged as an effort to place limits on the behaviour of belligerent forces during armed conflict. The convergence of the interests of human rights and humanitarian communities with respect to protecting victims of atrocity crimes (crimes against humanity, large-scale killings, ethnic cleansing, genocide) is a logical extension of their original impulses. At the same time, it produces the paradox of humanitarianism – 'an endless struggle to contain war in the name of civilization'[7] – encouraging, even demanding, the use of force, when it originated as a movement to limit and constrain the use of force.

The Red Cross prototype of 'neutral humanitarianism' was abandoned by some humanitarians in the aftermath of Rwanda and Srebrenica. The complex humanitarian emergencies of the 1990s had already begun to blur the border between military peace operations and the impartial delivery and distribution of emergency aid. In some cases in Africa and the Balkans military convoys were used to establish 'humanitarian corridors' through which relief supplies could be delivered to civilians trapped in zones of violent conflict. The humanitarian NGO Médecins Sans Frontières (MSF) concluded after Rwanda in 1994 that genocide cannot be stopped with medicines. A year later, other critics of neutral humanitarianism referred derisively to the 'well fed dead' of Srebrenica. The result was 'political humanitarianism' or 'humanitarian intervention': the use of military force to come to the rescue of civilians being killed in large numbers in acute conflict zones.

Yet the defenders of the traditional neutrality of humanitarians in the field also had their counter-slogans, talking, for example, of the 'operation shoot to feed' absurdity of Somalia in the early 1990s. Especially after Afghanistan and Iraq, they adapted the Irish dramatist Brendan Behan's comment about police to conclude that there is no humanitarian disaster so dismal that a military intervention could not make it worse. It was not until 'the challenge of humanitarian intervention' was reformulated as 'the responsibility to protect' that the two sides came together again.

## Peacekeeping

With respect to UN peace operations – one of the most visible symbols of the UN role in international peace and security – in addition to all the local actors, there are at least six different sets of external actors with overlapping spheres of activity: those who authorize such operations in the Security Council; those who contribute the military personnel; those who provide the financial funds; those who possess the necessary enforcement capabilities; UN humanitarian agencies; and NGOs in the field. The UN Office for the Coordination of Humanitarian Affairs (OCHA) has civilian protection as its core mission.[8]

Traditional peacekeeping was under UN auspices, command and control and aimed to contain and stabilize volatile regions and interstate conflicts until such time as negotiations produced lasting peace agreements. The number of UN operations increased dramatically after the end of the cold war as the UN was placed centre-stage in efforts to resolve outstanding conflicts. The newer generations of peacekeeping, for example in Namibia and Cambodia, were integral components of the peace agreement and meant to complete the peace settlement by providing third party international military reinforcement for the peace process. Reflecting the changing nature of modern armed conflict, UN operations expanded not just in numbers but also in the nature and scope of their missions, undertaking additional types of tasks such as military disengagement, demobilization and cantonment; policing; human rights monitoring and enforcement; observation, organization and conduct of elections; rehabilitation and repatriation; and temporary administration.[9]

In other words, these complex operations began to involve several military and civilian actors working to a common purpose under one overarching mandate. The Brahimi Report recommended that in order to defeat 'the lingering forces of war and violence' and protect innocent victims from warlords, UN peace operations must be equipped and authorized to use force. The UN should avoid falling into the trap of establishing a de facto moral equivalence between the perpetrators and victims of armed violence by embracing a posture of political neutrality in New York that translates into operational military timidity on the ground when confronted with armed challenges to its authority.[10]

Typically, peace operations are inserted into environments where there is a fragile peace process but not yet a peace settlement. Peacekeeping missions are often the most critical prop upon which fragile governments lean as they seek to build capacity and legitimacy – and therefore the only bulwark between collapse and resilience – in the transition from armed conflict to sustainable peace. This explains why they have been transformed from a relatively modest instrument on the margins of international affairs to a key tool for conflict management and post-conflict transition from war to peace: 110,000 deployed personnel (75,000 military, 11,500 police and 23,500 civilians) in eighteen operations across five continents in 2009.

In order to arrest and reverse the sense of drift, UN approaches to peace-keeping were transformed to reflect the multifaceted nature of UN action in countries afflicted by mostly civil wars. This meant promoting the rule of law and economic recovery by integrating the military, policing, institution building, reconstruction and civil administration functions of peacekeeping operations to a much greater degree than in the past. The UN became involved increasingly in post-conflict reconstruction, 'building' peace in order to prevent a relapse into conflict. Modern peacekeeping demands a very broad range of skills and competence, including 'innovation, flexibility, initiative and moral courage'.[11] Peacekeepers have to determine the application of relevant domestic, international humanitarian and human rights law to their conduct and operation. Civilian, police and military elements have to cooperate willingly and coordinate effectively with one another and with NGOs in the pursuit of common objectives. They have to be adaptable as the focus changes from security in one mission to humanitarian assistance in another and peacebuilding in yet a third. The last has led to growing recognition of the importance of instilling and institutionalizing the rule of law and justice systems that avoid a 'one-size-fits-all' approach on the one hand, and encompass the entire criminal justice process on the other – from police, prosecutors and defence lawyers to judges, court officials and prison officers – in a whole-of-legal-chain approach.

The use of force depends (i) on the mandate as written in the authorizing Security Council resolution; (ii) on the rules of engagement (ROE); and (iii) on the decision of military commanders on the ground. For UN operations, the use of force is restricted to self-defence, protecting UN personnel and property against attacks and protecting civilians targeted by spoilers. With UN-authorized but non-UN-led operations, as in Kosovo and Afghanistan, the rules of engagement are approved by the coalition or by NATO. The restrictions are far less stringent and the resources are far more robust. The Security Council gives them international legitimacy but has no say over the ROE nor does it exercise any effective authority over these forces. NATO countries who provide the troops, equipment and logistics have the military capability and the political clout to act independently of the UN; they have leverage over the UN, not the other way round. The Security Council is not the oversight body to which NATO forces in Afghanistan report.

In Kosovo, legislative, executive and judicial powers were vested in the single office and person of the Special Representative of the Secretary-General (SRSG) who could, for example, appoint international judges or prosecutors to any criminal case, at any level of jurisdiction and in any phase of the proceedings, anywhere in the territory. Marginalizing the local judiciary like this could only have the effect of undermining the goal of creating a credible national judicial system and other democratic institutions in Kosovo. The Serbs who remained in Kosovo after the initial exodus have stayed outside the new self-government structures and instead set up parallel structures linked to Serbia.

East Timor represented the most recent evolution in UN peacekeeping. The UN-authorized multinational force was prepared for combat action if necessary and was given the mandate, troops, equipment and robust rules of engagement required for such a mission. However, the military operation was but the prelude to a de facto UN administration that engaged in state-making for a transitional period.[12] That is, a 'nation' was granted independence as a result of UN-organized elections. But the nation concerned had no structures of 'state' to speak of. It was not even, like Somalia, a case of a failed state; in East Timor a state had to be created from scratch. In the latter the UN finally confronted and addressed the dilemma that haunted it in the Congo in the 1960s and Somalia in the 1990s, namely that peace-restoration is not possible without the establishment of law and order. In a country where the writ of government has either collapsed or is non-existent, the law that is made and enforced so as to provide order can only be that of the UN or of another foreign power (or coalition).

The older certitudes of traditional peacekeeping no longer apply when peacekeepers find themselves operating with the executive authority of transitional administrators inside societies characterized by criminality, corruption, political instability and armed power struggles. They have to ensure their own security in an environment in which far from being an emblem of safety, the blue helmet can be a target. They must learn to use modern information and communications tools to their advantage while being conscious of hostile elements also exploiting the newer opportunities to maximize mayhem. All this and more must be done in harmony with professional colleagues in a truly multinational, multicultural and multilingual effort operating in highly localized and particularized theatres.

Cedric de Coning makes the point that 'complicated' is different from 'complex'. In the former, for example a space mission, the causal factors are linear, can be mastered by different people working together and are therefore predictable. A complex system, for example climate, has dynamic and nonlinear relationships among its constituent elements. They evolve and change over time, adapt to their environment, do not follow a specific cause-and-effect path and can flip with dramatic suddenness in a highly volatile environment. Complexity is a function of the interaction between the elements, each of which is dynamic and nonlinear in its own right. UN peace operations are complex.[13] They are required to perform multiple tasks in pursuit of multiple goals. They have to work and interact with numerous actors at the global, regional, national and subnational levels, each with its own agenda. Typically, they must operate in insecure environments and tenuous political contexts, with 'spoilers' only too alert to any opening to exploit managerial, political and legal weaknesses and vacuums to paralyse the mission. This is why participants in a GCSP–IPI seminar concluded that the success of UN peace operations 'depends on the UN's ability to leverage its partnerships with other organizations and groups, coordinate activities among them, bring spoilers into the political process, and enable and strengthen host governments'.[14]

Different organizations have different mandates, standard operating procedures and chains of command. This amplifies the possibility of confusion, diffusion of authority and accountability, with units and individuals working at cross-purposes, and so provides an opening for divide-and-conquer strategies by spoilers. Humanitarian actors, for example, often seek to maintain their distance from military partners and protectors in order to proclaim and maintain their neutrality. But if there is an important military component to a mission, rare is the mission that can resist mission success being defined through the prism of military operations. How then can humanitarian and military 'partners' come to a common understanding and shared purpose of the mission?

## Responsibility to prevent

The twin protection–prosecution agenda lies at the crossroads of the global trends since 1945 that have heightened real-time awareness of depredations and atrocities, increased pressures to respond effectively, expanded the toolkit to do so, and fenced in the exercise of both internal and external sovereignty with innumerable threads of global norms and treaties.

If protection measures are instituted only after the onset of grave harm to at-risk populations, they will be costlier and less efficacious in ameliorating the harm than if preventive measures are instituted at an earlier point after risk is detected or apprehended. If civilian preventive measures are instituted and prove successful, military deployment may not be needed. The need to call on the military is therefore a self-indictment of the feebleness of intervention-before-the fact by civilian authorities and actors, including civil society. Of course, this charge is not relevant for those very rare cases where the international community is caught genuinely by surprise.

Armed conflicts can neither be understood nor muted without reference to such 'root' causes as poverty, political repression, institutional fragility and uneven distribution of resources, especially horizontal inequality. Preventive strategies must therefore work to promote human rights, protect minority rights and institute political arrangements for equitable power-sharing; promote economic growth and equity; strengthen the rule of law in its legislative and institutional forms; and bring security forces under firm civilian control and judicial accountability. Ignoring these underlying factors amounts to addressing the symptoms but neglecting the causes of deadly conflict.

Resources devoted to prevention are dwarfed by resources devoted to preparation for war, war-fighting, coercive intervention, humanitarian assistance to the victims of conflict and catastrophe, post–intervention reconstruction, and peacekeeping. The result, according to the Carnegie Commission on Preventing Deadly Conflict, was that the international community spent approximately $200 billion on conflict *management* in seven major interventions in the 1990s,[15] when it could have saved $130 billion through a more effective *preventive* approach.

Structural prevention support measures may come in the form of development assistance and other efforts to help address the root cause of potential conflict; or efforts to provide support for local initiatives to advance good governance, human rights, or the rule of law; or in the form of good offices missions, mediation efforts and other efforts to promote dialogue or reconciliation. In some cases international support for prevention efforts may take the form of inducements; in others, it may involve a willingness to apply tough and perhaps even punitive measures.

Direct prevention measures may include the direct involvement of the UN Secretary-General, as well as fact-finding missions, friends groups, eminent persons commissions, dialogue and mediation through good offices, international appeals, and non–official 'second track' dialogue and problem-solving workshops, and positive inducements such as new funding or investment and more favourable trade terms. At the negative end of the scale, direct prevention might encompass the threat or application of sanctions, 'naming and shaming', curtailment of aid, mediation, arbitration or adjudication, the threat of international criminal prosecution.

## Responsibility to protect

As noted in Chapter 9, the use of military force on the territory of a state without its consent with the goal of protecting innocent victims of large-scale atrocities differs from traditional warfare, collective security and peace operations, in that it refers to the use of military force by outsiders for the protection of victims of atrocities: us between perpetrators and victims. For an R2P operation, protecting populations at risk of mass killings using coercive means in a non–permissive environment is the primary goal. For most UN peace operations, protecting civilians in what has been negotiated to be a permissive environment but may have threatening components is an implied or derivative goal, often a moral but not a mandated duty.

In the 2009 UN General Assembly debate, discussed in the last chapter, it became clear that support for R2P is widespread and deep in the Western world and broad if shallower in the developing countries. In part the reason for the lack of deep support for R2P is lack of clarity about its operational principles. The protection of victims from mass atrocities requires different guidelines and rules of engagement as well as different relationships to civil authorities and humanitarian actors. These differences need to be identified, articulated and incorporated into officer training manuals and courses.[16] For example, recalling the tragedy of Rwanda in 1994: how does a UN peace operation, sent to supervise a peace agreement and process, recast its task on the fly to prevent an unfolding genocide?

The relationship between R2P and the protection of civilians in armed conflict could do with theoretical and conceptual clarification.[17] The latter has been a regular item on the Security Council's agenda since 1999 when it received the first Report of the Secretary-General on the subject. Some states fear that the agenda risks being politicized unnecessarily with the intrusion of R2P. The two agendas are complementary and mutually reinforcing, neither synonymous with nor unrelated to each other. They share legal underpinnings, normative weight and Security Council commitments under human rights, international humanitarian and refugee laws. The protection of civilians in armed conflict embraces (i) all measures to protect the safety, dignity and integrity of all human beings, but only (ii) in times of war. The first part is thus considerably broader and less precise than the four specific acts under R2P. But R2P is broader in being concerned with the prevention and protection of atrocity crimes in all circumstances, not merely during armed conflict.

Operationalizing R2P with respect to the protection agenda in the field will mean adopting a bottom-up approach that brings together the humanitarian actors on the ground in conflict zones.[18] Each context requires its own specific protection actions against threats to the people at risk there. The UN can provide the normative mandate at the global level for their protection and the forces necessary for intervention if need be. By its very nature a mandate is a brief, high-level policy document that cannot address the details of on-the-ground operational reality in each specific context. The action to prevent and rebuild has to be undertaken by UN agencies acting collaboratively with local civil society actors, NGOs and representatives of the Red Cross and Red Crescent Movement. They can be brought together in a distinct protection cluster to assess needs and priorities for each vulnerable group requiring protection and identifying, in advance, the custom-tailored responses for prevention and rebuilding.

## Responsibility to rebuild

Peacebuilding seeks to reduce the risk of a resumption of conflict and contribute to creating conditions most conducive to reconciliation, reconstruction and recovery. Post-conflict societies have special needs in order to avoid a return to conflict while laying a solid foundation for development. They need to emphasize critical priorities:

- reconciliation, political inclusiveness and national unity;
- respect for human rights;
- the safe, smooth and early repatriation and resettlement of refugees and internally displaced persons;
- the reintegration of former combatants;
- the elimination of small arms;

- the mobilization of domestic and international resources for reconstruction and economic recovery through economic growth, the recreation of markets and sustainable development.

The institutional reconstruction of a war-torn country often needs a prior reconciliation process to address the wounds of a traumatic and deeply unjust past. Intrastate conflicts often arise from inherited and accumulated hatred, transmitted across generations and focused around group-identity issues of dispossession, access to land, economic, cultural and religious resources, and the memory of prior aggression. External support for reconciliation efforts must be conscious of the need to encourage this cooperation and linked dynamically to joint development efforts between former adversaries.

## Regional peacekeeping and the protection agenda

There is renewed interest in regional peacekeeping, that is, peace operations undertaken by regional organizations such as NATO, the African Union, and the Economic Community of West African States (ECOWAS). Already in 1992 UN Secretary-General Boutros Boutros-Ghali called in *An Agenda for Peace* for greater involvement of regional organizations in UN activities regarding peace and security. His proposed division of labour envisioned using regional arrangements for different mechanisms such as preventive diplomacy, peacekeeping, peacemaking and post-conflict peacebuilding. Since then, formal cooperation between regional organizations and the UN has been consolidated further.

The UN Security Council also has given more attention to regional organizations. In July 2004, it invited regional organizations 'to take the necessary steps to increase collaboration with the United Nations in order to maximise efficiency in stabilization processes, and encouraged enhanced cooperation and coordination among regional and subregional organizations'.[19] The High-Level Panel urged that, if the Security Council is to be more active and effective in preventing and responding to threats, it needs to utilize Chapter VIII provisions more, and more productively. Its report advised the UN to promote the establishment of such regional and subregional groupings, particularly in view of their important contributions to peace and security. Their efforts neither contradict those of the UN, nor absolve the United Nations of its primary responsibility for the maintenance of international peace and security. Regional action should be organized within the framework of the UN Charter and be consistent with its purposes and principles; and the UN and regional organizations should work together in a more integrated fashion than hitherto.[20]

Kofi Annan accepted the broad thrust of this analysis.[21] At the sixth high-level meeting between the UN and regional organizations in July 2005, he affirmed that strengthening UN relations with regional and other intergovernmental organizations is a critical part of the effort to reform the multilateral system. The aim is to create 'a truly interlocking system that guarantees greater coordination in both policy and action' with partnerships that 'build on the comparative strengths of each organization'.[22]

Regional peacekeeping offers a solution to the UN's lack of capacity to meet growing demand. National and intergovernmental actors have a bigger stake in ensuring security and stability in their own region. They are less driven by heterogeneity of forces in skills, equipment and doctrines. They are more sensitive to local mores and nuances and better placed to receive and recognize early warning signals of imminent flare-ups. Against this, of course, there is the risk of regional actors, especially a regional hegemon, pursuing their vested interests instead of the regional public good. As such, regional operations are vulnerable to cross-infection by rivalry among regional powers.

Most importantly for present purposes, they lack institutional policies on the protection of civilians in armed conflict and knowledge of and training in the relevant principles of IHL.[23] Victoria Holt and Tobias Berkman noted that none of the African Union, European Union, ECOWAS and NATO 'has an institutional concept of civilian protection for their military missions'. Conversely, reflecting its 'humanitarian orientation, the UN has focused more on non-coercive forms of protection – legal, humanitarian, and political – than on military roles or the use of force to offer protection'.[24] There is the very real risk, therefore, that regional peace operations will neither be aware of nor be able to adhere to international standards like R2P and IHL. The risk of variable standards across different regional operations needs to be acknowledged and addressed. The verisimilitude among regional actors can only be offset by incorporating the rules of IHL and analyses of R2P into national legislation, military manuals and peacekeeping courses. In turn this requires the development of joint standards for regional and UN operations, common principles for accountable governance, harmonization of institutional concepts of protection of civilians in armed conflict, and the adoption of appropriate governance protocols between the United Nations and regional organizations.[25] Otherwise, there will be a debilitating fragmentation of multilateral responses to conflict.

## Afghanistan

The regional–global interface has not been particularly propitious in Afghanistan. Post-9/11 politics gave the major Western powers motivation and space to go beyond international consensus into over-securitization of international policies. Immediate military action overtook diplomacy and third-party negotiations. The fusion of the separate stages of peacemaking, peacekeeping and peacebuilding, even while international forces are still engaged in combat, raised difficult questions of sequencing, jurisdiction, accountability, delineation of responsibilities and timing of negotiations.[26] Thus in Afghanistan, the Security Council's initial resolutions were broad and generic, in effect outsourcing the task to NATO and leaving it to decide on details of the mandate and the rules of engagement. This was subsequently refined by adding new and more ambitious tasks to the mandate of the UN Assistance Mission in Afghanistan (UNAMA) as the political and peace-building mission. Such changes on the fly both strain the UN capacity to respond effectively to crises and erode its credibility as an instrument of international security. There is obvious discord in Afghanistan between the competing imperatives of state building and stabilization, between negotiation and combat and over stabilization and securitization methods and sequences. Nordic countries, with the support of other European Union (EU) countries, have tried to keep the human rights and humanitarian situation in Afghanistan, including the death of Afghan civilians caused by international military operations (collateral deaths), on the Security Council's watch against US reluctance. The very public spat over the presidential election in August 2009 between the Special Representative of the Secretary-General, the Norwegian Kai Eide, and his American deputy Peter Galbraith, was in one sense a symptom of these underlying differences in civilian versus military led nation building.

As the International Security Assistance Force (ISAF) was progressively transformed from a peacekeeping into a self-defence and counter-insurgency mission and force, and as it came under direct NATO command, it became correspondingly integrated into NATO doctrine. As the military operations intensified and caused growing civilian casualties and destruction, the UN legitimacy and credibility was held hostage to decisions by NATO military commanders and governments over whom the UN had zero authority. The three pillars of the international community's engagement in and with Afghanistan – fighting the insurgency, protecting the population and promoting development – sometimes collided with one another. In particular, the pressing but short-term goal of fighting the revived insurgency has often undermined the vital but longer-term goal of state and peace building.

The model of UN-authorized non-UN military operations alongside UNAMA as the UN political and peace-building mission has led to the curious result of the United Nations being saddled with global responsibility without local power, while NATO and ISAF exercise power in the conflict theatre without international accountability. The Security Council's decision to delegate military functions to NATO has ensured the deployment of professionally trained and well equipped fighting forces of a quality and in numbers not normally available for UN operations. But the Council lacks authority over the forces and has had no role in shaping their rules of engagement. This lack of NATO forces' accountability to the Security Council in turn has impacted adversely on UNAMA's political and peacebuilding goals.

The two pressing priorities in Afghanistan are to transform the mission from a militarized into a civilianized operation and shift it from an externally directed into a locally owned enterprise. At present, the capital and the country are fortified garrisons and Afghanistan under foreign occupation feels quasi-colonized, with real power divided between the Afghan warlords and the American overlords.[27] The result is that by March 2010, the percentage of Afghans who viewed ISAF troops as 'good' or 'very good' had dropped to twenty-nine.[28] The offensive military operations in Afghanistan had also pushed the Taliban and jihadists across the border into Pakistan in what is in reality an integrated battle space in the volatile and porous border region.

The Rumsfeld instrument of combining security, development and governance was the provincial reconstruction teams. While the logic of this is understandable and the individual PRTs do a marvellous job in unforgiving environments, it militates against moving from the military to the civilian end of the spectrum of international engagement. The PRT-led effort means that everything is seen through the security lens and results in the militarization of all efforts. To the extent that attempts are underway to devolve power to the provincial level, this also means that real power is appropriated by the PRTs at the local level.

The retreat from nation-building could prove fatal to the cause of creating and leaving behind a stable polity and a sound economy. This includes strengthening the police, judicial and criminal justice systems, instilling discipline and professionalism, paying adequate salaries so they don't take bribes out of economic necessity as opposed to corrupt character, and accentuating national as opposed to sectarian identity. History shows that to succeed, a counter-insurgency operation must be led by the police, not the military. The number of Afghan police killed in 2008 was around 2,000, double the number of soldiers.

The strengthened US military profile and role may be necessary, for no other country has stepped up to fill the security slack. But it does come with heightened risk of increased civilian casualties and culturally offensive behaviour. By May 2010 the number of US soldiers killed in Afghanistan had crossed the psychologically important threshold of 1,000; the monthly cost of the Afghanistan war ($6.7 billion) had overtaken that of the Iraq war ($5.5 billion); and a majority of Americans had turned against it, with 52 per cent saying it was not worth the cost in lives and treasure.[29] Even the Pentagon conceded that of Afghanistan's 121 critical districts, only 29 were sympathetic to the government.[30] At some stage the lead international actor should be the United Nations. For all its faults, it has no peer in nation building. The UN would also be better than NATO at engaging the necessary regional players such as China, Russia, Iran, Pakistan and India.

The UN's light footprint in Afghanistan was a reaction to the earlier experiences in Kosovo and East Timor, where the UN had assumed the burden of heavy public administration functions and deployed international personnel in large numbers. If the task of providing a secure environment could be left to the coalition of the willing (later largely subsumed under NATO) and the functions of governing could be left to the Afghans, then the international civilian presence could be limited to a political advisory role and a few key high-level positions. But the net effect was to weaken the UN mission, reducing its leveraging capacity and undermining its ability to influence policy, process and events.

While the international NGOs in Afghanistan focused mainly on short-term humanitarian needs, UNAMA lacks the resources and field presence to carry out development programmes in all provinces. Some of the most under-developed areas in Afghanistan are outside the 'hot' insurgency areas, and thus receive less international attention.

The protection of civilians is fundamental and must be a key strategic goal of any stabilization effort in Afghanistan. Failure to protect the Afghan civilians will doom the international counterinsurgency effort to failure. There is no doubt that the high-threat security environment in the country necessitates a strong military presence, particularly in the south and east. This cannot excuse the morally questionable and strategically counter-productive reality of a 40 per cent increase in 2008 of civilian casualties as a result of air strikes and air support to night-time raids. There is an unmistakable 'us–them' dichotomy between international forces and Afghans, where the burden of risk has been shifted from 'our' soldiers to 'their' civilians.

Most humanitarian workers seek humanitarian space to ensure the neutrality and safety of their activities. NGOs and military forces are often compelled to operate in the same geographical areas and must learn to coexist. In parts of Afghanistan the NGOs need, depend on and are grateful for the stability and protection that only the military can provide. Problems arise and intensify, however, the more that humanitarian and battle spaces begin to overlap. NGOs described it as a major achievement when ISAF agreed to stop using white vehicles (the traditional colour of UN missions).

Related to this is a lesson from Africa that could be carried over to Afghanistan: sustainable domestic security requires the reassuring presence of a robust, competent, effective and corruption-free police force. In the context of numerous other challenges faced in Afghanistan, this is a daunting task. The Afghan National Police face daily, deadly attacks. Their levels of education, training, professionalism and pay are such as to turn far too many of them from protectors of to predators on their own people.

## Conclusion

We must narrow the gap between policies, resolutions and practices, for example by providing female police units in international peace operations as in Sierra Leone, encouraging the introduction of gender units in national police forces, urging gender sensitization courses and training and funding medical support for victims of sexual violence. In addition to such measures on the civilian protection side of the ledger, we must also make sure that perpetrators of such violence and crimes are identified, apprehended, tried and punished. Impunity – de jure for commanders and government leaders, de facto for foot soldiers – must give way to accountability, national in the first instance but global if need be. At the same time, women are not simply victims and survivors of conflict. In addition, and just as importantly, they are actors and should be brought into the decision-making process as part of the peace process with regard to the protection of civilians and promotion of human rights.

The separate and variable capabilities and tools of protection available to the different actors and agencies need to be brought together under an integrated and cohesive strategy that strengthens the collective capacity to act in defence of civilians trapped in zones of conflict and danger. One possible means of entrenching the protection norm in public and policy discourse would be to cite paragraphs 138 and 139 of the Outcome Document on R2P in the preambular paragraphs of all relevant Security Council resolutions creating or renewing UN peace operations, while the operative paragraphs could contain the protection of civilians in armed conflict as part of the mandate of UN missions. This could help to generate the sort of norm entrapment that is familiar from the human rights literature. Norm–violating governments can choose to deny the validity of global norms and reject critics as agents or stooges of ignorant or ill-intentioned foreigners. But if vulnerable and subjected to sufficient pressure, they may begin to make tactical concessions in order to mollify domestic and international critics, lift aid suspensions and so on. The discourse has shifted from denying to accepting the validity of the norm, but rejecting specific allegations of norm-violation by questioning the facts and evidence presented by critics, or else insisting that these are isolated incidents and the cases will be investigated and perpetrators will be punished, etc. Every time that a state protests that R2P is not applicable to it, that critics have mis-understood the facts or not taken due account of the context, it acknowledges and reinforces the global norm even while questioning its applicability in the specific case to hand.[31] Similarly, much as imitation is the sincerest form of flattery, Russia's invocation of the R2P norm in its 2008 invasion of Georgia was a tribute to the moral power of R2P. By such a process of 'self-entrapment'[32] will the war for R2P be won though many skirmishes might remain to be fought.

What role can the humanitarian community play? David Kennedy argues that by and large, it has failed to confront the reality of bad consequences flowing from good intentions, preferring to retreat into denial, or intensifying efforts to do good, or pointing the finger of accountability at others. The growing influence and power of humanitarian actors mean that they have effectively entered the realm of policy making, at the same time as their emancipatory vocabulary has been captured by governments and other power brokers.[33] International humanitarians are participants in global governance as advocates, activists and policy makers. Their critiques and policy prescriptions have demon-strable consequences in the governmental and intergovernmental allocation of resources and the exercise of political, military and economic power. With influence over policy should come responsibility for the consequences of policy. When things go wrong or do not happen according to plan, the humanitarians share the responsibility for the suboptimal outcomes.

The explanation for the humanitarians' denial of responsibility is the refusal to acknowledge that they have crossed over from the world of ideas and ideals into the realm of power and policy making. Human rights has become the universal vocabulary of political legitimacy and humanitarian law of military legitimacy. But rather than necessarily constraining the pursuit of national interests in the international arena by military means, human rights and humanitarian law provide the discourse of justification for the familiar traditional means of statecraft. Much as humanitarians might want to believe that they still hold up the virtue of truth to the vice of power, the truth is that the vocabulary of virtue has been appropriated in the service of power. The fault line between activists and policy makers is no longer as sharp as it used to be.

Moreover, both the military strategist and the humanitarian activist retreat into abstract principles at the very point where the application of rules (humanitarian law) and standards (human rights) become conceptually and operationally interesting. For instance, if an Iraqi insurgent is hiding among the civilian populace in Fallujah, how many civilians may a US soldier kill without violating the principles of distinction between soldiers and noncombatants? And how many Iraqi civilians may legitimately be killed in order to save one American soldier without violating the principle of proportionality? This is a contemporaneous restatement of the dilemma familiar from the atomic bombings of Hiroshima and Nagasaki in August 1945: were they justified on the twin principles of distinction and proportionality? Rather than answer these difficult questions with any degree of clarity, both the humanitarian and the strategist retreat into restatements of abstract rules and standards, or the vocabulary of absolute normative commitment: the use of force must always be proportional; civilians may never be targeted; we will do our utmost to protect our soldiers; etc.

# 12  Conclusion

## Normative contestation, incoherence and inconsistency

The birth and continuing evolution of the responsibility to protect (R2P) – the mobilizer of last resort of the world's conscience to prevent and stop mass killings – is a clear illustration of how the United Nations has provided an essential space in which powerful normative and policy agendas have been articulated. Is R2P well-meaning enough to be attractive for its promise of making a difference, yet so vague as to be potentially threatening by being open to abuse? Is it in danger of falling prey to the fatal organizational paradox syndrome, where the effort to preserve the fragile diplomatic consensus in the international community is privileged over the call to protect vulnerable populations that led to the consensus being forged in the first place? That is, can the global consensus on R2P, necessary for the world to be able to translate it from noble principle to actual deeds, be stopped from fraying only at the cost of the integrity of R2P that precludes the need to act? Darfur is often the poster child for collective helplessness from the sidelines that translates as institutionalized international indifference.

Alternatively, is R2P a norm in search of a self-justifying crisis? Which does more harm – an endless stream of alibis for inaction in the face of humanitarian crises or misapplying and extending R2P beyond the 2005 consensus? Fortunately, atrocity crimes on the scale of the Holocaust, the Cambodian killing fields and the Rwanda genocide are rare events in human history. This is why R2P in its intervention avatar will be needed but rarely, in extremis. But when such horrific events do occur, standing on the sidelines leaves an indelible stain on our collective conscience that not all the perfumes of Arabia can remove. Which is why we must not shy away from implementing R2P when it is justified and necessary.

The chapters of this book are largely about the *politics* of contested norm shifts in international affairs. Where conceptual essays in scholarly journals might isolate one key argument and refine it, drawing out all the fine nuances, political debates emphasize cross-linkages among related issues and are reluctant to lose sight of the total picture. Where scholarly discourse puts a premium on new and original arguments, in the world of international politics old and familiar arguments are repeatedly cited and recited. All this is true of the shift underway from the old norm of non-intervention to the new norm of the responsibility to protect. How far has the shift occurred? Is it irreversible? Can we rightfully speak of R2P as the new norm in either the legal or political (a weaker claim) sense of the term?

In the absence of credible, reliable, prompt and preponderant coercive institutions and instruments for enforcing international law, the most common instrument for regulating international behaviour is global, regional and regime-specific norms. Social behaviour can be norm-breaking or norm-complying. Behaviour that breaks a norm in a particular instance, but seeks to explain normative noncompliance by pointing to extenuating or special circumstances, neither negates nor challenges the norm but instead acknowledges and revalidates it. When the United States argued that its military activity in Vietnam was not intervention, and when India argued that the 1971 war against Pakistan was self-defence against demographic aggression from East Pakistan in the form of ten million refugees and the threat of wider regional destabilization, both implicitly reaffirmed the norm of non-intervention.

Until the end of 1998, few analysts and even fewer diplomats and political leaders would have quibbled with the assertion that the norm of non-intervention remained firmly ensconced. To be sure, some attributes of state sovereignty had been qualified in practice and, in some regions like Europe, perhaps even in legal theory. It is equally indisputable that the norm of non-intervention had often been breached in practice, and not just by the Western powers. Vietnam's military intervention to overthrow the Pol Pot regime in Cambodia, Tanzania's intervention to eject Idi Amin from power in Uganda and India's intervention to secure the independence of Bangladesh from Pakistan are among the iconic episodes of recent international history. Nevertheless, these were considered deviations from the norm, not challenges to or replacements of the norm.

Neither the Western nor the non-Western intervening powers argued for an abrogation of non-intervention by challenging the foundational doctrine of state sovereignty. This is why the NATO intervention in Kosovo was different: the norm itself was centrally challenged by postulating an alternative norm of 'humanitarian intervention'. In these circumstances, efforts to legitimize and codify a new norm of 'humanitarian intervention' struck at the heart of the collective political identity of most developing countries and was an attempt, from their point of view, to renegotiate the essential terms of their engagement with the international community. The prospect of a fundamental challenge to the effort to craft a new norm of 'humanitarian intervention' was heightened by perceptions of bias, selectivity and strategic imperatives animating actual examples of intervention.

The groundwork for the normative challenge had been prepared by the genocide in Rwanda in 1994 as well as the unfolding tragedy in many acts in the Balkans throughout the 1990s. The 1999 international interventions in Kosovo and East Timor changed the discourse radically. This was the background against which the ICISS was set up, deliberated and promulgated the principle of the responsibility to protect.[1] Although the principle was unanimously endorsed at the UN World Summit in 2005, as several of the preceding chapters demonstrate, its precise meaning, legal status and applicability to various test cases remain contentious and, in some quarters at least, controversial. The contestation over the norm shift from non-intervention to R2P reflects continuing fundamental philosophical dissent from R2P by some states; dissent over its applicability or inapplicability to particular cases such as Darfur, Zimbabwe, Myanmar, Georgia, Gaza, Kashmir, Sri Lanka, Chechnya and so on; disagreements over the types of transgressions and the threshold at which international intervention is warranted; disputes over who may lawfully and legitimately authorize interventions; the circumstances, if any, in which states may unilaterally or in a group act without such prior authorization; and dissatisfaction at instances of normative incoherence and inconsistency.

Moreover, as of mid-2010, with the sole exception of Kenya with some unusual features, R2P has yet to be operationalized in a single case. A major reason for the continued uncertainty over the legal status and political utility of R2P is perceptions of inconsistency in invoking and applying it, with variable responses to seemingly like situations depending on the relations of the offending country or regime to the dominant powers rather than on the gravity of the atrocities being committed. A second major explanation is the clash between the intervention-prescribing R2P principle/norm and a host of intervention-proscribing other norms. The net result is to promote, sometimes furiously, contestation over the emerging or new norm. Until these issues are resolved and R2P is both established as the new norm and internalized by members of the international society of states, its capacity to regulate the internal and international behaviour of states with respect to the use of force – proscriptive for domestic and prescriptive for international – will remain severely limited. At the same time, the transformation of the discourse from 'humanitarian intervention' to 'the responsibility to protect' helps to answer, mute and deflect some key components of the contestation.

## Normative contestation

At any given time, incompatible norms may exist in different segments of human society around the world. In such a situation, norm displacement (of an existing standard of behaviour), establishment (of a new standard) and prominence (the diffusion of the new standard to all members of international society) will occur either because the state in which the mutant norm first arose is especially conspicuous, or because a state is actively championing the new norm. But, to the extent that not everyone is instantly won over by the brilliance of the argument in favour of the proposed new norm, the effort will encounter pockets of resistance. Successful norm promotion requires the attributes of norm entrepreneurship and international leadership skills. Conversely, success in vetoing or blocking the replacement of one norm with another also depends on a combination of structural power and coalition-forming skills: international 'spoilership' as the corollary to international leadership. When

President George W. Bush refused to implement the Kyoto Protocol on greenhouse gas emissions, he demonstrated US asymmetric ability to challenge the emerging international environmental norm on global warming.

Norms are effective as a behaviour-regulating mechanism only if they are accepted as legitimate by the target actor and internalized in its cognitive processes – whether Israel, India, Japan or the United States. Normative contestation occurs when some actors question either the existence of a particular norm or else its applicability to any particular situation; complain about double standards in its application and enforcement; or agitate and organize to overthrow an existing norm. Normative contestation reflects the fact that the international normative architecture is polymorphic, not isomorphic. In such contestation, mutually reinforcing and logically consistent norms have an advantage over discordant and inconsistent norms.

Existing norms are already codified in international law. This was true of non-intervention. New norms must therefore make the case that they are either logical extensions of the law, or necessary changes to it. Ann Florini argues that when there are contested norms, the selection made from them will depend on the relative prominence of each, their relative compatibility or coherence with other prevailing norms, and the extent to which they fit the existing environmental conditions. She remarks too on the importance of the supporting normative structure in norm generation and norm displacement. She notes that of the major norm shifts since the Second World War, two include multilateralism ('meaning that all relevant actors are expected to play by the same set of rules') and restrictions on the use of force.[2] On both counts, many developing countries have had continuing problems with R2P. But several potential intervening states too are uncomfortable at suggestions that under R2P, they can be required to deploy their troops into conflict zones that may trigger combat operations, at the behest of the UN Security Council, even when their vital interests are not engaged. In other words, both the potential targets and agents of international military intervention remain concerned at R2P's implied erosion of policy autonomy of sovereign states.

### Sovereignty vs intervention

Interventions by India in East Pakistan in 1971 and by Vietnam in Cambodia in 1978 removed two regimes that were clearly guilty of having committed gross humanitarian atrocities. But neither action was incompatible with the national security interests of the two intervening powers. In Kosovo, in circumventing the anticipated UN veto NATO repudiated the universally agreed-on rules of the game when the likely outcome was not to its liking. One of the peculiar aspects of the NATO countries' handling of the Kosovo conflict was their stress on the formal sovereignty and territorial integrity of Yugoslavia even while violating the same. Sovereignty in effect became 'fluid and contingent'.[3] After the war, the maintenance of sanctions on Serbia constrained its political and economic independence and efforts at reconstruction.

Most countries agree on the concept of sovereignty as an abstract principle and on the derivative norm of non-intervention. They also agree that sovereignty cannot be an absolute defence against humanitarian atrocities such as genocide and ethnic cleansing. But they hold competing conceptions of the circumstances in which the principle of sovereignty can be suspended and the norm of non-intervention violated. This is why questions of validation, validator and process are crucially important in determining the legitimacy of interventions.

An order secures habitual compliance either through perception of legitimacy, in which case it is a just order; or through fear, in which case it rests on coercion. The post-1945 'international' system was in essence the European states system write large with decisions on inclusion and exclusion of states made on the basis of 'standards of civilization' criteria that included state capacity to ensure law and order, contract sanctity, protection of rights of foreigners, administrative integrity and the like.[4] Japan was one of the few countries considered to have the appropriate table manners to belong at the table of this polite international society. With the colonized countries not admitted to that society during colonialism, it is hardly surprising that in the postcolonial era, many of them rejected the norms underpinning it even while holding fast to the foundational norm of state sovereignty that was rooted in European experience and philosophical tradition.[5]

Amitav Acharya argues that this explains why one key strand of norm subsidiarity is the developing countries' challenge to exclusion and marginalization from the institutions and sites of global governance, both formal and informal.[6] Regionalism was an important means to assert local ownership over the process, agenda and content against efforts by outsiders to define these for the locals. In this context, Acharya specifically identifies non-intervention as a robust regional norm in reaction to the 'managerial rules of great powers' such as the Monroe and Brezhnev doctrines as emblematic of the hypocrisy of great powers in demonstrating self-servingly selective fidelity to global norms. Or, to put it another way, regional norm subsidiarity seeks to fill 'the legitimacy deficit of great power-led institutions'. In channelling their normative resistance to the great powers and their global institutions, local actors claim the right to live by their own rules; levels of authority higher than the regional may only perform those tasks that cannot be carried out at the regional level.

At the same time, Acharya emphasizes the simultaneously norm-strengthening effects of subsidiarity when global norms are locally embedded as tools to secure and entrench autonomy against encroachments by great powers and global institutions.[7] The list of such norms includes self-determination, sovereignty, territorial integrity, political independence, legal equality of states, racial equality, and, of course, non-intervention. Another prominent subsidiary norm, first articulated in Latin America but rapidly adopted by Africa and Asia as well, was the doctrine of *uti possidetis juris*, or the inviolability of and respect for the political boundaries inherited from colonial empires. This therefore supported the global norm of territorial integrity. In reaction to the Monroe

Doctrine as well as to European claims to the right to intervene to protect their citizens and to compel target states to honour sovereign debts, Latin America also developed the counter-norm of absolute non-intervention in the hemispheric community. The slogan of regional solutions to regional problems was a logical extension of these animating impulses.

There is a political significance to conceptualizing norm diffusion in these terms. Countries of the Global South contesting so-called global norms cannot summarily be dismissed as norm spoilers. Instead, they are claiming agency and rejecting efforts by the Global North to deny them agency for ordering their own affairs. With respect to humanitarian intervention in particular, they contested the morality of the claim, whereas for some Western constructivist scholars, the point of demonstrating that non-intervention is a constructed norm is to detach it from a putative morality. Or, to invert another common perception, lacking material strength, developing countries are far more reliant on ideational and normative agency for empowerment as state actors. Ideas are the 'weapons of the weak'.[8]

Nor is sovereignty as responsibility necessarily limited to the domestic realm. Rather, the reality is one of systemic brittleness where shocks cascade across sectors and among countries. The contemporary international system exhibits systemic risks and vulnerabilities, both horizontally from one sector to another (the subprime crisis, mortgage meltdown and individual banks' crisis led inexorably to a global financial crisis), and vertically from firms and nations to the world. Sovereignty understood and jealously guarded as financial autonomy behind political frontiers becomes a risk multiplier for the system of sovereign states.[9] Conversely, systemic resilience lies in supranational regulatory/surveillance mechanisms, coordinating mechanisms, and sanctioning mechanism sans sovereignty for the core countries of global capitalism, not merely for developing countries. In other words, sovereignty entails global responsibility for the extra-territorial impacts of national decisions.

### Great power responsibility for world order

The formal authority for maintaining international peace and security is vested in the UN Security Council. The burden of responsibility, from having the power to make the most difference, often falls on the United States and other leading powers. Great powers play particular roles both in relations with one another and in relations among themselves and the lesser powers. Mutually, they help to promote order by preserving the general balance of power, controlling crises, and containing wars; unequally, they exploit their preponderance over lesser states by unilateral intervention, tacit respect of spheres of influence, and concerted action. Great powers claim and are granted the right to a determining role in issues of world peace and security; but they also are burdened by the corresponding duty to modify national policies in the light of international managerial responsibilities.[10] Permanent membership of the Security Council consecrated the special position of the five major powers (P5) in the UN scheme of helping to shape and safeguard international peace. The veto clause conferred the further competence to protect international encroachments upon their own vital interests. In return, as part of their obligations towards a responsible management of international order, the great powers agreed to eschew unilateral interventions in favour of concerted action through the UN system. Consequently, even great power concert today needs the legitimizing approbation of the UN for optimum effectiveness in regulating international behaviour.

The veto clause in the decision-making procedures of the Security Council was meant to correlate power more precisely to responsibility and to encourage the search for great power consensus as the prerequisite for enforcement action authorized by the UN. Many regard the use and abuse of the veto by the P5 as likely to be the principal obstacle to effective international action in cases where quick and decisive action is needed to stop or avert a significant humanitarian crisis. Those states who insist on the right to retaining permanent membership of the Security Council and the entrenched veto power, which amounts to 'sovereignty plus', have a questionable claim to act outside the UN framework as a result of the Council being paralysed by a veto cast by another permanent member. Those who insist on keeping the existing rules of the game unchanged, have a correspondingly less compelling claim to reject any specific outcome when the game is played by those very rules.

There is a second – and increasingly important – strand of delegitimization of Security Council-authorized interventions on the justification of the special responsibility and role of great powers. The simple fact is that the Security Council is increasingly misaligned with the distribution of power in the real world. As such, it is suffering an as-yet unchecked erosion of legitimacy and a resulting weakening of authority on the core logic of its composition that vests the major powers of the states system with permanent membership and the veto.

## US exceptionalism and triumphalism

The state actor with the greatest contemporary capacity to play the roles of norm entrepreneur and spoiler is the United States. We began the twenty-first century with the convergence of US global dominance in military might, economic dynamism and information technology without precedent in human history. To this list can be added the soft power hegemony in the major multilateral institutions, especially the International Monetary Fund and the World Bank but including also the United Nations; the collective action dominance of the G7 and NATO; and the many globally influential media and NGO conglomerates located in the United States.

The United States has unmatched structural assets in institutionalizing its preferences in negotiated global regimes. Its norm entrepreneurship and spoilership roles are helped by:

- the sheer size of its foreign policy and international trade bureaucracy;
- much greater scientific-technical depth of knowledge, especially useful as many of today's negotiations involve complex questions of contested science – the subject of global warming being a very good example;
- the superior ability to leverage information and knowledge to the pursuit of one's narrow commercial, political and strategic interests;
- the greater capacity to leverage legal resources – the United States can field a formidable team of technically skilled legal specialists in any branch of law;
- the considerable advantages of wealth – the United States can exact pre-emptive compliance by the threat of denying access to its vast market; its wealth and affluence mean that on one side, its own officials can expect reasonable salary levels as a shield against bribes, while US firms can offer vast inducements to individuals negotiating on the other side. Conversely, poor countries lack the wealth to bribe foreign officials, while their own officials can be tempted because of low wages and salaries;
- the immeasurably greater capacity of the United States to deploy national assets, including intelligence, to monitor compliance by others;
- the much more numerous, substantial and sophisticated information and communications technology and skills available to Washington.

Perhaps because of the possession of the above assets in abundance, the United States under the Bush administration lost sight of the importance of norms in regulating international behaviour. The political reputation of the norm advocate is also relevant in norm entrepreneurship. In turn, consistency and coherence affect political standing. On all counts, US behaviour was found wanting and its leadership credentials waned. On issues ranging from global warming to arms control and international criminal courts, the Bush administration pulled back from multilaterally negotiated agreements in a remarkably short period of time. It is not possible to construct a world in which all others have to obey universal norms and rules, but Washington can opt out whenever, as often, and for as long as it likes on specific global norms.

In many ways the US veto of the UN police training mission in Bosnia in July 2002, because its peacekeepers would not be granted blanket immunity from the jurisdiction of the International Criminal Court (ICC) that came into effect the same month, epitomized US unilateralism and exceptionalism. The message being transmitted was as simple as it was powerful: Washington would not hold itself to standards that other nations, including some of its closest friend and allies, are prepared to accept. Not surprisingly, this significantly degraded the US capacity to set international standards of behaviour in general. Fitful US arrogance had seemingly turned into habitual exceptionalism and triumphalism. The country founded in opposition to tyranny institutionalized this opposition in a form of government based on separation of powers. The same country had acquired the most concentrated power in world affairs yet had difficulty comprehending others' worries about the tyranny of total power.

The US–UN relationship and the international image of the United States improved dramatically with the election of Barack Obama as president and his early overtures aimed at repairing the battered US reputation. But actions have not necessarily matched words. With the US refusal to join the universal justice of the ICC, it is hardly surprising that many developing countries should view the moral imperialism of human rights as the handmaiden to judicial colonialism with respect to international criminal justice. African countries have been at the forefront of complaining at the Africans-only prosecution of alleged war criminals by the ICC.[11]

The West has often softened its commitment to international criminal justice when Israel is the target. The Goldstone Report 'is an important ethical challenge not only to Israel but to Western countries that have empowered Israel and remain insensitive to the suffering caused by Israel's occupation of the West Bank and its blockade of Gaza'.[12] On 16 October 2009, the forty-seven-member Human Rights Council endorsed the Goldstone Report by a vote of twenty-five to six, with the United States being one of the six to vote against. Britain and France were among five countries that did not vote, while eleven countries abstained.[13] On 5 November, the General Assembly voted 114–18 to endorse the Goldstone Report. While most Western countries abstained, Australia, Canada, Germany, Italy and the United States joined Israel in voting against it.[14]

### Legality vs legitimacy

The rule of law ideal has been diffused from the West to become an international norm. It asserts the primacy of law over the arbitrary exercise of political power by using law to tame power; the protection of the citizen from the arbitrary actions of the government by making both, and their relationship to each other, subject to impersonal and impartial law; and the primacy of universalism over particularism through the principle of equal in law, whereby individuals coming before the law are treated as individuals, divorced from their social characteristics.[15]

The Independent International Commission on Kosovo, chaired by Richard Goldstone and Carl Tham, concluded that NATO's intervention was illegal but legitimate.[16] The intervention was illegal because the use of force is prohibited by the UN Charter except in self-defence or when authorized by the Security Council. It was legitimate, nevertheless, because of the scale of human rights atrocities by the Milosevic regime, the failure of other means used to try to stop those atrocities and the political stalemate in the Security Council created by Russia and China.

There is a problem, nevertheless. Suppose I have witnessed a murder. Suppose further that for reasons to do with courtroom techniques of expensive trial lawyers who exploit every technicality, the murderer is acquitted. Can I claim legitimacy in inflicting vigilante justice on the murderer?[17] A normative commitment to the rule of law implies a commitment to the principle of relations being governed by law, not power. It also implies a willingness to accept the limitations and constraints of working within the law, in specific instances if necessary against individual notions of just or illegitimate outcome. To the extent that the UN Security Council has the monopoly on the legitimate use of coercive measures in international affairs, it is a symbol of what individual member states may *not* do.

Supporters of illegal–but–legitimate turn the normal process of reasoning upside down. The Kosovo war was illegal, yet necessary and justified. Therefore the war highlighted defects in international law, not shortcomings in NATO behaviour. And the (anticipated) failure of the Security Council to authorize the war was a reflection on flaws in the Council's functioning, not on the invalidity of NATO bombing. The moral urgency underpinning NATO actions, and the military success of those actions, would in due course shape legal justification to match the course of action.[18] Therefore NATO neither flouted international legitimacy nor challenged Security Council authority; rather, the Security Council failed to meet the challenge of international moral authority.

The legality–legitimacy distinction rests on an implicit hierarchy of norms, which too poses a fundamental challenge to the existing basis of state order.[19] The international order, being a society of sovereign states, has only a horizontal system of rules derived logically from the principle of sovereign equality. If the UN Charter's proscriptions on the threat and use of force can be set aside, the justification for this must necessarily rest on the existence of a higher order of norms that override Charter clauses. The *use* of force may be lawful or unlawful; the *decision* to use force is a political act; almost the only channel between legal authority and political legitimacy with regard to the international use of force is the Security Council. The Uniting for Peace resolution transferred the locus to the General Assembly in case of deadlock in the Council. Conceding to any – and therefore every – regional organization the authority to decide when political legitimacy may override legal technicality would make a mockery of the entire basis of strictly limited and increasingly constricted recourse to force for settling international disputes.

The Security Council's record is relevant to an assessment of the claim that it has exclusive authority over military intervention.[20] Its performance legitimacy suffers from two strikes: an uneven record, and a selective record. It lacks unquestioned representational legitimacy. And its procedural legitimacy is suspect on grounds of lack of democratization and transparency in decision-making.[21] Unlike NATO, which unilaterally transferred the legal capacity to authorize enforcement operations from the Security Council to NATO, most developing countries urge reform of the Security Council. Only the UN can legitimately authorize military action on behalf of the entire international community, instead of a select few. Efforts by the major Western powers, in Iraq as much as in the Balkans, to stretch the permissive scope of existing Security Council resolutions effectively rewrote carefully negotiated Security Council resolutions and thereby diminished the legal authority of the Security Council.[22]

The net message of the Kosovo war to the rest of the world was that 'the West continues to script international law . . . . The West assumes that its wealth, power and assurance bestow a normative authority that discounts alternative views'.[23] This is why the Indian representative argued that 'NATO believed itself to be above the law'.[24] The British in particular developed a new doctrine of overwhelming humanitarian necessity to justify the war in Kosovo. But no government addressed the obvious anomaly that arises, namely does any regional organization or ad hoc collection of countries have a parallel right to interpret and apply evolving customary international law for itself? This is why ICISS concluded that 'The task is not to find alternatives to the Security Council as a source of authority, but to make the Security Council work much better than it has'. It therefore recommended that in all cases, Security Council authorization must be sought prior to any military intervention.[25]

But even ICISS conceded that if an intervention is carried out despite the failure of Security Council authorization to popular approbation around the world, then it is the authority and credibility of the United Nations that will suffer still further damage.[26] UN authorization is neither a necessary nor a sufficient condition of international legitimacy. In national systems, bills passed into law by the legislature and actions of the executive arm of government can be found, by judicial review, to violate constitutionally guaranteed rights of citizens. In principle, Security Council resolutions could similarly violate the rights of member states guaranteed by the UN Charter. But there is no mechanism to hold the Council to independent international judicial account. Given its unrepresentative nature, there are occasional tremors of apprehension among developing countries about the potential for the UN, which they see as the best protection that the weak have against the strong in international affairs, to become instead the instrument for legitimating the actions of the strong against the weak. This is but one among several reasons why there has occurred a dangerous widening of the gulf between law and legitimacy across the UN system.[27]

## Normative incoherence

Normative coherence requires compatibility among a cluster of cognate norms. A new norm of intervention would run against the proscription on war as an instrument of state policy, reducing and eliminating weapons of mass destruction, international law as the basis of world order, the United Nations as the custodian of world order, and create friction between realism and idealism.

### War as an instrument of policy

Until the First World War, war was an accepted means of 'settling' international disputes and going to war was an acknowledged part of state sovereignty with its own stable sets of practices and etiquette. The only effective deterrent against it was the armed might of rivals, which raised both the chances of defeat and the costs of victory. Over the course of the twentieth century, the international community emplaced many legislative, normative and operational fetters on the rights of states to go to war without international authorization.[28] Progress was slow, difficult and protracted. After the Second World War, the focus of all such efforts was centred on the UN.[29] The Kosovo war was a major setback to the cause of slowly but steadily outlawing the use of force in solving disputes except under UN authorization. Alexei Arbatov, deputy chair of the Russian State Duma (Parliament) Defence Committee, argued explicitly that NATO's attack on Serbia removed the Russian taboo against the use of military force in Chechnya.[30]

There is a contradiction between war as the historical method of settling conflicts and its contemporary illegitimacy. The international community may sometimes have to choose between war and peace and, if war is the choice, impose the terms of the political settlement. Limited impartial intervention is a delusion.[31] Parties go to war in order to settle on the battlefield the question that could not be resolved around the negotiating table: who gets to control and rule over part or all of a territory. Limited intervention can succeed if it supports one side over the other and tilts the balance decisively in its favour. Alternatively, impartial intervention can succeed by imposing its will and authority over all sides through total commitment, not through limited means. Intervention that is impartial and limited may impose a truce, but cannot bring about a peace settlement. It stops decisive victory by either side, precludes mutual military exhaustion that can form the basis of a durable negotiated compromise, prolongs the military stalemate and perpetuates the underlying political power struggle.

Another difficulty in Kosovo was that the main rebel group provoking Serb atrocities itself had an unsavoury identity. The Kosovo Liberation Army, which included people with past connections to political terrorism,[32] incited reprisals from Serbian security forces through a variety of provocative acts. Even the Secretary-General acknowledged the moral hazard argument in this, of encouraging ethno-national groups everywhere to demand independence and back it with violence that provokes state retaliation, which then promotes external intervention.[33]

The dilemma faced by NATO in Kosovo in 1999 was but a specific example of a larger problem, namely providing an additional justification for the use of force for settling international disputes and thereby promoting a new militarism.[34] The great reluctance of NATO leaders to label actions in Kosovo as 'war' shows their own unease at the actions. British Defence Secretary George Robertson insisted in a House of Commons select committee debate on 24 March 1999 that 'It is not a war'.[35] Instead, various spokespersons used words such as air campaign, air strikes, and humanitarian intervention. NATO Secretary-General Javier Solana used truly Orwellian language at a press conference on 25 March: 'We are engaged in this operation in order not to wage war against anybody but to try to stop the war and to guarantee that peace is a reality.'[36] From this to humanitarian intervention, a humanitarian war, and even humanitarian bombing was but a short lexicological leap. One of the few exceptions was Tony Blair, prime minister of the country that was probably the most hawkish on the subject. He defended the action on the grounds that it was 'a just war, based not on any territorial ambitions but on values', and justified it with reference to a 'doctrine of the international community'.[37] Solana justified NATO behaviour with reference to 'the unique allied cohesion of 19 democracies'.[38]

Equally, though, China, India and Russia, who between them represented half the world's peoples, had strongly opposed the war launched by NATO. The conflation of the international community into NATO rested on a tautological definition of the international community in the image of the *values* represented by NATO. The international community is *defined* as the broad normative community that subscribes to the values on which NATO is founded. The alliance was prosecutor, judge, jury and executioner. It was not just founded on democracy, human rights and the rule of law, but was to be the custodian, interpreter and enforcer of these principles and values.

The justification resting on NATO as the alliance of democratic countries was extended to the need to preserve the credibility of NATO. But as the UK Select Committee noted afterwards, this begged the question of how and why NATO had become embroiled in the situation to the point where its credibility was on the line. Moreover, the credibility argument, being essentially a strategic justification, necessarily undermines the humanitarian justification: 'It is difficult to imagine a legal justification based upon the need to support any organization's credibility.'[39] The credibility argument also inverts cause and effect, goals and means. Collective defence organizations exist to deter and fight wars launched by others; wars are not – or should not be – the means to keep alliances intact.

### Nuclear proliferation

If alliances are going to launch aggressive wars against others, many countries will look to all means necessary to leverage the calculus of military decision-making in order to inject more caution. The force of this argument can be demonstrated convincingly with reference to the three countries that opposed NATO most strongly. In the case of China, Sha Zukang, its chief arms control negotiator, used NATO's actions in Kosovo as the alibi for missiles exports. The United States 'wantonly bombed Yugoslavia' because the latter 'had no means to retaliate', he said, adding: 'Once the United States believes it has both a strong spear and a strong shield, it could lead them to conclude that nobody can harm the United States and they can harm anyone they like anywhere in the world. There could be many more bombings like what happened in Kosovo.'[40]

Rebecca Johnson of the London-based Acronym Institute reported that at the Third Preparatory Committee (PrepCom) meeting of the NPT 2000 Review Conference in New York in May 1999, 'though the Chinese were the only ones publicly to wonder if NATO would have bombed Belgrade if Yugoslavia had also been nuclear armed, there were many in the corridors who made the obvious connection'.[41] Including in India: a former foreign secretary noted that: 'If it is Iraq and Yugoslavia today, it could very well be India tomorrow. This demonstrates convincingly the importance of India's nuclear deterrent.'[42]

### Order vs justice

Justice and order are logical and empirical correlates. A just order is one that defines and protects entitlements to legitimate expectations and, in cases of conflict, resolves them through procedures that are generally regarded as legitimate. Of course, order can be maintained without justice, through coercion. But an order based on force merely checks grievances, does not resolve them: the dissatisfied and the revisionists have the will but lack the means and the capacity to challenge the entrenched defenders of the status quo. Equally, however, justice cannot obtain in conditions of disorder and anarchy. Law is a means, albeit imperfect, and especially imperfect at the international level, of mediating between justice and order. For neither justice nor order will prevail in the absence of a lawful society: we always speak of law and order, never the reverse.

The difficulty is that 'existing principles of justice that govern international relations today are too weak, too abstract, and enjoy too little legitimacy to be determinative in hard cases'.[43] Both Serbia and NATO viewed their own cause as just, the opponent's as unjust, and believed their claim to be grounded in a legitimate entitlement. Their rival justifications were not merely competing; they were *parochial*. NATO used the justificatory vocabulary of 'humanitarian intervention'. Serbia used the language of defence of sovereignty against armed external aggression. NATO governments succeeded in justifying their actions to one another because they already gave greater weight to popular sovereignty; Serbia's claim resonated among developing countries because, in their international moral order, they were predisposed to privilege national sovereignty over military intervention by coalitions of the willing, even for humanitarian purposes.

Mohammed Ayoob argues that since the international system is highly stratified, there is a high probability of interventions being seen as instruments of depredation by the strong against the weak. In particular, for developing countries they will conjure up visions of the nineteenth-century doctrine of 'standard of civilization', with human rights being the new standard.[44] But the Western construction of the new standard is ahistorical, airbrushing the role of violence in the making of most Western states. The role of violence, conflict and conquest was integral to the historical enterprise of constructing modern US society and war made the modern European states as well. Ayoob asks how seriously delayed or distorted the Western state-making enterprise would have been if the likes of Amnesty International, Human Rights Watch, the UN Human Rights Commission and the Security Council had been monitoring their actions during the violent phases of their state making process.[45]

The claim of developing country governments to monopoly over the legitimate use of violence is resisted by many armed groups from within; is the state in the contemporary developing world to be denied the right to use force against those who would challenge its authority as the lawful guardian of domestic order? As Peter Popham comments on Sri Lanka, in 2009 'the West had no business trying to dictate peace terms to the legitimate government of the island, faced with an astonishingly brutal insurgency'.[46] And of course, outside intervention on behalf of groups resisting state authority by force encourages other recalcitrant groups in other places to resort to ever-more violent challenges, since that is the trigger to internationalizing their power struggle. Mahmoud Mamdani takes the attack on R2P to another extreme, describing it as 'a right to punish . . . without being held accountable – a clarion call for the recolonization of "failed" states in Africa'.[47]

### Realism vs idealism

The logic of power is inconsistent with that of justice. There is a logical slippage between normative idealism and realpolitik in picking and choosing which elements of the existing order are to be challenged and which retained. If ethical imperatives and calculations of justice are to inform, underpin and justify international interventions, then there is a powerful case for reforming the composition of the Security Council and eliminating the veto clause. To self-censor such calls for major reform on the grounds that they are unacceptable to the major powers, and therefore unrealistic, is to argue in effect that the motive for intervention is humanitarian, not strategic; but the agency and procedure for deciding on intervention must remain locked in the strategic logic of realpolitik. 'Eroding the existing normative basis of international society in order to provide major powers the facility to intervene selectively in the domestic affairs of weaker states ought not to form a part of the humanitarian intervention argument.'[48]

Power political calculations were inseparable from decisions on Kosovo. The collapse of the Soviet Union left a dangerous power vacuum throughout central and eastern Europe. The relentless expansion of NATO can be interpreted as a surge to fill the power vacuum. The end of the cold war reduced NATO to an alliance looking for an enemy and a role. It embarked on a triple transformation: enlargement of membership, an eastward expansion of geographical borders, and a change of role from collective defence of member states against armed attack from a non-member, to a more diffuse role of peace maintenance throughout Europe. The continued anchoring of the US military presence in Europe would be helped by all three changes. The Kosovo war validated the triple change and ground the US military to Europe for the foreseeable future.

The logics of peace and peaceful coexistence can be in collision. The terms of the defeat of Serbia had to be negotiated with the discredited and criminally indicted, but internationally still the only legitimate, Milosevic regime. Must different groups of people, each with its own powerful myths and history, be compelled to live together in one territorially defined 'nation-state'? Would peace in the Balkans have been easier if the region had been reconstituted territorially along ethnic lines at the start of the 1990s? Has not East Timor been more peaceful since its separation from Indonesia in 1999? In other words, should borders be drawn and redrawn with a view to congruence between political community and ethno-national identity?

## Normative inconsistency

Normative inconsistency refers to unevenness in the application of any one particular norm, for example non-intervention or non-proliferation either in different locations or cases around the same time, or in like cases and even the same place over time. The 'norm' of 'humanitarian intervention' in Kosovo and East Timor in 1999; the invocation of the new emerging norm of R2P in Iraq in 2003; and largely Western efforts to invoke it in Sri Lanka in 2009, in Myanmar (although it was less widely supported) in 2008; calls for its application to Darfur and Zimbabwe; and the international criminal prosecution of Africans but no others, are all inconsistent with the reality of non-intervention and non-prosecution in other comparable cases in the developing countries, with the continuing impunity of Westerners and their allies for possible war crimes and crimes of aggression, with the rejection of international scrutiny of human rights abuses inside Western countries, and with parts of international humanitarian law.

According to Charles Simic:

> . . . there's an unwritten understanding that crimes committed by the United States and a few other Western powers go unpunished . . . the United States regards itself as a country whose exceptional moral standing exempts it from accountability for the war crimes it commits. The trouble with that is that everybody else feels the same way. The belief that one ought to be able to kill one's enemies and live happily after is nearly universal.[49]

The major Western states – and those reliant on them for protection from the reach of international criminal justice – have been able to enjoy de facto impunity because of their dominant position in the international power hierarchy for several centuries. Today's laws reflect the will and wishes of the victors of yesterday's power struggles; today's international rules and global norms reflect yesterday's power distribution.

International indictments, criminal prosecutions and convictions for war crimes committed by the various parties in the ongoing Balkan wars since the dissolution of Yugoslavia do not appear to reflect the balance of perpetrations,[50] instead singling out Serbs disproportionately. The 1999 Kosovo war was between Serbia and NATO. Yet, located physically in a NATO country, its budget paid mostly by NATO countries, and reliant on NATO troops for collection of evidence and enforcement of warrants, the International Criminal Tribunal for former Yugoslavia (ICTY) has tried several Serbs and some other Balkan leaders, but no NATO national.

In a stinging indictment of the ICTY, Robert Hayden argued that it delivered biased justice: prosecutorial decisions have been based on the national characteristics of the accused rather than on an objective assessment of the available evidence with regard to cluster bombs and war crimes, wanton destruction of property, intentional targeting of civilian infrastructure that caused civilian deaths in a policy designed to avoid casualties among one's own military that would have resulted from attacking enemy military assets, etc.; the supposedly independent ICTY prosecuted only those whom Washington wanted prosecuted; Washington in turn used the threat of ICTY prosecution to secure compliance from political actors in the Balkans; its judicial decisions have trampled on the rights of accused to obtain a fair trial; and it has shown a lack of interest in investigating prosecutorial misconduct.[51] There is also the troubling element of the chief prosecutor who issued the indictment being appointed to her country's highest court very shortly thereafter.[52]

Nuremberg was supposedly about who started the war, not who lost. We know who started the Iraq war; they have not been called to account for it in any criminal jurisdiction. No US general or cabinet member is likely to face international criminal prosecution for the abuses of Abu Ghraib and Guantanamo. Nor has the world been given an honest accounting of what happened in Fallujah in April 2004, how many were killed, and whether any criminality was involved, including the use of illicit chemical weapons.

The rejection of the ICC by Washington – described by Sweden's ambassador to the UN as reminiscent of George Orwell's immortal line in *Animal Farm* that 'we are all equal but some are more equal than others'[53] – highlights the irony that the United States 'is prepared to bomb in the name of human rights but not to join institutions to enforce them'.[54] NATO bombed Serbia for over two months, and from their great height its planes were in a position to choose their targets at will with very little risk to themselves. The result was to make conditions significantly worse for the 'protected' population of Kosovo, on the one hand, and to cause damage to the lives and livelihoods of the unprotected Serbian population, on the other. After the war the latter became the new victims of revenge ethnic cleansing. According to Christine Chinkin, NATO bombing amounted to 'unauthorized reprisals against the civilian population for the Yugoslav Government's refusal to accept imposed terms at Rambouillet'.[55] Expanding the list of bombing targets, such as water and electricity infrastructure and broadcasting stations, reversed progressive trends in the laws of war and international humanitarian law over the course of the twentieth century.

Thus normative inconsistency lies in the selectivity of international intervention and prosecution. Selectivity per se may well be inevitable, for the international community simply cannot intervene everywhere, all the time. But for the sake of normative consistency, intervention should occur where and when it can make the difference between atrocities and human rights protection. Unfortunately, the criterion of selection tends to be material self-interest or discrimination between friends/allies (where the norm of non-intervention is privileged) versus adversaries and rogue states (where intervention has norm prominence).

Compared to the language of humanitarian intervention, R2P makes it more difficult to mask the failure to privilege the protection of victims over that of one's own military personnel through the adoption of particular tactics like high altitude bombing; it directs attention to questions of the costs and results of action.

## Conclusion

The dangers of a complete fraying of the existing normative consensus are magnified because of the potentially competing and conflicting norms and principles at play on most controversial/important issues. There is also resentment that, yet again, non-Westerners seem to be consigned to being norm-and-law-takers, not setters. Much of the twentieth century advances in globalizing norms and international law has been progressive and beneficial. But their viability will be threatened if developing countries are not brought more attentively into the process of norm formation, promulgation, inter-pretation and articulation; that is, made equal partners in the management of regimes in which international norms and laws are embedded. Otherwise, norms will become the major transmission mechanism for embedding structural inequality in international law, instruments and regimes.

When a person under ICC indictment is welcomed to Egypt by the president himself and attends an Arab League summit in the presence of UN Secretary-General Ban Ki-moon, the net result is to bring the system of international criminal justice into disrepute. Unlike Bashir or the other Africans in the dock, whose alleged atrocities were limited to national jurisdictions, the Bush administration asserted and exercised the right to kidnap suspected enemies in the war on terror anywhere in the world and take them anywhere else, including countries known to torture suspects.[56] Many Western allies colluded in the extraordinary rendition. To date the only convictions came in November 2009 when an Italian court convicted, in absentia, twenty-three Americans, most of them working for the CIA, of abducting Muslim cleric Osama Moustafa Hassan Nasr (also known as Abu Omar) off a Milan street on 17 February 2003.[57] In a surreal twist worthy of Kafka, some leading Western countries sent terror suspects to be tortured to countries that they then branded as human rights abusers. Even the US lawyers who wrote the justifications providing legal cover for torture will not be charged.[58] Instead, patriotic public intellectuals write opinion articles pleading against prosecution on the grounds that they acted out of a sincere desire to keep America safe.[59]

To dismiss the concerns on the shortcomings of normative inconsistency, incoherence and contestation over R2P and international criminal justice as being entirely without merit would jeopardize the achievements and discredit the twin sovereignty-challenging enterprise. Instead, for the progressive trend to be consolidated, the genuineness of the concerns must be acknowledged, responded to and mitigated.

The UN's political agenda is controlled largely by the Western states who are its most powerful and wealthy members. This is exacerbated by UN officials at policy-influencing ranks being disproportionately Westerners as well.[60] How successfully and speedily will the newly empowered big players of the Global South manage their transformation from perennial spoilers to responsible globalizers? In particular, will they act as norm spoilers, continuing to reject such major normative advances as the prohibition on antipersonnel landmines, the responsibility to protect, and the International Criminal Court? Or will they also begin to demonstrate the willingness to become norm entrepreneurs, champions, brokers and carriers?

The Western world could be in for a period of turbulence as it adjusts to the reversion to the historical norm of China and India being major world actors. The BASIC countries (Brazil, South Africa, India and China) are likely to be sympathetic to developing countries' complaints that excessive attention to the military intervention component of R2P and international justice structures reflect past power equations and take away agency from developing countries in deciding how to balance peace, justice and reconciliation. One would expect that the global players of the South will tweak the norms and practices, along with the clauses and institutions, of international law and order such as to transform them from instruments of selective justice to universal justice. Alternatively, if they are uninterested in or fail in that goal, they will indict and break critical components of the system of international law, order and justice because of its discriminatory selectivity as the discredited instrument of the virtuous West against the evil rest.

# Notes

## 1 Introduction: norms and laws in international relations

1 International Commission on Intervention and State Sovereignty, *The Responsibility to Protect* (Ottawa: International Development Research Centre, 2001).

2 *2005 World Summit Outcome*, adopted by UN General Assembly Resolution A/RES/60/1, 24 October 2005, paras 138–40.

3 The definition of a *norm* isolates a single standard of behaviour, whereas *institutions* emphasize a collection of rules and practices and do not capture the 'oughtness' of the norm definition.

4 F. V. Kratochwil, *Rules, Norms, and Decisions: On the conditions of practical and legal reasoning in international relations and domestic affairs* (Cambridge: Cambridge University Press, 1989), pp. 10–11.

5 For an argument on how shaming is an effective instrument in underpinning the efficacy of the European human rights regime, see A. Moravcsik, 'Explaining International Human Rights Regimes: Liberal Theory and Western Europe', *European Journal of International Relations* 1:2 (June 1995), pp. 157–89. For a slightly different interpretation of the domestic impact of norms embedded in the European human rights regime, see J. T. Checkel, 'International Norms and Domestic Politics: Bridging the Rationalist–Constructivist Divide', *European Journal of International Relations* 3:4 (December 1997), pp. 473–95. See also his 'Norms, Institutions, and National Identity in Contemporary Europe', *International Studies Quarterly* 43:1 (March 1999), pp. 83–114.

6 B. Greenhill, 'The Company You Keep: International Socialization and the Diffusion of Human Rights Norms', *International Studies Quarterly* 54:1 (March 2010), pp. 127–45.

7 A. Florini, 'The Evolution of International Norms', *International Studies Quarterly* 40:3 (September 1996), pp. 363–89 at p. 366.

8 M. Finnemore and K. Sikkink, 'International Norm Dynamics and Political Change', *International Organization* 52:4 (Autumn 1998), p. 894.

9 T. Risse, '"Let's Argue!": Communicative Action in World Politics', *International Organization* 54:1 (Winter 2000), pp. 1–39 at p. 5.

10 A. Björkdahl and S. McMahon, 'Market Shares for Conflict Prevention and Human Security: Sweden and Canada as Norm Entrepreneurs', Paper presented at the annual conference of the Academic Council on the UN System (ACUNS), Oslo, 16–18 June 2000.

11 Finnemore and Sikkink, 'International Norm Dynamics and Political Change', p. 906.

12 A. Acharya, 'How Ideas Spread: Whose Norms Matter? Norm Localization and Institutional Change in Asian Regionalism', *International Organization* 58:2 (2004),

pp. 239–75. See also A. Acharya, *Whose Ideas Matter: Agency and power in Asian regionalism* (Ithaca, NY: Cornell University Press, 2009).

13   A. Acharya, 'Norm Subsidiarity and Regional Orders: Sovereignty, Regionalism and Rule-making in the Third World', *International Studies Quarterly* 55 (2011, forthcoming). I am not convinced that this is the correct adaptation of the principle of subsidiarity, most famous in the context of the European Union, which locates governance at the lowest possible level for resolving a problem. That aside, the substance of Acharya's argument is powerfully persuasive.

14   Finnemore and Sikkink, 'International Norm Dynamics and Political Change'.

15   R. Malnes, '"Leader" and "Entrepreneur" in International Negotiations', *European Journal of International Relations* 1:1 (March 1995), pp. 88–90.

16   Quoted in ibid., p. 90.

17   For a collection of essays examining the Ottawa Treaty, the ICC, codes of conduct and the nature and development of new diplomacy, see A. F. Cooper, J. English, and R. Thakur, eds, *Enhancing Global Governance: Towards a new diplomacy?* (Tokyo: United Nations University Press, 2002).

18   See A. F. Cooper, J. Heine and R. Thakur, eds, *The Oxford Handbook of Modern Diplomacy* (Oxford: Oxford University Press, forthcoming).

19   Finnemore and Sikkink, 'International Norm Dynamics and Political Change', p. 901.

20   See R. Thakur and W. Maley, 'The Ottawa Convention on Landmines: A Landmark Humanitarian Treaty in Arms Control?', *Global Governance* 5:3 (July–September 1999), pp. 273–302.

21   A. P. Cortell and J. W. Davis, Jr, 'How Do International Institutions Matter? The Domestic Impact of International Rules and Norms', *International Studies Quarterly* 40:4 (December 1996), pp. 451–78.

22   Risse, '"Let's Argue!"', p. 5.

23   D. Türk, 'Humanitarian Interventions: Balancing Human Rights and National Sovereignty', *International Policy Perspectives* No. 2002.1 (St. Louis, MO: University of Missouri-St. Louis, January 2002), p. 20.

24   Risse, '"Let's Argue!"', p. 32. In a subsequent refinement with colleagues, Risse developed the five-stage spiral model of norm generation, diffusion and domestication by the target state: repression, denial, tactical concessions, prescriptive status (when the state accepts the international norm and incorporates it into domestic legislation), and rule-consistent behaviour. T. Risse and K. Sikkink, 'The Socialization of International Human Rights Norms into Domestic Practices: Introduction', in T. Risse, S. C. Ropp and K. Sikkink, eds, *The Power of Human Rights: International norms and domestic change* (Cambridge: Cambridge University Press, 1999), pp. 17–35.

25   L. McCarthy, *Justice, the State, and International Relations* (Houndmills: Macmillan, 1998), pp. 67–69.

26   T. Nardin, 'Introduction', in T. Nardin, ed., *The Ethics of War and Peace: Religious and secular perspectives* (Princeton, NJ: Princeton University Press, 1996), pp. 6–7.

27   T. Nardin, 'The Comparative Ethics of War and Peace', in Nardin, ed., *Ethics of War and Peace*, p. 245.

28   D. A. Welch, *Justice and the Genesis of War* (Cambridge: Cambridge University Press, 1993), p. 216.

29   Risse and Sikkink, 'The Socialization of International Human Rights Norms into Domestic Practices', p. 5.

30   T. Risse and S. C. Ropp, 'International Human Rights Norms and Domestic Change: Conclusions', in Risse, Ropp and Sikkink, eds, *The Power of Human Rights*, p. 277.

31 See R. Thakur, *Towards a Less Imperfect State of the World: The gulf between north and south* (Berlin: Friedrich Ebert Stiftung, Dialogue on Globalization Briefing Paper 4, April 2008).

32 See R. H. Jackson, 'The Weight of Ideas in Decolonization: Normative Change in International Relations', in J. Goldstein and R. O. Keohane, eds, *Ideas and Foreign Policy: Beliefs, institutions, and political change* (Ithaca, NY: Cornell University Press, 1993), pp. 111–38.

33 For a study of the diffusion of the struggle against apartheid into a global norm, see A. Klotz, *Norms in International Relations: The struggle against apartheid* (Ithaca, NY: Cornell University Press, 1995).

34 See M. Mazower, *No Enchanted Palace: The end of empire and the ideological origins of the United Nations* (Princeton, NJ: Princeton University Press, 2009).

35 See R. Thakur, 'India After Nonalignment', *Foreign Affairs* 71:2 (Spring 1992), pp. 165–82.

36 R. Thakur, 'The Nuclear Option in India's Security Policy', *Asia Pacific Review* 5:1 (Spring/Summer 1998), pp. 39–60.

37 'Faced with US-led UN coercion, an isolated, sullen and resentful India is more likely to respond with an open nuclear programme, including a . . . series of nuclear tests.' R. Thakur, 'Nuclear India needs coaxing, not coercion', *Australian* (Sydney), 6 September 1996. The UN General Assembly vote on the CTBT was held on 10 September 1996.

38 See E. Newman, R. Thakur and J. Tirman, eds, *Multilateralism Under Challenge? Power, international order, and structural change* (Tokyo: United Nations University Press, 2006.)

39 D. Nayyar, *Developing Countries in the World Economy: The future in the past?* (Helsinki: UN University World Institute for Development Economics Research, WIDER Annual Lecture 12, 2009), p. 41.

40 Se Sung Won Kim, D. P. Fidler and S. Ganguly, 'Eastphalia Rising? Asian Influence and the Fate of Human Security', *World Policy Journal* 26:2 (Summer 2009), pp. 53–64.

41 As T. Garton Ash notes, 'in the market of geopolitics, as in financial markets, expectations are also realities'; 'Europe is sleepwalking to decline. We need a Churchill to wake it up', *Guardian*, May 20, 2010.

## 2 Non-intervention in international relations: a case study

1 Published originally in *Political Science* 42:1 (July 1990), pp. 26–61; reprinted with permission.

2 R. Naidu (spokesman for Bavadra), 'The Rise and Fall of Fijian Democracy', *Dominion* (Wellington), 26 January 1988. The best account of the many layered causes of the coup is to be found in B. V. Lal, *Power and Prejudice: The making of the Fiji Crisis* (Wellington: New Zealand Institute of International Affairs, 1988). See also R. Alley, 'The Military Coup in Fiji', *Round Table* 76 (October 1987); R. Thakur and A. Wood, 'Paradise Regained or Paradise Defiled? Fiji under Military Rule', *International Studies* 26 (January–March 1989).

3 *Otago Daily Times* (Dunedin), 20 January 1989.

4 H. Bull, 'Intervention in the Third World', in H. Bull, ed., *Intervention in World Politics* (Oxford: Oxford University Press, 1984).

5 D. Horovitz, 'Israel Proposed Joint Strike with India on Pakistani Reactor', *Jerusalem Post*, 22 February 1987; E. Silver, 'Israel Willing to Help India Raid Pak N-plant', *Statesman Weekly* (Calcutta), 19 September 1987.

6   For a sceptical assessment of the justifications advanced for the Grenada inter-
    vention, see W. C. Gilmore, *The Grenada Intervention: Analysis and documentation*
    (New York: Facts on File, 1984).

7   An influential news magazine defended the Tanzanian intervention while decrying
    the Vietnamese invasion of a few months earlier; 'Installed by Invasion', *Economist*
    (London), 21 April 1979, pp. 16–17. For a recent study which concludes that
    the Vietnamese invasion of Cambodia was essentially justifiable, see G. Klintworth,
    *Vietnam's Intervention in Cambodia in International Law* (Canberra: Australian
    Government Publishing Service, 1989).

8   See, in particular, R. A. Falk, ed., *The Vietnam War and International Law*
    (Princeton, NJ: Princeton University Press/American Society of International Law,
    1968).

9   H. Bull, 'Introduction', in Bull, ed., *Intervention in World Politics*, p. 4.

10  M. Ayoob, 'The Third World in the System of States: Acute Schizophrenia or
    Growing Pains?' *International Studies Quarterly* 33 (March 1989), p. 69.

11  *Times* (London), 10 December 1983.

12  J. E. Hare and C. B. Joynt, *Ethics and International Affairs* (London: Palgrave
    Macmillan, 1982), p. 152.

13  C. R. Beitz, *Political Theory and International Relations* (Princeton, NJ: Princeton
    University Press, 1979), p. 81.

14  Ibid., p. 82.

15  R. Cole and H. Hughes, *The Fiji Economy, May 1987: Problems and prospects*
    (Canberra: National Centre for Development Studies, Australian National
    University, 1988), pp. xii, 69–73. See also *Pacific Economic Bulletin* 3 (December
    1988), pp. 5–6. Fiji's economy experienced a remarkable recovery in 1988–9.

16  See K. Skubiszewski, 'Use of Force by States', in M. Sørensen, ed., *Manual of
    Public International Law* (London: Macmillan, 1968), pp. 758–64.

17  *Australia's Relations with the South Pacific*. Report of the Joint Committee on Foreign
    Affairs and Trade, Parliament of Australia (Canberra: Australian Government
    Publishing Service, 1989), p. 152.

18  Ibid., p. 153.

19  'There would appear to be no room in world diplomacy for genuine human anger
    over unspeakable acts, as the international conference on Cambodia in Paris seems
    to have attested once again'; S. Schanberg, 'Old Wounds, New Bones', *Guardian
    Weekly*, 10 September 1989, p. 11. The power of popular anger and the resulting
    erosion of regime legitimacy has been dramatically manifested across Eastern Europe
    in 1989–90.

20  R. Higgins, 'Intervention and International Law', in Bull, ed., *Intervention in World
    Politics*, p. 35.

21  M. Akehurst, 'Humanitarian Intervention', in Bull, ed., *Intervention in World Politics*.

22  T. J. Farer, 'The UN and Human Rights: More than a Whimper, Less than a
    Roar', in A. Roberts and B. Kingsbury, eds, *United Nations, Divided World*
    (Oxford: Oxford University Press, 1988), p. 97.

23  *UN Chronicle* 25 (March 1988), p. 45.

24  See L. Henkin, ed., *The International Bill of Rights: The covenant on civil and political
    rights* (New York: Columbia University Press, 1981).

25  Farer, 'UN and Human Rights', p. 99.

26  Ibid., p. 123.

27  D. P. Forsythe, 'The United Nations and Human Rights, 1945–1985', *Political
    Science Quarterly* 100 (Summer 1985), p. 252.

28  H. Tolley, 'The United Nations Commission on Human Rights', quoted in
    Forsythe, 'UN and Human Rights', p. 257.

29    S. Hoffmann, 'The Hell of Good Intentions', *Foreign Policy* 29 (Winter 1977–8), p. 8.

30    See, for example, A. W. Singham and S. Hune, *Non-Alignment in an Age of Alignments* (London: Zed, 1986), pp. 357–64.

31    R. Aron, *Peace and War: A theory of international relations*, translated by R. Howard and A. B. Fox (New York: Frederick A. Praeger, 1967), pp. 99–104, 147–9.

32    H. Bull, 'Conclusion', in Bull, ed., *Intervention in World Politics,* p. 189.

33    G. Schwarzenberger, 'Hegemonial Intervention', *Year Book of World Affairs* 13 (1959), p. 262.

34    S. Hoffmann, 'The Problem of Intervention', in Bull, ed., *Intervention in World Politics*, p. 25.

35    For an analysis of potential tension between indigenous rights and democratic principles, see R. Mulgan, 'Should Indigenous Peoples Have Special Rights?' *Orbis* 33 (Summer 1989).

36    See S. Ryan, 'Explaining Ethnic Conflict: The Neglected International Dimension', *Review of International Studies* 14 (July 1988).

37    'Some Developments in the Analytic Study of Pluralism', in M. G. Smith and L. Kuper, eds, *Pluralism in Africa* (Berkeley, CA: University of California Press, 1971).

38    L. Kuper, *Race, Class and Power: Ideology and revolutionary change in plural societies* (London: Aldine Transaction, 1974), p. 65.

39    By the end of 1989, the Bureau of Statistics reported that, for the first time since 1946, ethnic Fijians outnumbered Fiji-Indians 48.4:46.4 per cent. *Otago Daily Times*, 13 December 1989.

40    For the distinction between the two roles, see C. Pentland, 'International Organizations', in J. N. Rosenau, K. W. Thompson and G. Boyd, ed., *World Politics: An Introduction* (New York: The Free Press, 1976).

41    E. Luard, 'Collective Intervention', in Bull, ed., *Intervention in World Politics*, p. 157.

42    See *UN Chronicle* 25 (June 1988), p. 63.

43    See, for example, A. Eilan, *The General Assembly: Can it be salvaged?* (Washington, DC: Heritage Foundation, 1984); T. M. Franck, *Nation Against Nation: What happened to the UN dream and what the U.S. can do about it* (New York: Oxford University Press, 1985).

44    J. Donnelly, 'Human Rights at the United Nations 1955–85: The Question of Bias', *International Studies Quarterly* 32 (September 1988).

45    Forsythe, 'UN and Human Rights', p. 258.

46    Although to be fair, 'It might even be said that in the field of human rights there has been a notable departure on many occasions from the usually acquiescent attitude of . . . UN bodies'; A. Williams, 'The United Nations and Human Rights', in P. Taylor and A. J. R. Groom, eds, *International Institutions at Work* (London: Pinter, 1988), p. 120.

47    *Amnesty International Report 1988* (London: Amnesty International, 1988), pp. 156–7.

48    See J. G. Ruggie, 'Human Rights and the Future International Community', *Daedalus* 112 (Fall 1983).

49    M. W. Zacher, *International Conflicts and Collective Security, 1946–77* (New York: Praeger, 1979), p. 213.

50    Australia, the Cook Islands, the Federated States of Micronesia, Fiji, Kiribati, the Marshall Islands, Nauru, New Zealand, Niue, Papua New Guinea, the Solomon Islands, Tonga, Tuvalu, Vanuatu and Western Samoa.

51    Television New Zealand, *Eyewitness News*, 17 October 1988.

52    See Forsythe, 'UN and Human Rights'.

53  *Australian Foreign Affairs Record* (AFAR) 58 (September/October 1987), p. 456.

54  K. Bain in his book *Treachery at 10*; as reported in P. Hallwright, 'Was Lange Influenced by Indian Influx Threat?' *Otago Daily Times*, 27 March 1989.

55  For a survey of categories of reservations about recognizing sovereign states, see A. James, *Sovereign Statehood* (London: Allen & Unwin, 1986), Chapter 6.

56  The literature on sanctions is fairly considerable by now. For relatively recent works, see D. A. Baldwin, *Economic Statecraft* (Princeton, NJ: Princeton University Press, 1985); M. S. Daoudi and M. S. Dajani, *Economic Sanctions: Ideals and experience* (London: Routledge & Kegan Paul, 1983); G. C. Hufbauer and J. J. Schott, *Economic Sanctions Reconsidered: History and current policy* (Washington, DC: Institute for International Economics, 1985); K. R. Nossal, 'International Sanctions as International Punishment', *International Organization* 43 (Spring 1989).

57  D. A. Baldwin, 'Foreign Aid, Intervention, and Influence', *World Politics* 21 (April 1969), p. 426.

58  J. N. Rosenau, *The Scientific Study of Foreign Policy* (New York: Nichols Publishing Co., 1971), p. 93.

59  Quoted in P. Kelly, 'Minister for the Long Haul', *Weekend Australian*, 19–20 November 1988, p. 41.

60  In an address to the Foreign Correspondents' Association in Sydney on 23 September 1988; AFAR 59 (September 1988), pp. 348–50.

61  See M. Gubb, 'The Australian Military Response to the First Fijian Coup – An Assessment', *Australian Defence 2000* (January 1989), pp. 19–26.

62  R. Mandel, 'Gunboat Diplomacy', *International Studies Quarterly* 30 (March 1986), p. 73.

63  '. . . neither powers conferred by . . . the Constitution nor the implied emergency powers gave legal validity to the Governor-General's actions' of dissolving Parliament and dismissing Prime Minister and cabinet; F. M. Brookfield, 'The Fiji Revolutions of 1987', *New Zealand Law Journal* (July 1988), p. 251.

64  Even though elections had just been held in April and produced a clear verdict, Prime Minister Bob Hawke declared on 26 May that 'if there were a new election in Fiji on the basis of the existing Constitution . . . that would be acceptable to this Government'. AFAR 58 (May 1987), p. 270. Similar views had been expressed by New Zealand Prime Minister Lange; *Post-cabinet Press Conference*, 18 May 1987, pp. 10–11: this is not a process he would advocate but 'clearly it would be a constitutionally proper course' – and could lead to reversal of the April election results.

65  S. Harden, ed., *Small is Dangerous: Micro states in a macro world* (New York: St. Martin's Press, 1985), p. 88.

66  *Pacific Islands Monthly* (February 1990), p. 34.

67  Speculation along these lines was reported in Hallwright, 'Was Lange Influenced by Indian Influx Threat?'.

68  In an address to the Wellington branch of the UN Association on 15 March 1989; text supplied to author by the office of the Minister of Foreign Affairs.

69  *Australia's Relations with the South Pacific*, pp. 215–17.

70  For the text of the statement, see AFAR 59 (January 1988), p. 21.

71  For the text of B. Hayden's news release, see AFAR 59 (March 1988), p. 114.

72  Cited in A. Bergin, 'The New Australian Policy on Recognition of States Only', *Australian Outlook* 42 (December 1988), p. 152.

73  Television New Zealand, *Eyewitness News,* 17 October 1988.

74  *Otago Daily Times,* 9 November 1988.

75  D. D. Raphael, 'Human Rights, Old and New', in D. D. Raphael, ed., *Political Theory and the Rights of Man* (London: Macmillan, 1967).

76    *Economist*, 9 April 1988, p. 30; *Otago Daily Times*, 31 March 1988.
77    A member of the Bavadra delegation to London after the coup was left with the impression that while the Queen's sympathy lay with the elected government, the Thatcher government's did not; confidential interview, February 1988.
78    *Observer* (London), 4 October 1987.
79    Ministry of External Affairs, Government of India, *Annual Report 1986–87* (New Delhi, 1987), p. 94.
80    For reports of Rajiv Gandhi's statements on the subject, see the *Statesman* (Calcutta), 22 and 23 May 1987. For a report of a statement to the Lok Sabha (the House of People, the lower house of India's Parliament) on 16 November 1987 by Minister of State for External Affairs K. Natwar Singh, see 'India May Take More Steps Against Fiji', *Statesman Weekly,* 21 November 1987, p. 4.
81    Confidential interviews, New Delhi, February 1988.
82    Rabuka denies charges of racism. In his view, there is a commercial need for Indians in Fiji, so long as they accept being out of political power. He would also like them to convert to Christianity, since at present they are 'heathens'. Nor can he tell with Indians 'if they're lying or not'. E. Dean and S. Ritova, *Rabuka: No other way – his own story of the Fijian Coup* (Sydney: Doubleday, 1988) pp. 120–1, 123, 125. With non-racists like this . . . .
83    Radio New Zealand, *Midday Report,* 20 November 1987.
84    M. Wight, 'Why Is There No International Theory?' in H. Butterfield and M. Wight, ed., *Diplomatic Investigations: Essays in the theory of international politics* (Cambridge, MA: Harvard University Press, 1966), p. 33.
85    For example A. Linklater, *Men and Citizens in the Theory of International Relations* (London: Palgrave Macmillan, 1982).
86    Akehurst, 'Humanitarian Intervention', p. 111.
87    Harden, ed., *Small is Dangerous,* p. 102.
88    For an Indian account of the intervention, see S. Gupta, 'Maldives: A Close Shave', *India Today,* 30 November 1988, pp. 28–32.
89    The coup was 'a mission that God has given me'; in *Rabuka: No other way*, p. 11. Claims of having God on his side are sprinkled throughout the 'authorized' biography.
90    W. F. Mackey, quoted in Ryan, 'Explaining Ethnic Conflict', p. 171.
91    S. Hoffmann, *The Political Ethics of International Relations* (New York: Carnegie Council on Ethics and International Affairs, 1988), p. 4.
92    S. Hoffmann, *Duties Beyond Borders* (Syracuse, NY: Syracuse University Press, 1981), p. 23.
93    Ibid., p. 11.
94    London: Macmillan, 1977.
95    See, for example, Beitz, *Political Theory and International Relations*; Linklater, *Men and Citizens in International Relations*; J. Mayall, ed., *The Community of States* (London: Allen & Unwin, 1982).

## 3 Kosovo, humanitarian intervention and the challenge of world order

1    Published originally as A. Schnabel and R. Thakur, 'Kosovo, the Changing Contours of World Politics and the Challenge of World Order' and 'Unbridled Humanitarianism: Between Justice, Power and Authority' in A. Schnabel and R. Thakur, eds, *Kosovo and the Challenge of Humanitarian Intervention: Selective indignation, collective action and international citizenship* (Tokyo: United Nations University Press, 2000), pp. 1–16 and 496–504; reprinted with permission.

2   R. Falk, 'Reflections on the Kosovo War', *Global Dialogue* 1:2 (Autumn 1999), p. 93.

3   'The Future of Kosovo: An Indefinite NATO Presence', *IISS Strategic Comments* 6:1 (January 2000), p. 1.

4   The most recent and authoritative statement of the dilemma is K. A. Annan, *Facing the Humanitarian Challenge: Towards a culture of prevention* (New York: United Nations Department of Public Information, 1999).

5   *Report of the Secretary-General Pursuant to General Assembly Resolution 53/35 (1998)* (New York: UN Secretariat, November 1999), para. 503. The text of the report is available on the Internet at www.un.org/News/ossg/srebrenica.html

6   Falk, 'Reflections on the Kosovo War', p. 93.

7   Ibid., p. 94. In fact Falk goes a lot further, arguing that the air war was a form of electronic blood sport. It was structurally similar to torture, he believes, in that the perpetrator chose the method by which to inflict pain while the victim was helpless to retaliate. Ibid., p. 96.

8   *Report of the Secretary-General Pursuant to General Assembly Resolution 53/35 (1998)*, para. 502.

9   For a succinct account of the KLA strategy, as well as a discourse on the many 'sub-texts' underlying NATO campaign, see M. McGwire, 'Why did we bomb Belgrade?', *International Affairs* 76:1 (January 2000), pp. 1–24. In answering his question, McGwire is sceptical of the claim that humanitarianism had displaced geopolitical interests as the principal motive.

10  K. A. Annan, *We the Peoples: The role of the United Nations in the twenty-first century*. Report of the Secretary-General (New York: UN General Assembly, Doc. A/54/2000, 27 March 2000), para. 216.

11  For a short but authoritative claim of the achievements, see M. K. Albright, 'U.S. Should be Proud', *International Herald Tribune*, 31 March 2000.

12  'Edging Toward the Exit in Kosovo', editorial, *Los Angeles Times*, 17 March 2000. See also C. Layne and B. Schwarz, 'A Brutal Quagmire', *International Herald Tribune*, 31 March 2000.

13  'The future of Kosovo: An indefinite NATO presence', *IISS Strategic Comments* 6:1 (January 2000), p. 1.

## 4 Global norms and international humanitarian law: an Asian perspective

1   Published originally in *International Review of the Red Cross* 83: 841 (March 2001), pp. 19–44; reprinted with permission.

2   *Basic Facts about the United Nations* (New York: United Nations, 1998), pp. 267–8.

3   For yet another recent documentation of this, see E, Aydinli and J. Mathews, 'Are the Core and Periphery Irreconcilable? The Curious World of Publishing in Contemporary International Relations', *International Studies Perspectives,* December 2000, pp. 289–303.

4   This subsection is adapted from R. Thakur and W. Maley, 'The Ottawa Convention on Landmines: A Landmark Humanitarian Treaty in Arms Control?', *Global Governance* 5:3 (July–September 1999), pp. 275–77.

5   The classic statement of the apparent paradox remains that of H. Bull, *The Anarchical Society: A study of order in world politics* (London: Macmillan, 1977).

6   See M. Walzer, *Just and Unjust Wars: A moral argument with historical illustrations* (New York: Basic Books, 1992), and Geoffrey Best, *Humanity in Warfare: The modern history of the international law of armed conflicts* (London: Weidenfeld & Nicolson, 1983).

7   H. Dunant, *A Memory of Solferino* (Geneva: ICRC, 1986).

8    F. Kalshoven, *Constraints on the Waging of War* (Geneva: ICRC, 1991), pp. 8–18. There is, of course, a significant overlapping of these streams; see G. Best, *War and Law Since 1945* (Oxford: Oxford University Press), 1994, pp. 183–4.

9    For a compilation of relevant instruments, see A. Roberts and R. Guelff, eds, *Documents on the Laws of War*, 3rd edn (Oxford: Oxford University Press, 2000).

10   See the views of the majority of the International Court of Justice in *Legality of the Threat or Use of Nuclear Weapons, Advisory Opinion*, ICJ Reports 1996, p. 226, and 35 ILM 814.

11   R. A. Falk, *The Status of Law in International Society* (Princeton, NJ: Princeton University Press, 1970), p. 177.

12   P. C. Szasz, 'General Law-making Processes', in C. C. Joyner, ed., *The United Nations and International Law* (Cambridge: Cambridge University Press, 1997), pp. 32–3.

13   D. W. Greig, 'Sources of International Law', in S. Blay, R. Piotrowicz and B. M. Tsamenyi, eds, *Public International Law: An Australian perspective* (Melbourne: Oxford University Press, 1997), p. 86.

14   J. Linehan, 'The Law of Treaties', in ibid., p. 107.

15   Thakur and Maley, 'Ottawa Convention on Landmines'.

16   Convention on the Prohibition of the Use, Stockpiling, Production and Transfer of Anti-personnel Mines and on their Destruction, 18 September 1997.

17   I had the privilege of chairing the four-day conference in Sydney.

18   International Convention on Economic, Social and Cultural Rights, and International Convention on Civil and Political Rights, both 16 December 1966.

19   Nelson Mandela notes in his autobiography, for instance, that sanctions were the best lever to force changes on South Africa's apartheid regime, and even in the early 1990s he was still urging the US Congress not to loosen US sanctions as favoured by the Bush Administration. N. Mandela, *Long Walk to Freedom* (London: Abacus, 1994), pp. 697–9. He was unhappy that '[e]ven during the bleakest years on Robben Island, Amnesty International would not campaign for us on the ground that we had pursued an armed struggle'. Ibid., p. 734.

20   Rome Statute of the International Criminal Court, 17 July 1998.

21   For a discussion of the origins, evolution and limitations of geographical representation in the United Nations, see R. Thakur, ed., *What is Equitable Geographic Representation in the Twenty-first Century?* (Tokyo: United Nations University, 1999).

22   The seat of Europe today is Brussels. For a recent account of the scale of humanitarian atrocities committed by Belgium in its African colony, see A. Hochschild, *King Leopold's Ghost*, (Boston, MA: Houghton Mifflin, 1999).

23   *Bringing Them Home: Report of the National Inquiry into the Separation of Aboriginal and Torres Strait Islander Children from Their Families* (Sydney: Human Rights and Equal Opportunity Commission, 1997).

24   See A. Saikal, 'Afghans are Mistreated in Australia', *International Herald Tribune*, 4 January 2001.

25   I. L. Claude, 'The Evolution of Concepts of Global Governance and the State in the Twentieth Century', paper delivered at the annual conference of the Academic Council on the United Nations System (ACUNS), Oslo, 16–18 June 2000. Claude does note, however, that the new norm 'has been no less challenged in principle and dishonoured in practice than was the old norm of non-intervention'.

26   J. Mueller and K. Mueller, 'Sanctions of Mass Destruction', *Foreign Affairs*, May/June 1999, pp. 43–53.

27   See J. Gordon, 'A Peaceful, Silent, Deadly Remedy: The Ethics of Economic Sanctions', *Ethics & International Affairs* 13 (1999), pp. 123–42; D. Christiansen and G. F. Powers, 'Economic Sanctions and Just-War Doctrine', in D. Cortright

and George A. Lopez, eds, *Economic Sanctions: Panacea or peacebuilding in a post-cold war world* (Boulder, CO: Westview, 1995), pp. 97–120; A. C. Pierce, 'Just War Principles and Economic Sanctions', *Ethics & International Affairs* 10 (1996), pp. 99–113; and A. Winkler, 'Just Sanctions', *Human Rights Quarterly* 21 (1999), pp. 133–55.

## 5 Intervention, sovereignty and the responsibility to protect: experiences from ICISS

1   Published originally in *Security Dialogue* 33:3 (September 2002), pp. 323–40; reprinted with permission.

2   For a full treatment of the Kosovo debate from a variety of perspectives, see A. Schnabel and R. Thakur, eds, *Kosovo and the Challenge of Humanitarian Intervention: Selective indignation, collective action and international citizenship* (Tokyo: United Nations University Press, 2000). See also *The Kosovo Report: Conflict, international response, lessons learned.* Report of the Independent International Commission on Kosovo (Oxford: Oxford University Press, 2000).

3   On Rwanda, see in particular A. J. Kuperman, *The Limits of Humanitarian Intervention: Genocide in Rwanda* (Washington, DC: Brookings, 2001); L. Melvern, *A People Betrayed: The role of the West in Rwanda's genocide* (London: Zed Books, 2000); and G. Prunier, *The Rwanda Crisis: History of a genocide* (New York: Columbia University Press, 1997).

4   *The Responsibility to Protect: Report of the International Commission on Intervention and State Sovereignty* (Ottawa: International Development Research Centre for ICISS, 2001). The Report is available also on the website at www.iciss.gc.ca.

5   Clearly, as a Commissioner, I am writing as a partisan advocate, not an independent critic.

6   The Commission's own supplementary volume (see n9 below) provides sixteen pages of bibliographic entries under 'Humanitarian Intervention' and 'Sovereignty and Intervention', plus many more entries under specific case studies including Kosovo and East Timor.

7   The co-chairs were Gareth Evans and Mohamed Sahnoun, the remaining ten Commissioners being Gisele Côté-Harper, Lee Hamilton, Michael Ignatieff, Vladimir Lukin, Klaus Naumann, Cyril Ramaphosa, Fidel Ramos, Cornelio Sommaruga, Eduardo Stein and R. Thakur. Their biodata can be found in the Report or on the Commission's website (n4 above).

8   Commission meetings were held in Ottawa (Nov 2000), Maputo (March 2001), New Delhi (June 2001), Wakefield, Canada (August 2000) and Brussels (September 2001). Round tables and consultative meetings were held, in chronological order, in Ottawa, Geneva, London, Maputo, Washington, DC, Santiago, Cairo, Paris, New Delhi, Beijing and St. Petersburg.

9   *The Responsibility to Protect: Research, bibliography, background.* Supplementary Volume to the Report of the International Commission on Intervention and State Sovereignty (Ottawa: International Development Research Centre for ICISS, 2001).

10   See H. Shinoda, *Re-examining Sovereignty: From classical theory to the global age* (New York: St. Martin's Press, 2000).

11   M. Ayoob, 'Humanitarian Intervention and State Sovereignty', *International Journal of Human Rights*, 6:1 (Spring 2002), pp. 81–102.

12   On this we owe an intellectual debt to F. M. Deng *et al.*, *Sovereignty as Responsibility: Conflict management in Africa* (Washington, DC: Brookings, 1996). See also F. M. Deng, 'Reconciling Sovereignty with Responsibility: A Basis for

International Humanitarian Action', in J. Harbeson and D. Rothchild, eds, *Africa in World Politics: Post-cold war challenges* (Boulder, CO: Westview, 1995), pp. 295–310.

13    As the Report puts it, 'While there is not yet a sufficiently strong basis to claim the emergence of a new principle of customary international law, growing state and regional organization practice as well as Security Council precedent suggest an emerging guiding principle – which in the Commission's view could properly be termed "the responsibility to protect"' (p. 15, para. 2.24).

14    These are clearly derived from the just war doctrine. But because the doctrine is rooted in the Christian tradition, acknowledging its religious roots would not necessarily have been the wisest political decision. This is just one example, albeit an interesting one, of the clash of academic and policy cultures.

15    For a review of this debate, see in particular S. Chesterman, *Just War or Just Peace? Humanitarian intervention and international law* (Oxford: Oxford University Press, 2001), pp. 226–32 and N. Wheeler, *Saving Strangers: Humanitarian intervention in international society* (Oxford: Oxford University Press, 2000), pp. 33–51.

16    See D. Freestone and E. Hey, eds, *The Precautionary Principle and International Law: The challenge of implementation* (London: Kluwer Law International, 1996); J. Cameron, 'The Precautionary Principle', in G. P. Sampson and W. B. Chambers, eds, *Trade, Environment and the Millennium*, 2nd edn (Tokyo: United Nations University Press, 2002), pp. 287–319.

17    This normative inconsistency is fatal to the moral majority proponents of coalitions of the willing. Yet it is an obvious flaw – so much so that one may question whether failure to address it reflects intellectual laziness or moral duplicity. Can an intellectually coherent or morally consistent argument be advanced for any one or several of the P5 to lead such coalitions when faced with an actual or apprehended Security Council veto, if they are not prepared to give up the veto right?

18    J. Dhanapala, 'The Canberra Commission: Lessons Learned for a Future Commission', keynote address at the UN University and University of Waterloo Conference on the Ideas-Institutional Nexus, Waterloo, Ontario, 18 May 2002; and J. Dhanapala and R. Thakur, 'Let's Get Together Against Terrorism', *International Herald Tribune*, 4 June 2002.

## 6 In defence of the responsibility to protect

1    Published originally in *International Journal of Human Rights* 7:3 (Autumn 2003), pp. 160–78; reprinted with permission.

2    G. Evans and M. Sahnoun, 'The Responsibility to Protect', *Foreign Affairs* 81:6 (November/December 2002), p. 100.

3    We concluded that there must be a reasonable chance of success in halting or averting the suffering that has justified the intervention, with the consequences of action not likely to be worse than the consequences of inaction.

4    See the section on the 1971 Indian intervention in *The Responsibility to Protect: Research, bibliography and background.* Supplementary volume to the Report of the International Commission on Intervention and State Sovereignty. (Ottawa: International Development Research Centre, 2001), pp. 54–6.

5    See R. Thakur, 'Global Norms and International Humanitarian Law: An Asian Perspective', *International Review of the Red Cross* 83: 841 (March 2001), pp. 19–44.

6    See, for example, J. Hoagland, 'Time for Bush to Cast War Aims in Iron', *Japan Times,* 28 October 2002, reprinting an article from the *Washington Post* (where Hoagland is a columnist).

7    R. Haass, 'When Nations Forfeit their Sovereign Privileges', *International Herald Tribune*, 7 February 2003.

8    My views on this can be found in a series of three op-ed articles in the *Japan Times*: R. Thakur, 'Peril of Pre-emptive Thinking', 20 October 2002; 'US Test of UN Relevance', 9 February 2003; and 'US Bears Costs as UN is Challenged', 12 March 2003.

9    Of course, this does not address other parts of the Bush administration's justification, from the threat to regional and international security posed by Iraqi weapons of mass destruction to allegations of Iraqi complicity in international terrorism.

10   Summaries of the roundtable discussions can be found in *The Responsibility to Protect: Research, bibliography and background*, III.3, pp. 349–98.

## 7 Collective security and the use of force: reflections on the report of the high-level panel on threats, challenges and change

1    Published originally in N. Azimi and Chang Li Lin, eds, *United Nations as Peace-keeper and Nation-Builder: Continuity and change – what lies ahead* (Leiden: Martinus Nijhoff for the UN Institute for Training and Research, Geneva and the Institute of Policy Studies, Singapore, 2005), pp. 31–48; reprinted with permission.

2    Full disclosure: As well as being a serving and senior UN official, I was a Commissioner of the International Commission on Intervention and State Sovereignty (ICISS) and indeed one of the principal authors of its report, *The Responsibility to Protect* (2001), whose main normative conclusions are incorporated into the report of the high-level panel that is the subject of this chapter; and the principal writer (but not author) of the UN Secretary-General's second reform report in 2002, which too gets a strong endorsement from the high-level panel.

3    *Hindu*, 4 January 2005.

4    For example the *Japan Times*, 7 January 2005.

5    *Japan Times*, 7 January 2005.

6    The text of his address can be found at www.un.org/apps/sg/printsgstats.asp?nid=517.

7    No one has questioned the eminence and distinction of any one of the members individually; it is the balance among the group that raised many eyebrows.

8    There was similar dissatisfaction at the choice of an American professor to head the Millennium Development Goals project. When very good people with experience of living and working in poor developing countries are readily available, it struck some as curious that the project should be led by someone whose knowledge of poverty is solely academic. On the same vein, finally, people at ministerial and senior ambassadorial levels have commented that, starting with the Secretary-General and moving down the list, the ranking Asian UN official with the senior line responsibility for dealing with Asia is at the sixth or seventh rung in the hierarchy.

9    *A More Secure World: Our shared responsibility*. Report of the High-level Panel on Threats, Challenges and Change. (New York: United Nations, document A/59/565, 2 December 2004), p. 54, para. 184.

10   *The Responsibility to Protect: Report of the International Commission on Intervention and State Sovereignty* (Ottawa: International Development Research Centre for ICISS, 2001). The Report is also available on the website at www.iciss.gc.ca.

11   Along the same line, see S. Chesterman, M. Ignatieff and R. Thakur, eds, *Making States Work: State failure and the crisis of governance* (Tokyo: United Nations University Press, 2005).

12   The United Nations University is already engaged in an exploration of this in partnership with two Canadian think tanks. See R. Thakur, 'Time is Ripe to Establish G-20', *Japan Times,* 12 June 2004.

13   See R. Thakur, 'Knives out for Kofi Annan', *Japan Times,* 4 December 2004.

## 8 The responsibility to protect and prosecute: the parallel erosion of sovereignty and impunity

1   Published originally in G. Z. Capaldo, ed., *The Global Community: Yearbook of international law and jurisprudence 2007*, Vol. 1 (New York: Oxford University Press, 2008), pp. 39–61; reprinted with permission.

2   One of the best studies to map the changes in armed conflict since 1945 is A. Mack *et al.* eds, *Human Security Report 2005* (Oxford: Oxford University Press, 2005).

3   K. A. Annan, 'Two Concepts of Sovereignty', *The Economist*, 18 September 1999, pp. 49–50.

4   For an exploration of the changes from classical peacekeeping to peace operations by the United Nations, see R. Thakur and A. Schnabel, eds, *United Nations Peacekeeping Operations: Ad hoc missions, permanent engagement* (Tokyo: United Nations University Press, 2001) and A. J. Bellamy, P. Williams and S. Griffin, *Understanding Peacekeeping* (Oxford: Polity Press, 2004).

5   *Report of the Panel on United Nations Peace Operations* (A/55/305-S/2000/809), 21 August 2000, p. viii. For a comment on the Brahimi Report, see D. M. Malone and R. Thakur, 'UN Peacekeeping: Lessons Learned?' *Global Governance* 7:1 (January–March 2001), pp. 11–17.

6   *Report of the Panel on United Nations Peace Operations*, para. 51.

7   The language and the argument of the Brahimi Report here borrowed from a speech of Kofi Annan himself to the Council on Foreign Relations in New York in 1999; see I. Johnstone, 'The Role of the UN Secretary-General: The Power of Persuasion Based on Law', *Global Governance* 9:4 (October–December 2003), p. 444.

8   M. Ignatieff, *Human Rights as Politics and Idolatry*, edited and introduced by A. Gutmann (Princeton, NJ: Princeton University Press, 2001), p. 163.

9   J. Donnelly, 'Human Rights and Asian Values: A Defense of Western Universalism', in J. R. Bauer and D. A. Bell, eds, *The East Asian Challenge for Human Rights* (Cambridge: Cambridge University Press, 1999), p. 68.

10   See R. Gellately and B. Kiernan, eds, *The Spectre of Genocide: Mass murder in historical perspective* (Cambridge: Cambridge University Press, 2003) and M. Shaw, *War and Genocide: Organized killing in modern society* (Cambridge: Polity Press, 2003).

11   Lemkin was discovered weeping in a UN corridor at the news and described the convention as an epitaph for his mother who had been among many members of his family killed in the Holocaust; M. Ignatieff, 'The Legacy of Raphael Lemkin', lecture delivered at the US Holocaust Memorial Musuem Washington, DC, 13 December 2001, available at: www.ushmm.org/conscience/events/ignatieff/ignatieff.php.

12   United Nations, *Press Release* SG/SM/7842, 13 June 2001.

13   One of the best single studies of human security is S. N. MacFarlane and Yuen Foong Khong, *Human Security and the United Nations: A critical history* (Bloomington, IN: Indiana University Press for the UN Intellectual History Project, 2006).

14   T. Benner, W. H. Reinecke and J. M. Witte, *Shaping Globalization: The role of global public policy networks* (2002), p. 4; downloadable from: www.globalpublic policy.net.

15    R. H. Jackson, *Quasi-States: Sovereignty, international relations and the Third World* (Cambridge: Cambridge University Press, 1990). See also S. D. Krasner, *Sovereignty: Organized hypocrisy* (Princeton, NJ: Princeton University Press, 2001).

16    F. M. Deng *et al.*, *Sovereignty as Responsibility: Conflict management in Africa* (Washington, DC: Brookings, 1996) and F. M. Deng, 'Frontiers of Sovereignty', *Leiden Journal of International Law* 8, no. 2 (1995): 249–86. See also, T. G. Weiss and D. A. Korn, *Internal Displacement: Conceptualization and its consequences* (London: Routledge, 2006).

17    See B. D. Lepard, *Rethinking Humanitarian Intervention* (University Park, PA: Pennsylvania State University Press, 2002), pp. 7–23.

18    International Commission on Intervention and State Sovereignty, *The Responsibility to Protect* (Ottawa: International Development Research Centre, 2001).

19    *2005 World Summit Outcome*, adopted by UN General Assembly as Resolution A/RES/60/1, (24 October 2005), paras 138–40.

20    See 'The Princeton Principles on Universal Jurisdiction', adopted by distinguished jurists around the world in 2001, published by the Program in Law and Public Affairs, Princeton University, available at: www.law.uc.edu/morgan/newsdir/unive_jur.pdf.

21    This still casts a shadow over East Asian regional relations. The annual visit by Prime Minister Junichiro Koizumi to Tokyo's Yasukuni Shrine to honour Japan's 2.4 million soldiers killed in war aroused fierce opposition from China and the Koreas because 14 Class A convicted war criminals are also interred there. Defenders of his visit retorted that the convictions were based on victors' justice. See 'Separation of War Criminals "Will Never Happen": Yasukuni', *Japan Times*, 5 June 2005. Parliamentary secretary Masahiro Morioka asked 'What tribunal was the Tokyo tribunal? Both sides do wrong in a war. It is erroneous to label only countries that win as right and nations that lose as wrong'; 'Morioka again slams war tribunal', *Japan Times*, 23 June 2005.

22    See Y. Beigbeder and T. Van Boven, *Judging War Criminals: The politics of international justice* (New York: St. Martin's Press, 1999); S. R. Ratner and J. S. Abrams, *Accountability for Human Rights Atrocities in International Law: Beyond the Nuremberg legacy*, 2nd edn (Oxford: Clarendon Press, 2001); D. Scheffer, 'The United States and the International Criminal Court', *American Journal of International Law* 93:1 (January 1999), pp. 12–22; and S. B. Sewall and C. Keysen, eds, *The United States and the International Criminal Court: National security and international law* (Lanham, MD: Rowman & Littlefield, 2000).

23    G. J. Bass, *Stay the Hand of Vengeance: The politics of war crimes tribunals* (Princeton, NJ: Princeton University Press, 2000), p. 283.

24    C. Bassiouni, 'Negotiating the Treaty of Rome on the Establishment of the I.C.C.', *Cornell International Law Journal* 32:3 (1999), p. 457.

25    W. Schabas, 'Balancing the Rights of the Accused with the Imperatives of the Accountability', in R. Thakur and P. Malcontent, eds, *From Sovereign Impunity to International Accountability: The search for justice in a world of states* (Tokyo: United Nations University Press, 2004), pp. 154–68.

26    J. Alvarez, 'The UN Security Council: Are There Checks to Provide Balance?', *Law Quadrangle Notes* (University of Michigan Law School) (Fall 1994), p. 43.

27    K. A. Annan, *Report of the Secretary-General on the Work of the Organization* (New York: United Nations, 2004), para. 223.

28    H. Owada, 'The Creation of the International Criminal Court: A Critical Analysis', in R. K. Dixit and C. Jayaraj, eds, *Dynamics of International Law in the New Millennium* (New Delhi: Manak, for the Indian Society of International Law, 2004), p. 101. Owada was a member of the Japanese delegation to the Rome conference and has since been elected as a Judge of the ICJ.

29    M. H. Morris, 'Democracy, Global Governance and the International Criminal Court', in Thakur and Malcontent, eds, *From Sovereign Impunity to International Accountability*, p. 191.

30    C. Chinkin, 'Gender-related Crimes: A Feminist Perspective', in Thakur and Malcontent, eds, *From Sovereign Impunity to International Accountability*, p. 128.

31    The growing literature on the subject includes Bass, *Stay the Hand of Vengeance*; R. J. Goldstone, *For Humanity: Reflections of a war crimes investigator* (New Haven, CT: Yale University Press, 2001); M. Minow, *Between Vengeance and Forgiveness: Facing history after genocide and mass violence* (Boston, MA: Beacon Press, 1998).

32    For a study of the issue, see Y. Shany, *The Competing Jurisdictions of International Courts and Tribunals* (Oxford: Oxford University Press, 2003).

33    See, for example, P. X. Kelley and R. F. Turner, 'War Crimes and the White House', *Washington Post*, 26 July 2007, p. A21. Their concern was about tortures authorized by the White House and committed by US personnel. General (retired) Kelley was appointed commandant of the Marine Corps (1983–7) by President Ronald Reagan; Turner served as legal counsel in the Reagan White House.

34    See R. Johansen, ed., *A United Nations Emergency Peace Service to Prevent Genocide and Crimes Against Humanity*, Global Action to Prevent War, Nuclear Age Peace Foundation, World Federalist Movement (2006) available at: www.globalaction pw.org/uneps/UNEPS_PUBLICATION.pdf.

## 9 R2P: from idea to norm – and action?

1    Published originally in *Global Responsibility to Protect* 1:1 (January–March 2009), pp. 22–53; reprinted with permission.

2    Pope Benedict XVI, 'Address to the General Assembly of the United Nations', UNO, New York (Vatican City: Holy See Press Office, 18 April 2008).

3    International Commission on Intervention and State Sovereignty, *The Responsibility to Protect* (Ottawa: International Development Research Centre, 2001).

4    H. Bull, *The Anarchical Society: A study of order in world politics* (New York: Columbia University Press, 1977).

5    K. A. Annan, 'A Progress Report on UN Renewal', speech to the UN Association – UK, London, 31 January 2006, *New World* (journal of UNA-UK), April–June 2006, p. 8.

6    Pope Benedict XVI, 'Address to the General Assembly of the United Nations'.

7    For details, see T. G. Weiss and D. A. Korn, *Internal Displacement: Conceptualization and its consequences* (London: Routledge, 2006).

8    The examples are drawn from R. Thakur, *The Government and Politics of India* (London: Macmillan, 1995).

9    L. Axworthy, *Navigating a New World: Canada's global future* (Toronto: Alfred A. Knopf Canada, 2003), 414. Gareth Evans has made clear this historical link in *The Responsibility to Protect: Halting mass atrocity crimes* (Washington, DC: Brookings Institution, 2008).

10    See, for example, F. M. Deng and I. W. Zartman, eds, *Conflict Resolution in Africa* (Washington, DC: Brookings Institution, 1991); F. M. Deng and T. Lyons, eds, *African Reckoning: A quest for good governance*, (Washington, DC: Brookings Institution, 1998); and F. M. Deng, 'Reconciling Sovereignty with Responsibility: A Basis for International Humanitarian Action', in J. W. Harbeson and D. Rothschild, eds, *Africa in World Politics: Post-cold war challenges* (Boulder, CO: Westview, 1995), pp. 295–310.

11    R. Cohen, *Human Rights Protection for Internally Displaced Persons* (Washington, DC: Refugee Policy Group, 1991), p. 1.

12   See K. J. Holsti, *War, the State and the State of War* (Cambridge: Cambridge University Press, 1996).

13   See R. Thakur and C. A. Thayer, eds, *A Crisis of Expectations: UN peacekeeping in the 1990s* (Boulder, CO: Westview, 1995).

14   *Report of the Panel on United Nations Peace Operations*, UN doc., A/55/305-S/2000/809, 21 August 2000, para. 50.

15   For further details, see T. G. Weiss, *Military-Civilian Interactions: Humanitarian crises and the responsibility to protect* (Lanham, MD: Rowman & Littlefield, 2004), 2nd edn, pp. 191–214.

16   Greenberg Research, *The People on War Report* (Geneva: ICRC, 1999), p. xvi.

17   A. Donini, L. Minear, I. Smillie, T. van Baarda and A. C. Welch, *Mapping the Security Environment: Understanding the perceptions of local communities, peace support operations and assistance agencies* (Medford, MA: Feinstein International Famine Centre, June 2005), p. 53.

18   See R. Thakur, *The United Nations, Peace and Security: From collective security to the responsibility to protect* (Cambridge: Cambridge University Press, 2006), Chapter 14, 'The Political Role of the Secretary-General'; and S. Chesterman, ed., *Secretary or General? The UN Secretary-General in world politics* (Cambridge: Cambridge University Press, 2007).

19   R. Thakur's notes from that event.

20   K. A. Annan, *The Question of Intervention: Statements by the Secretary-General* (New York: UN, 1999), p. 7.

21   K. A. Annan, *The Question of Intervention* and '*We the Peoples': The United Nations in the 21st century* (New York: UN, 2000). For a discussion of the controversy surrounding the speech in September 1999, see T. G. Weiss, 'The Politics of Humanitarian Ideas', *Security Dialogue* 31:1 (2000), pp. 11–23.

22   For an overview, see M. Ayoob, 'Humanitarian Intervention and International Society', *Global Governance* 7:3 (2001), pp. 225–30; and R. Jackson, *The Global Covenant: Human conduct in a world of states* (Oxford: Oxford University Press, 2000).

23   For elaboration, see Thakur, *The United Nations, Peace and Security*, Chapter 12, 'Developing Countries and the Eroding Non-intervention Norm'.

24   T. G. Weiss, T. Carayannis, L. Emmerij and R. Jolly, *UN Voices: The struggle for development and social justice* (Bloomington, IN: Indiana University Press, 2005), p. 378.

25   *Report of the Secretary-General on the Work of the Organization*, UN document A/54/1 (1999), p. 48.

26   Commission meetings were held in Ottawa (November 2000), Maputo (March 2001), New Delhi (June 2001), Wakefield, Canada (August 2000) and Brussels (September 2001). Round tables and consultative meetings were held, in chronological order, in Ottawa, Geneva, London, Maputo, Washington, DC, Santiago, Cairo, Paris, New Delhi, Beijing and St. Petersburg.

27   They are reflected in T. G. Weiss and D. Hubert, *The Responsibility to Protect: Research, bibliography and background* (Ottawa: IDRC, 2001), Part III.

28   G. Evans, 'Humanity Did Not Justify this War', *Financial Times*, 15 May 2003; R. Thakur, 'Chrétien Was Right: It's Time to Redefine a "Just War"', *Globe and Mail*, 22 July 2003 and 'Iraq and the Responsibility to Protect', *Behind the Headlines* 62:1 (Toronto: Canadian Institute of International Affairs, October 2004). However, one of the commissioners, Michael Ignatieff, a member of Parliament in Canada, justified the war.

29   The full list of Evans's extensive speeches and writings on R2P can be found on the website of the International Crisis Group: www.crisisgroup.org. Thakur's writings encompass a wide range of products from newspaper op-eds and scholarly articles to his book, *The United Nations, Peace and Security*. Weiss's writings are

mainly academic, especially *Humanitarian Intervention: Ideas in action* (Cambridge: Polity Press, 2007).

30   High-level Panel on Threats, Challenges and Change, *A More Secure World: Our shared responsibility* (New York: United Nations, A/59/565, December 2004), para. 201.

31   Ibid., para. 207.

32   *Position Paper of the People's Republic of China on the United Nations Reforms* (Beijing: 7 June 2005), downloaded from: http://news.xinhuanet.com/english/2005-06/08/content_3056817_3.htm, Part III.1, 'Responsibility to Protect'.

33   *American Interests and UN Reform: Report of the Task Force on the United Nations* (Washington, DC: US Institute of Peace, 2005), p. 15.

34   K. A. Annan, *In Larger Freedom: Towards development, security and human rights for all*. Report of the Secretary-General (New York: United Nations, document A/59/2005, 21 March 2005), paras 122–35.

35   *2005 World Summit Outcome*, adopted by UN General Assembly Resolution A/RES/60/1, 24 October 2005, paras 138–40.

36   For an assessment, see A. J. Bellamy, 'What Will Become of the Responsibility to Protect?' *Ethics and International Affairs* 20:2 (2006), pp.143–69.

37   ICISS, *R2P*, p. xi.

38   US Committee for Refugees, *World Refugee Survey 2005* (Washington, DC: USCR, 2005), p. 11.

39   M. Ayoob, 'Humanitarian Intervention and International Society', *The International Journal of Human Rights* 6:1 (2002), p. 84. For the context that drives Ayoob's scepticism, see S. Chesterman, M. Ignatieff and R. Thakur, eds, *State Failure and the Crisis of Governance: Making states work* (Tokyo: UN University Press, 2005).

40   D. Rieff, *A Bed for the Night: Humanitarianism in crisis* (New York: Simon & Schuster, 2002), p. 15.

41   A. J. Bellamy, 'Responsibility to Protect or Trojan Horse? The Crisis in Darfur and Humanitarian Intervention after Iraq', *Ethics & International Affairs* 19:2 (2005), p. 53.

42   Email to T. G. Weiss, 11 October 2005.

43   T. G. Weiss, 'The Sunset of Humanitarian Intervention? The Responsibility to Protect in a Unipolar World', *Security Dialogue* 35:2 (2004), pp. 135–53.

44   See R. Thakur, 'Humanitarian Intervention', in T. G. Weiss and S. Daws, eds, *Handbook of the United Nations* (Oxford: Oxford University Press, 2007), pp. 387–403; and Weiss and Hubert, *The Responsibility to Protect*, pp. 57–63.

45   A. Lewis, 'The Challenge of Global Justice Now', *Dædalus* 132:1 (2003), p. 8.

46   See T. G. Weiss, T. Carayannis and R. Jolly, 'The "Third" United Nations', *Global Governance* 15:1 (2009), pp. 123–42.

47   See R. Thakur and P. Malcontent, eds, *From Sovereign Impunity to International Accountability: The search for justice in a world of states* (Tokyo: United Nations University Press, 2004); and E. Hughes, W. A. Schabas and R. Thakur, eds, *Atrocities and International Accountability: Beyond transitional justice* (Tokyo: UN University Press, 2007).

48   Reissued in 2005 by Lawbook Exchange.

49   United Nations, *Press Release* SG/SM/7842, 13 June 2001.

50   See K. C. Moghalu, *The Politics of Justice for Rwanda's Genocide* (New York: Palgrave Macmillan, 2005); and *Global Justice: The politics of war crimes trials* (Westport, CT: Praeger International, 2006).

51   See R. S. Clark and M. Sann, eds, *The Prosecution of International Crimes: A critical study of the international tribunal for the former Yugoslavia* (New Brunswick, NJ.: Transaction, 1996).

52   See W. A. Schabas, *An Introduction to the International Criminal Court* (Cambridge: Cambridge University Press, 2001); and B. Broomhall, *International Justice and the International Criminal Court: Between state consent and the rule of law* (Oxford: Oxford University Press, 2003).

53   See R. Goldstone and A. Smith, *International Judicial Institutions: The architecture of international justice at home and abroad* (London: Routledge, 2008).

54   See the discussion in the Fifth Committee of the General Assembly at its twenty-eighth meeting on 4 March 2008 (GA/AB/3837) in the context of the publicly announced intention of the Secretary-General to appoint Professor Edward C. Luck as his special adviser with a focus on R2P.

55   Quoted in G. Evans, 'Delivering on the Responsibility to Protect: Four Misunderstandings, Three Challenges and How to Overcome Them', Address to SEF Symposium 2007, 'The Responsibility to Protect (R2P): Progress, Empty Promise or a License for "Humanitarian Intervention"', Bonn, 30 November 2007. See also 'Int'l Diplomatic Coup to Erode SL's Sovereignty?' *The Nation on Sunday* (Colombo), 27 January 2008, available at: www.nation.lk/2008/01/27/newsfe5.htm.

56   H. L. D. Mahindapala, 'Peace Secretariat Calls for UN Inquiry into Radhika Coomaraswamy, UN Under Secretary General, Stuck in NGO Scandal', *Lanka Times*, 29 January 2008, downloaded from: www.lankatimes.com/fullstory.php?id=7218.

57   See G. Evans, 'Humanity Did Not Justify this War', *Financial Times*, 15 May 2003; and R. Thakur, 'The Responsibility to Protect and the War on Saddam Hussein', in R. Thakur and Waheguru Pal Singh Sidhu, eds, *The Iraq Crisis and World Order: Structural, institutional and normative challenges* (Tokyo: United Nations University Press, 2006), pp. 464–78.

58   Weiss and Hubert, *The Responsibility to Protect*, 49–77. See also S. Krasner, *Sovereignty: Organized hypocrisy* (Princeton, NJ: Princeton University Press, 1999).

59   Ibid., pp. 79–126.

60   K. Naumann, J. Shalikashvili, L. Inge, J. Lanxade and H. van den Breemen, *Towards a Grand Strategy for an Uncertain World: Renewing transatlantic partnership* (Lunteren, Germany: Noaber Foundation, 2007).

61   See A. Zaw, 'Ballot for a Tyrant', *Guardian*, 12 May 2008.

62   K. A. Annan, '*We the Peoples*': The role of the United Nations in the twenty-first Century. Report of the Secretary-General (New York: UN, 2000), document A/54/2000, para. 216.

63   See www.GlobalCentre2p.org.

64   Daily Press Briefing by the Office of the Spokesperson for the Secretary-General, 28 January 2008; available at: www.un.org/News/briefings.

65   D. Tutu, 'Taking the Responsibility to Protect', *International Herald Tribune*, 19 February 2008.

## 10 The responsibility to protect and the North–South divide

1   This is a revised version of a chapter previously published in S. R. Silverburg, ed., *International Law: Readings on contemporary problems and future issues* (Boulder, CO: 2011) and used by permission of Westview Press, a member of the Perseus Books Group. All rights reserved.

2   In a CNN opinion poll shortly after the incident, 59 per cent of blacks but only 29 per cent of whites said Crowley acted stupidly; 58 per cent of whites said that of Gates, with African-Americans evenly split. 'CNN Poll: Did Obama Act Stupidly in Gates Arrest Comments', *CNN*, 4 August 2009, http://politicalticker.blogs.cnn.com/2009/08/04/cnn-poll-did-obama-act-stupidly-in-gates-arrest-comments/ (accessed 4 August 2009).

3    M. Ayoob, 'Humanitarian Intervention and State Sovereignty', *International Journal of Human Rights* 6:1 (Spring 2002), pp. 98–9.
4    See R. Thakur, *Towards a Less Imperfect State of the World: The gulf between North and South* (Berlin: Friedrich Ebert Stiftung, Dialogue on Globalization Briefing Paper 4, April 2008).
5    N. D. Kristof, 'Obama and Race', *New York Times*, 20 March 2008.
6    'African Nations Unite to Defend Sudanese Leaders', *Independent* (London), 4 July 2009.
7    A. Mack *et al.*, eds, *Human Security Report 2005: War and peace in the 21st century* (New York: Oxford University Press, 2005).
8    T. G. Weiss and D. Hubert *et al.*, *The Responsibility to Protect: Research, bibliography, and background.* Supplementary volume to the Report of the International Commission on Intervention and State Sovereignty. (Ottawa: International Development Research Centre, 2001), pp. 162, 357. See also P. Nel, 'South Africa: The Demand for Legitimate Multilateralism', in A. Schnabel and R. Thakur, eds, *Kosovo and the Challenge of Humanitarian Intervention: Selective indignation, collective action, and international citizenship* (Tokyo: United Nations University Press, 2000), pp. 245–59.
9    'Look across Africa and see the major changes that are happening', *Time*, 13 July 2009, at www.time.com/magazine/article/0,9171,1908312,00.html (accessed 30 April 2010).
10   International Commission on Intervention and State Sovereignty, *The Responsibility to Protect* (Ottawa: International Development Research Centre, 2001).
11   L. Bourquien, in an article published in 1923 on the failed effort by Napoleon Bonaparte to take India from the British towards the end of the eighteenth century; quoted in W. Dalrymple, *The White Mughals: Love and betrayal in eighteenth century India* (New Delhi: Viking, 2002), pp. 147–8.
12   R. Thakur, *The United Nations, Peace and Security: From collective security to the responsibility to protect* (Cambridge: Cambridge University Press, 2006), p. 267.
13   See S. Chesterman, M. Ignatieff and R. Thakur, eds, *Making States Work: State failure and the crisis of governance* (Tokyo: United Nations University Press, 2005).
14   A. Acharya, 'Redefining the Dilemmas of Humanitarian Intervention', *Australian Journal of International Affairs* 56:3 (2002), pp. 377–80.
15   S. Petcharamesree, 'Rapporteur's Report, ICISS Round Table Consultation, New Delhi, 10 June 2001'; unattributed, 'Rapporteur's Report, ICISS Round Table Consultation, Beijing, 14 June 2001'. The reports from all the ICISS regional discussions are available on the Commission's website at www.iciss.gc.ca.
16   For a full-fledged discussion of the moral hazard argument, see A. J. Kuperman, 'The Moral Hazard of Humanitarian Intervention: Lessons from the Balkans', *International Studies Quarterly* 52:1 (March 2008), pp. 49–80.
17   At first glance, East Timor – an operation to which even China acquiesced – would appear to contradict this. But in fact, from a strictly technical point of view, East Timor was not a coercive intervention in the internal affairs of a member state. For one thing, the UN had never given formal consent to Indonesia's annexation of the territory and so the question of requiring Indonesian consent did not arise. For another, Indonesian consent was in fact secured.
18   Tokyo, 16 December 2002, Bangkok, 19 March 2003, Singapore, 20 March 2003, seventeenth Asia-Pacific Roundtable, Kuala Lumpur, 6–9 August 2003, Jakarta, 23–5 February 2004.
19   See L. Subianto, 'The Responsibility to Protect: An Indonesian View', and M. Anthony, 'The Responsibility to Protect: Southeast Asian Perspectives'; papers delivered at the seventeenth Asia-Pacific Roundtable, Kuala Lumpur, 9 August 2003.

20　M. Ayoob, 'Third World Perspectives on Humanitarian Intervention and Inter-national Administration', *Global Governance* 10:1 (2004), p. 112.

21　O. el-Shafie, 'Intervention and State Sovereignty', discussion paper for the ICISS Round Table consultation in Cairo, 21 May 2001.

22　See Ambassador (retired) A. T. Khalil, 'Rapporteur's Report, ICISS Round Table Consultation, Cairo, 21 May 2001'; available on the Commission's website at www.iciss.gc.ca.

23　The text of the Constitutive Act is available online at www.africa-union.org/home/Welcome.htm.

24　D. Kuwali, 'The End of Humanitarian Intervention: Evaluation of the African Union's Right of Intervention', *African Journal of Conflict Resolution* 9:1 (2009), p. 41.

25　A. Ayebare, 'Regional Perspectives on Sovereignty and Intervention', discussion paper prepared for the ICISS Round Table Consultation, Maputo, 10 March 2001.

26　E. K. Aning, 'Rapporteur's Report, ICISS Round Table Consultation, Maputo, 10 March 2001'; available on the Commission's website at www.iciss.gc.ca.

27　See J. Heine, 'The Responsibility to Protect: Humanitarian Intervention and the Principle of Non-intervention in the Americas', in R. Thakur, A. F. Cooper and J. English, eds, *International Commissions and the Power of Ideas* (Tokyo: United Nations University Press, 2005), pp. 221–45.

28　M. S. Alvear, 'Humanitarian Intervention: How to Deal with Crises Effectively', introductory remarks at the ICISS Round Table Consultation, Santiago, 4 May 2001 (unofficial translation).

29　L. Bitencourt, 'Rapporteur's Report, ICISS Round Table Consultation, Santiago, 4 May 2001'; available on the Commission's website at www.iciss.gc.ca.

30　High-Level Panel on Threats, Challenges and Change (HLP), *A More Secure World: Our shared responsibility* (New York: United Nations, A/59/565, December 2004).

31　K. A. Annan, *In Larger Freedom: Towards development, security and human rights for all*. Report of the Secretary-General (New York: United Nations document A/59/2005, 21 March 2005), paras 122–35.

32　*2005 World Summit Outcome*, adopted by UN General Assembly Resolution A/RES/60/1, 24 October 2005, paras 138–40.

33　Ban Ki-moon, *Implementing the Responsibility to Protect: Report of the Secretary-General* (A/63/677, 12 January 2009).

34　The same mistake is made by A. J. Bellamy, 'Realizing the Responsibility to Protect', *International Studies Perspectives* 10:2 (May 2009), pp. 111–28.

35　Conversely, there are some iconic cases of 'bad' interventions, such as that to remove the Marxist Allende regime in Chile, that could also be studied with respect to what, if any, difference R2P would or might have made. This would apply especially if legitimacy criteria could be approved by consensus.

36　The deployment of moral arguments to justify imperialist actions in Iraq in 2003 had a direct structural counterpart in the British annexation of the Indian kingdom of Awadh in the first half of the nineteenth century. See P. Chatterjee, 'Empire after Globalization', *Economic and Political Weekly*, 39:37 (11 September 2004), p. 4163.

37　For his own account, see H. Blix, *Disarming Iraq* (New York: Pantheon, 2004).

38　*BBC News*, 9 May 2008; http://news.bbc.co.uk/go/pr/fr/-/2/hi/uk_news/7391492.stm (accessed 9 May 2008).

39　J. Borger and I. MacKinnon, 'Bypass Junta's Permission for Aid, US and France Urge', *Guardian*, 9 May 2008.

40　In a different context, an investigation by a group of eighty-four local and inter-national organizations concluded that 'A UN-backed offensive to destroy a Hutu rebel group in eastern Democratic Republic of Congo has had disastrous humanitarian consequences, with more than 1,000 civilians killed, 7,000 raped, and 900,000 forced from their homes'. The organizations collectively described the human cost of the attempt to defeat the Democratic Forces for the Liberation of Rwanda as 'unacceptable and disproportionate to the results it has achieved'. Xan Rice, 'UN-backed Congo military offensive a "humanitarian disaster"', *Guardian*, 13 October 2009, www.guardian.co.uk/world/2009/oct/13/democratic-republic-of-congo-civilian-deaths (accessed 14 October 2009).

41    W. Kemp, 'Where Are the Borders? National Identity and National Security', in W. Kemp, V. Popovski and R. Thakur, eds, *Blood and Borders: The responsibility to protect and the problem of the 'kin state'* (Tokyo: United Nations University Press, forthcoming).

42    See Global Center for R2P, 'The Georgia-Russia Crisis and the Responsibility to Protect: Background Note', 19 August 2008, available at: www.globalr2p.org/pdf/related/GeorgiaRussia.pdf; (accessed 5 March 2009).

43    *Human Rights in Palestine and Other Occupied Arab Territories: Report of the United Nations Fact Finding Mission on the Gaza Conflict* (Geneva: United Nations Human Rights Council, A/HRC/12/48, 15 September 2009), available at: www2.ohchr.org/english/bodies/hrcouncil/specialsession/9/docs/UNFFMGC_Report.pdf (accessed 14 October 2009). See also, C. McGreal, 'Demands Grow for Gaza War Crimes Investigation', *Guardian*, 13 January 2009; R. Falk (UN Special Rapporteur on Palestinian Human Rights), 'Israel's War Crimes', *Le Monde Diplomatique* (English edn) (15 March 2009, available at: http://mondediplo.com/2009/03/03warcrimes (accessed 30 June 2009).

44    *Human Rights in Palestine and Other Occupied Arab Territories*, pp. 546–8.

45    A. Cassese (President of the Special Tribunal for Lebanon and past President of the International Criminal Tribunal for Former Yugoslavia), 'We Must Stand Behind the UN Report on Gaza', *Financial Times*, 14 October 2009. For discussions of R2P in relation to Darfur, see C. G. Badescu and L. Bergholm, 'The Responsibility to Protect and the Conflict in Darfur: The Big Let-Down', *Security Dialogue* 40:3 (June 2009), pp. 287–309; H. Adelman, 'Refugees, IDPs and the Responsibility to Protect (R2P): The Case of Darfur', *Global Responsibility to Protect* 2 (2010), pp. 1–22; R. W. Williamson, 'Sudan and the Implications for Responsibility to Protect', Stanley Foundation, *Policy Analysis Brief* (October 2009).

46    This paragraph is based on C. Philp, 'Sri Lanka Forces West to Retreat Over "War Crimes" with Victory at UN', *The Times*, 28 May 2009, www.timesonline.co.uk/tol/news/world/us_and_americas/article6375044.ece? (accessed 5 June 2009).

47    See International Crisis Group, *War Crimes in Sri Lanka* (Brussels: ICG, Asia Report No. 191, 17 May 2010).

48    Helpful summaries have been provided by two civil society organizations: Global Centre for the Responsibility to Protect, 'Implementing the Responsibility to Protect – The 2009 General Assembly Debate: An Assessment', GCR2P Report, August 2009, available at: www.GlobalR2P.org; and International Coalition for the Responsibility to Protect, 'Report on the General Assembly Plenary Debate on the Responsibility to Protect'(New York: ICRtoP, 15 September 2009), available at: www.Responsibilitytoprotect.org.

49    Quoted in N. Macfarquhar, 'Memo from the United Nations: When to Step In to Stop War Crimes Causes Fissures', *New York Times*, 22 July 2009.

50    'At the Opening of the Thematic Dialogue of the General Assembly on the Responsibility to Protect', UN Headquarters, New York, 23 July 2009, www.un.org/ga/president/63/statements/openingr2p230709.shtml (accessed 29 July 2009).

51   E. C. Luck, Special Adviser to the Secretary-General, 'Remarks to the General Assembly on the Responsibility to Protect', 23 July 2009, p. 3; www.un.org/ga/president/63/interactive/protect/luck.pdf (accessed 17 September 2009).

52   J. Bricmont, 'A More Just World and the Responsibility to Protect', statement to the Interactive Thematic Dialogue of the General Assembly on the Responsibility to Protect, United Nations, New York, 23 July 2009; www.un.org/ga/president/63/interactive/protect/jean.pdf (accessed 17 September 2009).

53   Statement by Professor Noam Chomsky to the United Nations General Assembly Thematic Dialogue on the Responsibility to Protect, United Nations, New York, 23 July 2009; www.un.org/ga/president/63/interactive/protect/noam.pdf (accessed 17 September 2009).

54   G. Evans, Statement to United Nations General Assembly Informal Interactive Dialogue on the Responsibility to Protect, New York, 23 July 2009; www.un.org/ga/president/63/interactive/protect/evans.pdf (accessed 17 September 2009).

55   Ngugi wa Thiong'o, 'Uneven Development is the Root of Many Crimes', statement to UN General Assembly Dialogue on the Responsibility to Protect, New York, 23 July 2009; www.un.org/ga/president/63/interactive/protect/ngugi.pdf (accessed 17 September 2009).

56   See 'Delegates Seek to End Global Paralysis in Face of Atrocities as General Assembly Holds Interactive Dialogue on Responsibility to Protect', General Assembly document GA/10847 (New York: United Nations, Department of Public Information, 23 July 2009), www.un.org/News/Press/docs/2009/ga10847.doc.htm (accessed 17 September 2009); 'More than 40 Delegates Express Strong Scepticism, Full Support as General Assembly Continues Debate on Responsibility to Protect', General Assembly document GA/10849 (New York: United Nations, DPI, 23 July 2009), www.un.org/News/Press/docs/2009/ga10849.doc.htm (accessed 17 September 2009); and 'Delegates Weigh Legal Merits of Responsibility to Protect Concept as General Assembly Concludes Debate', General Assembly document GA/10850 (New York: United Nations, DPI, 28 July 2009), www.un.org/News/Press/docs/2009/ga10850.doc.htm (accessed 17 September 2009).

57   S/PV.5577, 'Security Council Open Debate on Protection of Civilians in Armed Conflict', UN Security Council Verbatim Record, 4 December 2006, p. 8; quoted in S. Teitt, 'Assessing Polemics, Principles and Practices: China and the Responsibility to Protect', *Global Responsibility to Protect* 1:2 (2009), p. 216.

58   E. Aba and M. Hammer, *Yes We Can? Options and barriers to broadening the scope of the Responsibility to Protect to include cases of economic, social and cultural rights abuse* (London: One World Trust, Briefing Paper No. 116, March 2009).

59   Ban, *Implementing the Responsibility To Protect*, para. 67.

60   'More than 40 Delegates Express Strong Scepticism, Full Support.'

61   Ibid.

62   For an interesting argument on how even misuses and abuses of the R2P norm help to strengthen it, see C. G. Badescu and T. G. Weiss, 'Misrepresenting R2P and Advancing Norms: An Alternative Spiral' *International Studies Perspectives* 11:3 (August 2010).

63   S. J. Stedman, 'UN Transformation in an Era of Soft Balancing', *International Affairs* 83:5 (2007), pp. 933 and 938.

64   'Assembly President Warns on Doctrine to Intervene on War Crimes, Atrocities', UN News Centre, www.un.org/ga/news/news.asp?NewsID=31562&Cr=right+to+protect&Cr1=; (accessed 26 May 2010).

65   For an analysis of 'international community' as a contested concept, see D. C. Ellis, 'On the Possibility of "International Community"', *International Studies Review* 11:1 (March 2009), pp. 1–26.

66　Kofi Annan in an interview with R. Cohen, 'How Kofi Annan Rescued Kenya', *New York Review of Books*, 14 August 2008, pp. 51–53, at p. 52.

67　Daily Press Briefing by the Office of the Spokesperson for the Secretary-General, 28 January 2008; available at: www.un.org/News/briefings

68　D. Tutu, 'Taking the Responsibility to Protect', *International Herald Tribune*, 19 February 2008.

69　M. Sahnoun, 'Africa: Uphold Continent's Contribution to Human Rights, Urges Top Diplomat', *allAfrica.com*, http://allafrica.com/stories/printable/200907210 549.html (accessed 21 July 2009). For another African perspective that also strongly supports R2P, see S. Atuobi, 'The Responsibility to Protect: The Time to Act is Now', *KAIPTC Policy Brief* No. 1 (Accra: Kofi Annan International Peacekeeping Training Centre, July 2009).

70　I argued this in 'The Responsibility to Protect Revisited,' *Daily Yomiuri*, 12 April 2007.

71　See World Federalist Movement, *Global Consultative Roundtables on the Responsibility to Protect: Civil society perspectives and recommendations for action, interim report* (New York: WFM, January 2009), p. 8: 'At almost every roundtable, civil society emphasized how R2P principles already resonate with pre-existing cultural values.'

72　S. Krasner, *Sovereignty: Organized hypocrisy* (Princeton, NJ: Princeton University Press, 1999).

## 11 R2P and the protection of civilians in armed conflict

1　C. Clement and A. C. Smith, eds, *Managing Complexity: Political and managerial challenges in United Nations peace operations* (New York: International Peace Institute, 2009), pp. 3–4. Report of a joint IPI–Geneva Centre for Security Policy (GCSP) conference held in New York, 1–2 December 2008.

2　'Protection of Civilians and the Responsibility to Protect', keynote address at the seminar on 'Beskyttelse av sivile', organized by the Norwegian Institute of International Affairs (NUPI), Oslo, 6 October 2009.

3　L. Vieira de Mello, 'Unsung Heroes of the Battlefields', *Washington Post*, 19 August 2009.

4　International Commission on Intervention and State Sovereignty, *The Responsibility to Protect* (Ottawa: International Development Research Centre, 2001).

5　See R. Gellately and B. Kiernan, eds, *The Spectre of Genocide: Mass murder in historical perspective* (Cambridge: Cambridge University Press, 2003), and M. Shaw, *War and Genocide: Organized killing in modern society* (Cambridge: Polity Press, 2003).

6　K. A. Annan, *In Larger Freedom: Towards development, security and human rights for all*. Report of the Secretary-General (New York: United Nations, document A/59/2005, 21 March 2005).

7　D. Kennedy, *The Dark Sides of Virtue: Reassessing international humanitarianism* (Princeton, NJ: Princeton University Press, 2004), p. 323.

8　See http://ochaonline.un.org/HumanitarianIssues/ProtectionofCiviliansinArmed Conflict/tabid/1114/language/en-US/Default.aspx.

9　For an exploration of the changes from classical peacekeeping to peace operations, see R. Thakur and A. Schnabel, eds, *United Nations Peacekeeping Operations: Ad hoc missions, permanent engagement* (Tokyo: United Nations University Press, 2001).

10　*Report of the Panel on United Nations Peace Operations* (A/55/305-S/2000/809), 21 August 2000, p. viii. The language and the argument of the Brahimi Report here borrowed from a speech of Kofi Annan to the Council on Foreign Relations in New York in 1999; see I. Johnstone, 'The Role of the UN Secretary-General:

The Power of Persuasion Based on Law', *Global Governance* 9:4 (October–December 2003), p. 444.

11   *Challenges of Peace Operations into the 21st Century: Concluding report 1997–2002* (Stockholm: Swedish National Defence College, 2002), p. 17.

12   For a critical evaluation of the UN's record of transitional administration, see S. Chesterman, *You, the People: The United Nations, transitional administration, and state-building* (Oxford: Oxford University Press, 2004).

13   C. de Coning, 'Planning for Success', in Clement and Smith, eds, *Managing Complexity*, pp. 24–7.

14   Clement and Smith, eds, *Managing Complexity*, p. 2.

15   Bosnia and Herzegovina, Somalia, Rwanda, Haiti, Persian Gulf, Cambodia, El Salvador.

16   V. K. Holt and T. C. Berkman, *The Impossible Mandate? Military preparedness, the responsibility to protect and modern peace operations* (Washington, DC: Stimson Center, 2006).

17   See 'The Relationship Between the Responsibility to Protect and the Protection of Civilians in Armed Conflict', *Policy Brief* (New York: Global Centre for R2P, January 2009), http://globalr2p.org/pdf/GCR2PPolicyBrief-ProtectCivConflict.pdf (accessed 20 July 2009).

18   See J. Murthy, 'Mandating the Protection Cluster with the Responsibility to Protect: A Policy Recommendation Based on the Protection Cluster's Implementation in South Kivu, DRC,' *Journal of Humanitarian Assistance* (October 5 2008), downloaded from: http://jha.ac/2007/10/05/mandating-the-protection-cluster-with-the-responsibility-to-protect-a-policy-recommendation-based-on-the-protection-cluster%e2%80%99s-implementation-in-south-kivu-drc/ (accessed 1 October 2008).

19   UN Security Council, *Statement by the President of the Security Council*, 20 July 2004, S/PRST/2004/27.

20   High-Level Panel on Threats, Challenges and Change, *A More Secure World: Our shared responsibility* (New York: United Nations, A/59/565, December 2004) paras 270–3.

21   Annan, *In Larger Freedom*, paras 213–15.

22   Joint Statement by Participants in the Sixth High-Level Meeting between the United Nations and Regional and other Intergovernmental Organizations, held at United Nations Headquarters in New York, 25–26 July 2005.

23   See M. Bateman and M. Hammer, 'Don't Call Me, I'll Call You?', (London: One World Trust, Briefing Paper No. 107, October 2007).

24   Holt and Berkman, *The Impossible Mandate*, pp. 183–4.

25   Bateman and Hammer, 'Don't Call Me, I'll Call You?', pp. 7–8.

26   See B. Antonini, ed., *Security Council Resolutions under Chapter VII: Design, implementation and accountabilities* (Madrid: FRIDE, 2009).

27   These observations are based on a trip to Afghanistan in April 2009. See R. Thakur, 'Afghanistan: The High Costs of Failure', *Hindu* (Chennai), 30 April 2009.

28   K. vanden Heuvel, 'A Flawed Strategy and a Failed War in Afghanistan', *Washington Post*, 26 May 2010.

29   Ibid.

30   *Report on Progress Toward Security and Stability in Afghanistan and United States Plan for Sustaining the Afghanistan National Security Forces* (Washington, DC: Department of Defense, 28 April 2010); www.defense.gov/pubs/pdfs/Report_Final_SecDef_04_26_10.pdf (accessed 26 May 2010), pp. 7, 35.

31   For an interesting argument on how even misuses and abuses of the R2P norm help to strengthen it, see C. G. Badescu and T. G. Weiss, 'Misrepresenting R2P and Advancing Norms: An Alternative Spiral', *International Studies Perspectives* 11:3 (August 2010).

32   T. Risse, '"Let's Argue!": Communicative Action in World Politics', *International Organization* 54:1 (Winter 2000), p. 32. In a subsequent refinement with colleagues, Risse developed the five-stage spiral model of norm generation, diffusion and domestication by the target state: repression, denial, tactical concessions, prescriptive status (when the state accepts the international norm and incorporates it into domestic legislation), and rule-consistent behaviour. T. Risse and K. Sikkink, 'The Socialization of International Human Rights Norms into Domestic Practices: Introduction', in T. Risse, S. C. Ropp and K. Sikkink, eds, *The Power of Human Rights: International norms and domestic change* (Cambridge: Cambridge University Pres, 1999), pp. 17–35.

33   Kennedy, *The Dark Sides of Virtue*, pp. 327–32.

## 12 Conclusion: normative contestation, incoherence and inconsistency

1   International Commission on Intervention and State Sovereignty, *The Responsibility to Protect* (Ottawa: International Development Research Centre, 2001).

2   A. Florini, 'The Evolution of International Norms', *International Studies Quarterly* 40:3 (September 1996), pp. 377–8 and 382–3.

3   C. M. Chinkin, 'Kosovo: A "Good" or "Bad" War?', *American Journal of International Law* 93:4 (October 1999), p. 845.

4   H. Bull and A. Watson, 'Conclusion', in H. Bull and A. Watson, eds, *The Expansion of International Society* (Oxford: Clarendon, 1984), pp. 425–35.

5   The ambivalence was described by Ayoob as 'acute schizophrenia': M. Ayoob, 'The Third World in the System of States: Acute Schizophrenia or Growing Pains?', *International Studies Quarterly* 33:1 (1989), pp. 67–79.

6   A. Acharya, 'Norm Subsidiarity and Regional Orders: Sovereignty, Regionalism and Rule-making in the Third World', *International Studies Quarterly* 55 (2011, forthcoming).

7   Ibid.

8   Ibid.

9   This argument is hardly new, having been made, for example, by the late Susan Strange more than a decade ago; S. Strange, 'The Westfailure System,' *Review of International Studies* 25:3 (July 1999), pp. 345–54.

10   H. Bull, *The Anarchical Society: A study of order in world politics* (London: Macmillan, 1977), pp. 200–29.

11   See 'Sudan rejects ICC arrest warrant against president', *Xinhua*, 5 March 2009, http://news.xinhuanet.com/english/2009-03/05/content_10944809.htm (accessed 14 March 2010); and UN document S/2009/144, 6 March 2009, available at: www.securitycouncilreport.org/atf/cf/{65BFCF9B-6D27-4E9C-8CD3-CF6E4FF96FF9}/Sudan%20S%202009%20144.pdf (accessed 14 March 2010).

12   M. Lerner, 'A War Crime Whitewash', *Guardian*, 21 October 2009.

13   H. Schneider and C. Lynch, 'U.N. Panel Backs Gaza Report', *Washington Post*, 17 October 2009.

14   Document GA/10883, 5 November 2009, www.un.org/News/Press/docs/2009/ga10883.doc.htm (accessed 15 March 2010).

15   E. S. Cohn and S. O. White, 'Legal Socialization Effects on Democratization', *International Social Science Journal* No. 152 (June 1997), p. 165.

16   *Kosovo Report: Conflict, international response, lessons learned* (Oxford: Oxford University Press for the Independent International Commission on Kosovo, 2000).

17   The analogy of vigilante justice was used explicitly by the co-chairs of the Commission on Global Governance, one of whom is a former Prime Minister

of Sweden and the other the former Secretary-General of the Commonwealth. Writing of NATO bombing shortly after it started, they commented that 'This temptation to assume police powers on the basis of righteousness and military strength is dangerous for world order and world peace; what results is a world ordered by vigilante action'; I. Carlson and S. Ramphal, 'Air Strikes: Incalculable Damage to Peace Under Law', www.cgg.ch/kosovo.htm; edited versions were also published in the *International Herald Tribune*, 1 April 1999 and the *Guardian*, 2 April 1999.

18    For development of this line of argumentation, see in particular L. Henkin, 'Kosovo and the Law of "Humanitarian Intervention"', *American Journal of International Law* 93:4 (October 1999), pp. 824–8, and R. Wedgwood, 'NATO's Campaign in Yugoslavia', *American Journal of International Law* 93:4 (October 1999), pp. 828–34.

19    H. Shinoda, 'The Politics of Legitimacy in International Relations: A Critical Examination of NATO's Intervention in Kosovo', *Alternatives* 25:4 (October–December 2000), pp. 528–31.

20    A. Neier, 'The Quest for Justice', *New York Review of Books*, 8 March 2001, p. 34.

21    These issues are discussed in R. Thakur, ed., *What is Equitable Geographic Representation in the Twenty-first Century* (Tokyo: United Nations University, 1999).

22    Chinkin, 'Kosovo: A "Good" or "Bad" War?', p. 843.

23    Ibid., pp. 846–47.

24    Quoted in Shinoda, 'Politics of Legitimacy in International Relations', p. 519.

25    *The Responsibility to Protect*, pp. 49–50, paras 6.14 and 6.15.

26    Ibid., p. 55, para. 6.40.

27    See R. Thakur, 'Law, Legitimacy and the United Nations', *Melbourne Journal of International Law* 11:1 (May 2010), pp. 1–26.

28    See C. Gray, *International Law and the Use of Force*, 3rd edn (Oxford: Oxford University Press, 2008) and M. E. O'Connell, *International Law and the Use of Force, Cases and Materials*, 2nd edn (Eagan, MN: Foundation Press, 2008).

29    See V. Lowe, A. Roberts, J. Welsh and D. Zaum, eds, *The United Nations Security Council and War: The evolution of thought and practice since 1945* (Oxford: Oxford University Press, 2008).

30    A. G. Arbatov, *The Transformation of Russian Military Doctrine: Lessons learned from Kosovo and Chechnya* (Washington, DC: The George C. Marshall Center Papers, No. 2, 20 July 2000).

31    R. K. Betts, 'The Delusion of Impartial Intervention', C. A. Crocker and F. O. Hampson with P. Aall, eds, *Managing Global Chaos: Sources of and responses to international conflict* (Washington, DC: US Institute of Peace, 1996), pp. 333–41.

32    Thus a former US Ambassador to Yugoslavia (1977–81) and then Secretary of State (1992–3), in an article not exactly friendly to Slobodan Milosevic: 'The Kosovo Liberation Army *Earned* its Reputation as a Terrorist Group'; L. S. Eagleburger, 'Taking a Stand Against the Milosevics of the Future', *International Herald Tribune*, 5 April 1999 (emphasis added).

33    K. A. Annan, *We the Peoples: The role of the United Nations in the 21st century* (New York: UN Department of Public Information, 2000), p. 48.

34    See M. E. O'Connell, 'Responsibility to Peace: A Critique of R2P', *Journal of Intervention and Statebuilding* 4 (2010), pp. 39–52.

35    Quoted in Shinoda, 'Politics of Legitimacy in International Relations', p. 515.

36    Ibid., p. 516.

37    Ibid., pp. 521–2.

38    J. Solana, 'NATO's Success in Kosovo', *Foreign Affairs* 78:6 (November–December 1999), p. 118.

39    Shinoda, 'Politics of Legitimacy in International Relations', p. 524.

40   Quoted in M. R. Gordon, 'China Looks to Foil Missile Defense', *International Herald Tribune*, 30 April 2001.

41   R. Johnson, 'NPT Report', *Disarmament Diplomacy* 37 (May 1999), p. 16.

42   M. Dubey, 'The NATO Juggernaut: Logic of an Indian Defense Deterrent', *Times of India*, 8 April 1999. The sentiment was widely shared in India. The country's leading newspaper commented: 'The war unleashed by NATO against Serbia has implications for general staff establishments the world over . . . . The nations which want to retain their strategic autonomy and sovereignty are left with no choice but to sustain their nuclear arsenals and go in for missiles and try to develop RMA [the revolution in military affairs] capabilities for themselves'; 'Might on Show', *Times of India*, 2 April 1999.

43   D. A. Welch, *Justice and the Genesis of War* (Cambridge: Cambridge University Press, 1993), pp. 206, 209.

44   G. W. Gong, *The Standard of 'Civilization' in International Society* (Oxford: Clarendon, 1984).

45   M. Ayoob, 'Humanitarian Intervention and International Society', *Global Governance* 7:3 (July–September 2001), p. 227.

46   P. Popham, 'How Beijing Won Sri Lanka's Civil War', *Independent*, 23 May 2010.

47   Quoted in N. Kristof, 'What to Do About Darfur', *New York Review of Books*, 2 July 2009, p. 32.

48   Ayoob, 'Humanitarian Intervention and International Society', p. 229.

49   C. Simic, 'Connoisseurs of Cruelty', *New York Review of Books*, 12 March 2009, p. 23.

50   See C. Del Ponte with C. Sudetic, *Madame Prosecutor: Confrontations with humanity's worst criminals and the culture of impunity* (New York: Other Press, 2009); T. Judah, *Kosovo: What everyone needs to know* (Oxford: Oxford University Press, 2008); J. Subotic, *Hijacked Justice: Dealing with the past in the Balkans* (Ithaca, NY: Cornell University Press, 2009); and W. Tochman, *Like Eating a Stone: Surviving the past in Bosnia*, translated by A. Lloyd-Jones (New York: Atlas, 2008).

51   R. M. Hayden, 'Biased Justice: "Humanrightism" and the International Criminal Tribunal for the Former Yugoslavia', in R. G. C. Thomas, ed., *Yugoslavia Unraveled: Sovereignty, self-determination, intervention* (Lanham, MD: Lexington Books, 2003), pp. 259–85. See also 'NATO/Federal Republic of Yugoslavia: "Collateral Damage" or Unlawful Killings?', *Amnesty International Report* (London: AI, 6 June 2000), and 'Civilian Deaths in the NATO Air Campaign', *Human Rights Watch* 12, no. 1(D), February 2000.

52   See J. Hagan, *Justice in the Balkans: Prosecuting war crimes in the Hague Tribunal* (Chicago, IL: University of Chicago Press, 2003), Chapter 4. ICTY prosecutor Louise Arbour became a Judge of the Supreme Court of Canada effective 15 September 1999 (and the UN High Commissioner for Human Rights 2004–9). According to Hagan, her Supreme Court appointment was approved but undisclosed on 26 May 1999, the day before her announcement of the Milosevic indictment. Normally such appointments are announced in the week they are made. At her request, the official announcement was delayed until 11 June. Ibid., p. 127.

53   P. Schori, 'What We Need is a Cooperative America', *International Herald Tribune*, 6 August 2002.

54   Chinkin, 'Kosovo: A "Good" or "Bad" War?', p. 846.

55   Ibid., p. 844.

56   For details of the secret but leaked ICRC report on the Guantanamo detainees, see M. Danner, 'US Torture: Voices from the Dark Sites', *New York Review of Books*, 9 April 2009, pp. 69–77.

57   'Italy Convicts 23 Americans, Most Working for CIA', *New York Times*, 5 November 2009; C. Barry, 'Italian Judge Mulls CIA Renditions', *Globe and Mail* (Toronto), 4 November 2009.

58  See J. Heine and R. Thakur, 'A Global Taste for Justice', *Ottawa Citizen*, 30 April 2009.

59  For a contrary position with regard to former British Prime Minister Tony Blair, see G. Monbiot, 'Wanted: Tony Blair for War Crimes. Arrest Him and Claim Your Reward', *Guardian*, 25 January 2010. Unfortunately, Monbiot's is a voice in the wilderness. Blair's post-prime ministerial life has been extremely lucrative and even though he failed in his quest to be the inaugural EU president, he has served as an envoy for peace in the Middle East. Similarly, J. Howard, who took Australia to war in Iraq as prime minister, was chosen by the Australian cricket board to be the next president of the International Cricket Council but this was rejected by the ICC. 'Equal in, under and before the law' is not a principle that will apply to international criminal justice in the foreseeable future.

60  R. Thakur, *The United Nations, Peace and Security: From collective security to the responsibility to protect* (Cambridge: Cambridge University Press, 2006), Tables 13.1 and 13.2, pp. 311–12.

# Index